Malta

Neil Wilson

LONELY PLANET PUBLICATIONS
Melbourne • Oakland • London • Paris

MALTA

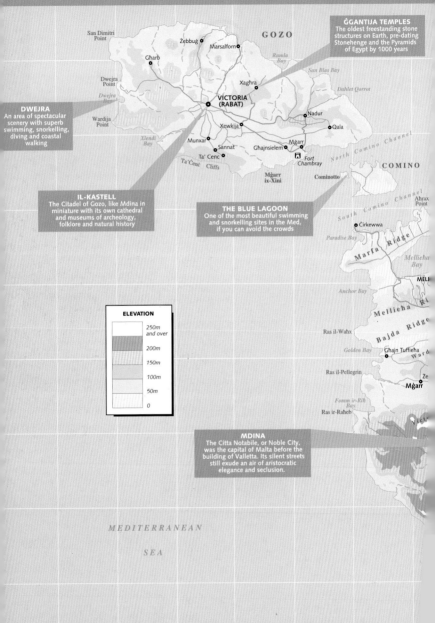

GOZO

San Dimitri Point

Żebbuġ

Marsalforn

Gharb

Dwejra Point

Ramla Bay

San Blas Bay

Xagħra

Dahlet Qorrot

DWEJRA
An area of spectacular scenery with superb swimming, snorkelling, diving and coastal walking

Dwejra Bay

VICTORIA (RABAT)

Wardija Point

Xlendi Bay

Nadur

Xewkija

Qala

Munxar

Sannat

Ghajnsielem

Mġarr

ĠGANTIJA TEMPLES
The oldest freestanding stone structures on Earth, pre-dating Stonehenge and the Pyramids of Egypt by 1000 years

Fort Chambray

Ta' Ċenċ Cliffs

Ta' Ċenċ

Mġarr ix-Xini

Cominotto

North Comino Channel

COMINO

IL-KASTELL
The Citadel of Gozo, like Mdina in miniature with its own cathedral and museums of archeology, folklore and natural history

THE BLUE LAGOON
One of the most beautiful swimming and snorkelling sites in the Med, if you can avoid the crowds

South Comino Channel

Abrax Point

Ċirkewwa

Paradise Bay

Marfa Ridge

Mellieħa Bay

ELEVATION

	250m and over
	200m
	150m
	100m
	50m
	0

Anchor Bay

MELI

Mellieħa Ri

Ras il-Wahx

Bajda Ridge

Golden Bay

Ghajn Tuffieħa

Ward

Ras il-Pellegrin

Że

Mġarr

Fomm ir-Riħ Bay

Ras ir-Raheb

Viċt

MDINA
The Citta Notabile, or Noble City, was the capital of Malta before the building of Valletta. Its silent streets still exude an air of aristocratic elegance and seclusion.

MEDITERRANEAN

SEA

14° 10' E   14° 12' E   14° 14' E   14° 16' E   14° 18' E   14° 20' E   14° 22'

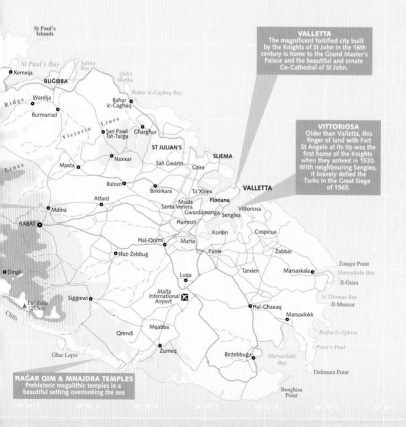

0   2   4km
0   1.25   2.5mi

MEDITERRANEAN

SEA

VALLETTA
The magnificent fortified city built
by the Knights of St John in the 16th
century is home to the Grand Master's
Palace and the beautiful and ornate
Co-Cathedral of St John.

VITTORIOSA
Older than Valletta, this
finger of land with Fort
St Angelo at its tip was the
first home of the Knights
when they arrived in 1530.
With neighbouring Senglea,
it bravely defied the
Turks in the Great Siege
of 1565.

St Paul's
Islands

St Paul's Bay   *Salina Bay*

Xemxija
BUĠIBBA

Ridge   Wardija

Burmarrad

Qalet Marku

Baħar iċ-Ċagħaq

Baħar iċ-Ċagħaq Bay

Victoria   *Lines*

San Pawl
Tat-Tarġa   Għargħur

ST JULIAN'S

Mosta

Naxxar

San Ġwann

Gżira

SLIEMA

Lines

Balzan

Attard

Birkirkara

Ta'Xbiex

VALLETTA

Mdina

Msida
Santa Venera
Gwardamanga

Floriana

Vittoriosa

RABAT

Hamrun

Senglea

Dingli

Ħal-Qormi   Marsa

Kordin

Cospicua

Ħaż-Żebbuġ

Paola

Żabbar

▲ *Ta' Zuta*
(253m)

Siġġiewi

Luqa

Tarxien

Marsaskala

Żonqor Point

Marsaskala Bay

Il-Gżira

Malta
International
Airport ✈

Ħal-Għaxaq

St Thomas Bay
Il-Munxar

Marsaxlokk

Cliffs

Qrendi

Mqabba

Hofra Iż-Żghira

Pater's Pool

Għar Lapsi

Żurrieq

Birżebbuġa

Marsaxlokk Bay

Delimara Point

ĦAĠAR QIM & MNAJDRA TEMPLES
Prehistoric megalithic temples in a
beautiful setting overlooking the sea

Benghisa
Point

Malta
1st edition – August 2000

Published by
Lonely Planet Publications Pty Ltd ABN 36 005 607 983
90 Maribyrnong St, Footscray, Victoria 3011, Australia

Lonely Planet Offices
Australia Locked Bag 1, Footscray, Victoria 3011
USA 150 Linden St, Oakland, CA 94607
UK 10a Spring Place, London NW5 3BH
France 1 rue du Dahomey, 75011 Paris

Photographs
Many of the images in this guide are available for licensing from
Lonely Planet Images.
email: lpi@lonelyplanet.com.au
Web site: www.lonelyplanetimages.com

Front cover photograph
The Eye of Osiris on a Maltese fishing boat (Bethune Carmichael)

ISBN 1 86450 119 7

Printed through Colorcraft Ltd, Hong Kong
Printed in China

Although the authors and Lonely Planet try to make the information as accurate as possible, we accept no responsibility for any loss, injury or inconvenience sustained by anyone using this book.

Contents – Text

Contents – Maps

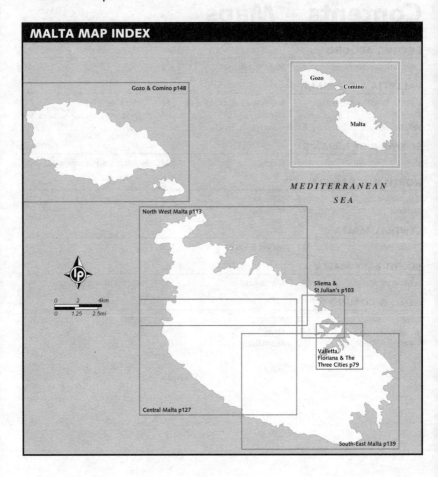

MALTA MAP INDEX

Gozo & Comino p148

Gozo

Comino

Malta

MEDITERRANEAN SEA

North West Malta p113

0   2   4km
0   1.25   2.5mi

Sliema &
St Julian's p103

Valletta,
Floriana & The
Three Cities p79

Central Malta p127

South-East Malta p139

The Author

Neil Wilson

After working as a geologist in Australia and the North Sea and doing geological research at Oxford University, Neil gave up the rock business for the more precarious life of a freelance writer and photographer. Since 1988 he has travelled in five continents and written some 25 travel and walking guides for various publishers. Although he was born in Glasgow, Neil defected to the east at the age of 18 and still lives in Edinburgh.

FROM THE AUTHOR

Thanks to Claude Muscat Doublesin, Sandra Aquilina and Joanna Dowling at NSTS in Valletta; and to James Azzopardi of the Malta Tourist Authority. Thanks also to Carol Downie for dedicated restaurant research.

This Book

From the Publisher

The first edition of *Malta* was produced in the Melbourne office, and was coordinated by Susie Ashworth (editorial) and Ann Jeffree (mapping and design). Thanks to Susannah Farfor who assisted with editing and proofing, and Chris Thomas and Yvonne Bischofberger who helped out with mapping. New illustrations were provided by Martin Harris and Ann Jeffree, Quentin Frayne prepared the Language chapter, the cover was designed by Maria Vallianos, Production Services helped with our font needs and Tim Uden provided valuable Quark support. All photographs were supplied by Lonely Planet Images.

Foreword

ABOUT LONELY PLANET GUIDEBOOKS

The story begins with a classic travel adventure: Tony and Maureen Wheeler's 1972 journey across Europe and Asia to Australia. Useful information about the overland trail did not exist at that time, so Tony and Maureen published the first Lonely Planet guidebook to meet a growing need.

From a kitchen table, then from a tiny office in Melbourne (Australia), Lonely Planet has become the largest independent travel publisher in the world, an international company with offices in Melbourne, Oakland (USA), London (UK) and Paris (France).

Today Lonely Planet guidebooks cover the globe. There is an ever-growing list of books and there's information in a variety of forms and media. Some things haven't changed. The main aim is still to help make it possible for adventurous travellers to get out there – to explore and better understand the world.

At Lonely Planet we believe travellers can make a positive contribution to the countries they visit – if they respect their host communities and spend their money wisely. Since 1986 a percentage of the income from each book has been donated to aid projects and human rights campaigns.

Updates Lonely Planet thoroughly updates each guidebook as often as possible. This usually means there are around two years between editions, although for more unusual or more stable destinations the gap can be longer. Check the imprint page (following the colour map at the beginning of the book) for publication dates.

Between editions up-to-date information is available in two free newsletters – the paper *Planet Talk* and email *Comet* (to subscribe, contact any Lonely Planet office) – and on our Web site at www.lonelyplanet.com. The *Upgrades* section of the Web site covers a number of important and volatile destinations and is regularly updated by Lonely Planet authors. *Scoop* covers news and current affairs relevant to travellers. And, lastly, the *Thorn Tree* bulletin board and *Postcards* section of the site carry unverified, but fascinating, reports from travellers.

Correspondence The process of creating new editions begins with the letters, postcards and emails received from travellers. This correspondence often includes suggestions, criticisms and comments about the current editions. Interesting excerpts are immediately passed on via newsletters and the Web site, and everything goes to our authors to be verified when they're researching on the road. We're keen to get more feedback from organisations or individuals who represent communities visited by travellers.

Lonely Planet gathers information for everyone who's curious about the planet – and especially for those who explore it first-hand. Through guidebooks, phrasebooks, activity guides, maps, literature, newsletters, image library, TV series and Web site we act as an information exchange for a worldwide community of travellers.

Research Authors aim to gather sufficient practical information to enable travellers to make informed choices and to make the mechanics of a journey run smoothly. They also research historical and cultural background to help enrich the travel experience and allow travellers to understand and respond appropriately to cultural and environmental issues.

Authors don't stay in every hotel because that would mean spending a couple of months in each medium-sized city and, no, they don't eat at every restaurant because that would mean stretching belts beyond capacity. They do visit hotels and restaurants to check standards and prices, but feedback based on readers' direct experiences can be very helpful.

Many of our authors work undercover, others aren't so secretive. None of them accept freebies in exchange for positive write-ups. And none of our guidebooks contain any advertising.

Production Authors submit their raw manuscripts and maps to offices in Australia, USA, UK or France. Editors and cartographers – all experienced travellers themselves – then begin the process of assembling the pieces. When the book finally hits the shops, some things are already out of date, we start getting feedback from readers and the process begins again …

WARNING & REQUEST

Things change – prices go up, schedules change, good places go bad and bad places go bankrupt – nothing stays the same. So, if you find things better or worse, recently opened or long since closed, please tell us and help make the next edition even more accurate and useful. We genuinely value all the feedback we receive. A well-travelled team reads and acknowledges every letter, postcard and email and ensures that every morsel of information finds its way to the appropriate authors, editors and cartographers for verification.

Everyone who writes to us will find their name listed in the next edition of the appropriate guidebook. They will also receive the latest issue of *Planet Talk*, our quarterly printed newsletter, or *Comet*, our monthly email newsletter. Subscriptions to both newsletters are free. The very best contributions will be rewarded with a free guidebook.

We may edit, reproduce and incorporate your comments in all Lonely Planet products, such as guidebooks, Web sites and digital products, so let us know if you don't want your comments reproduced or your name acknowledged.

Send all correspondence to the Lonely Planet office closest to you:

Australia: Locked Bag 1, Footscray, Victoria 3011
USA: 150 Linden St, Oakland, CA 94607
UK: 10a Spring Place, London NW5 3BH

Or email us at: talk2us@lonelyplanet.com.au

For news, views and updates see our Web site: www.lonelyplanet.com

HOW TO USE A LONELY PLANET GUIDEBOOK

The best way to use a Lonely Planet guidebook is any way you choose. At Lonely Planet we believe the most memorable travel experiences are often those that are unexpected, and the finest discoveries are those that you make yourself. Guidebooks are not intended to be used as if they provide a detailed set of infallible instructions!

Contents All Lonely Planet guidebooks follow roughly the same format. The Facts about the Destination chapters or sections give background information ranging from history to weather. Facts for the Visitor gives practical information on issues like visas and health. Getting There & Away gives a brief starting point for researching travel to and from the destination. Getting Around gives an overview of the transport options when you arrive.

The peculiar demands of each destination determine how subsequent chapters are broken up, but some things remain constant. We always start with background, then proceed to sights, places to stay, places to eat, entertainment, getting there and away, and getting around information – in that order.

Heading Hierarchy Lonely Planet headings are used in a strict hierarchical structure that can be visualised as a set of Russian dolls. Each heading (and its following text) is encompassed by any preceding heading that is higher on the hierarchical ladder.

Entry Points We do not assume guidebooks will be read from beginning to end, but that people will dip into them. The traditional entry points are the list of contents and the index. In addition, however, some books have a complete list of maps and an index map illustrating map coverage.

There may also be a colour map that shows highlights. These highlights are dealt with in greater detail in the Facts for the Visitor chapter, along with planning questions and suggested itineraries. Each chapter covering a geographical region usually begins with a locator map and another list of highlights. Once you find something of interest in a list of highlights, turn to the index.

Maps Maps play a crucial role in Lonely Planet guidebooks and include a huge amount of information. A legend is printed on the back page. We seek to have complete consistency between maps and text, and to have every important place in the text captured on a map. Map key numbers usually start in the top left corner.

Although inclusion in a guidebook usually implies a recommendation we cannot list every good place. Exclusion does not necessarily imply criticism. In fact there are a number of reasons why we might exclude a place – sometimes it is simply inappropriate to encourage an influx of travellers.

Introduction

In its long and turbulent history, the diminutive island nation of Malta has often assumed an importance out of all proportion to its size. It has served as a stepping stone between Europe and Africa, a policeman of the central Mediterranean sea lanes, a guardian of imperial trade routes and a launching pad for invasions.

When Malta gained its independence in 1964 it was the first time since prehistory that the islands had been ruled by the native Maltese, and not by some outside power. Since early in the 1st millennium BC Malta has been occupied successively by Phoenicians, Carthaginians, Romans, Byzantines, Arabs, Normans, Sicilians, the Knights of St John, the French and the British, yet in all this time its people have managed to preserve a distinctive identity and a strong sense of continuity with the past. The *luzzu,* the traditional Maltese fishing boat, still carries the watchful 'Eye of Osiris' on its bow, a custom thought to date back more than 2500 years.

Malta has long been regarded as an inexpensive destination for a family beach holiday. The weather is excellent, the food and accommodation are good value and the sea is clean and warm. However, the coastline is mainly rocky, the few sandy beaches are often crowded, and some of the older resort areas are ugly and over-developed. New five-star hotels and marina complexes are being built as the government tries to push the tourist industry upmarket, and the overcrowded environment is increasingly under pressure.

But there is much to discover in Malta – and its sister islands Gozo and Comino – that will appeal to the independent traveller. Beyond the beaches and bars there lies a fascinating history, dramatic coastal scenery and excellent opportunities for snorkelling, scuba-diving and other watersports. And there's the added attraction of cheap charter flights, reasonably priced accommodation (especially in the low season), good food and warm winter weather.

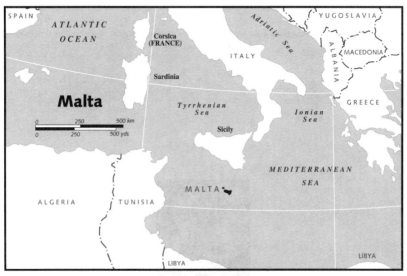

Malta's true highlights are not its beaches but the magnificent 16th-century fortified city of Valletta – 'history encased in golden stone' was how the novelist Nicholas Monsarrat described it – with its glorious harbour and bustling Mediterranean street life; the stone-built towns and villages with their idiosyncratic baroque churches and exuberant *festas*; the mysterious prehistoric temples and archaeological finds; the elegant, medieval fortress town of Mdina; and, if you want to get away from it all, the smaller and quieter island of Gozo with its quaint landscape of flat-topped hills and towering cliffs.

Facts about Malta

HISTORY

Malta has a fascinating history, and the island is crowded with physical and cultural reminders of the past. The fossilised bones of animals found in Ghar Dalam cave in the south-east suggest that Malta was once linked by a land bridge to Sicily and southern Europe. But Malta was not big enough to support a hunting-gathering lifestyle, and the earliest evidence of human habitation – the remains of primitive farming settlements – has been dated to the period 5200 to 4000 BC. Neolithic pottery fragments unearthed at Skorba are similar to those found in Sicily.

The Temple Builders

The Maltese Islands' oldest monuments are the beautifully preserved megalithic temples built between 3600 and 2500 BC, which are the oldest surviving freestanding structures in the world. About 1000 years before the construction of the Great Pyramid of Cheops in Egypt, the people of Malta were manipulating megaliths weighing up to 50 tonnes and creating elaborate buildings that appear to be oriented in relation to the winter solstice sunrise (see the boxed text 'Megalithic Temples' in the South-East Malta chapter).

No one knows whether the temple builders evolved out of the pre-existing farming communities of Malta, or whether they arrived from elsewhere bringing their architectural skills with them. Rock-cut tombs found on a hillside near Xemxija and dated to before 4000 BC display a 'trefoil' layout which may be a precursor to the three-lobed plan seen in the temples. The remains of around a dozen megalithic temples survive today, and some of them are remarkably well preserved.

Whatever their origins, the temple people seem to have worshipped a cult of fertility. Archaeologists have found large numbers of figurines and statues of wide-hipped, well-endowed female figures – the so-called 'fat ladies' of Malta – that have been interpreted as 'fertility goddesses'. These figures range in size from barely 10cm long to more than 1.5m.

The culmination of Malta's temple culture was the large temple complex at Tarxien and the subterranean burial chambers of the nearby Hypogeum (see the Valletta & Floriana chapter). These sites appear to have been abandoned sometime after 2500 BC, and then taken over by a noticeably different Bronze Age culture. The new inhabitants cremated their dead and used the Tarxien temple site as a cemetery. They also built dolmens like those seen at Ta'Ċenċ on Gozo.

Phoenicians & Romans

From around 800 to 218 BC, Malta was colonised by the Phoenicians and, for the last 250 years of this period, by Phoenicia's principal North African colony, Carthage. With their watchful eyes painted on the prow, the colourful Maltese fishing boats – the *luzzu* and the *kajjik* – seem little changed from the Phoenician trading vessels that once plied the Mediterranean. The islands may have served as a Carthaginian naval base during the First Punic War against Rome (264-241 BC).

During the Second Punic War (218-201 BC) Rome took control of Malta before finally crushing Carthage in the Third Punic War of 149-146 BC. The island was then given the status of a municipium, or free town, with the power to control its own affairs and to send an ambassador to Rome. However, there is evidence that Malta retained a Punic influence. The 1st-century BC historian Diodorus Siculus described the island as a Phoenician colony, and the biblical account of St Paul's shipwreck on Malta in AD 60 (see the boxed text 'St Paul in Malta' in the North-West Malta chapter) describes the islanders as 'barbarous' (ie, they did not speak the 'civilised' languages of Latin or Greek).

St Paul's shipwreck was certainly the most influential event of this period. According to tradition, during Paul's three-month stay both the Roman governor of Malta (later to become St Publius) and many of the islanders were converted to Christianity, making the Maltese one of the oldest Christian peoples in the world.

Malta seems to have prospered under Roman rule. The main town, called Melita, occupied the hilltop of Mdina but spread over an area around three times the size of the later medieval citadel. The excavated remains of townhouses, villas, farms and baths suggest that the inhabitants enjoyed a comfortable lifestyle, and occupied themselves with the production of olives, wheat, honey and grapes.

When the Roman Empire split into East and West in AD 395 Malta seems to have fallen under the sway of Constantinople. But very little is known of this period of Maltese history, when the islands seem to have been little more than a neglected Byzantine backwater.

Arabs & Normans

The rapid expansion of Islam in the 7th to 9th centuries saw an Arab empire extend from Spain to India. Arab armies invaded Sicily in 827 and finally conquered it in 878; Malta fell into Arab hands in 870. Both Malta and Sicily remained Muslim possessions until the end of the 11th century. The Arab rulers generally tolerated the Christian population, introduced irrigation and the cultivation of citrus fruits and cotton, and had a notable impact on Maltese customs and language. Apart from the names Malta and Gozo, which probably have Latin roots, there is not a single place name in the Maltese Islands that can be proved to pre-date the Arab occupation.

During the 11th century small groups of Norman adventurers from northern Europe arrived in Italy, formed allegiances with local leaders and set up a system of feudal lordships. One, Robert Guiscard, took over much of southern Italy and in 1060 his younger brother, Count Roger, captured Messina and used it as a base for the conquest of Sicily. It took 30 years of constant struggle, but by 1091 Count Roger had driven the Arabs out of Sicily. A year earlier, in 1090, he had captured Malta after a surprise attack. Tradition has it that, needing the support of the local people, Count Roger tore his red-and-white quartered banner in two and gave half to the Maltese contingent, thus inventing Malta's national flag.

For the next 400 years Malta's history was closely linked to Sicily's, and its rulers were a succession of Normans, Angevins (French), Aragonese and Castilians (Spanish). Malta remained a minor pawn on the edge of the European chessboard, and its relatively small population of downtrodden islanders paid their taxes by trading, slaving and piracy, and were repaid in kind by marauding Turks and Barbary corsairs. During this period a Maltese aristocracy began to form, and a few of their elegant townhouses survive in Mdina and Victoria. Their distinctive architectural style is referred to as Siculo-Norman (Sicilian-Norman), but it is almost entirely Sicilian – there is little if any Norman influence.

The marriage of the Catholic monarchs Ferdinand II of Aragon and Isabella of Castile led to the unification of Spain in 1479, and under their grandson, the Holy Roman Emperor Charles V, Malta became part of the vast Spanish Empire. One of the greatest threats to Charles' realm was the expanding Ottoman Empire of Suleyman the Magnificent in the east. Suleyman had driven the Knights of St John from their island stronghold of Rhodes in 1522-23. When the Knights begged Charles V to find them a new home, he offered them Malta along with the governorship of Tripoli, hoping that they might help to contain the Turkish naval forces in the eastern Mediterranean. The nominal rent was to be two falcons a year – one for the emperor and one for the viceroy of Sicily (see boxed text 'The Maltese Falcon' in the Gozo & Comino chapter).

The Knights Arrive

Grand Master Philippe Villiers de L'Isle Adam (1530-34) of the Knights of St John (see special section) was not particularly impressed by the gift of the Maltese Islands, which seemed to him barren, waterless and poorly defended. Neither were the 12,000 or so local inhabitants, who were given no say in the matter. Nor were the Sicilian aristocracy, who remained aloof in their palazzos in Mdina. However, determined to make the best of a bad job and hoping one day to return to Rhodes, in 1530 the Knights decided to settle in the fishing village of Birgu (now Vittoriosa) on the south side of the Grand Harbour and set about fortifying the harbour.

In Rhodes, the Knights had developed into a formidable marine fighting force and had been a constant thorn in the side of the Ottoman Turks. Their expulsion allowed Turkish corsairs to roam the central Mediterranean at will, raiding and pillaging and carrying off Christians to serve as slaves or to hold for ransom. Short of funds and lacking any real support from European powers, the Knights became pirates themselves, attacking Turkish trading ships and raiding along the Barbary Coast of North Africa.

Their greatest adversary was Dragut Reis, the Turkish admiral, who raided Gozo in 1551 and carried off almost the entire population of 5000 into slavery. Then in 1559 the Knights lost half their galleys in a disastrous attack on Dragut's lair on the island of Djerba off the Tunisian coast. With the power of the Knights at a low ebb, Suleyman the Magnificent saw an opportunity to polish off this troublesome crew once and for all, at the same time capturing Malta as a base for the invasion of Europe from the south.

The Great Siege of 1565

Jean Parisot de la Valette (1557-68; see boxed text 'The Founder of Valletta' in the Valletta & Floriana chapter) inherited the title of Grand Master in 1557. He was a stern disciplinarian and an experienced soldier who foresaw the threat of a Turkish siege and prepared for it well. Following the disaster of 1559, la Valette ordered the building of ditches and defensive walls around the peninsulas of Birgu and Isla.

Fort St Angelo on the tip of Birgu was rebuilt and strengthened, and Fort St Michael was built on Isla. A new fortress, Fort St Elmo, was constructed on the tip of the uninhabited Sceberras peninsula.

The Knights' galley fleet was taken into the creek below Birgu, and a great chain was stretched across the harbour entrance between Fort St Angelo and Fort St Michael to keep out enemy vessels. Food, water and arms were stockpiled, and la Valette sent urgent requests for aid to the emperor, the pope and the viceroy of Sicily. But no help came. In May 1565, when an enormous Ottoman fleet carrying more than 30,000 men arrived to lay siege to the island, la Valette was 70 years old, and commanded a force of only 700 knights and around 8000 Maltese irregulars and mercenary troops.

The Turkish force, led jointly by Admiral Piali and Mustafa Pasha, dropped anchor in the bay of Marsaxlokk, and its soldiers set up camp on the plain of Marsa. The entire population of Malta took refuge within the walls of Birgu, Isla and Mdina, taking their livestock with them and poisoning the wells and cisterns they left behind. The Turks took their time, digging out gun emplacements and setting up batteries, before beginning their campaign with an attack on Fort St Elmo, which guarded the entrance to both Grand and Marsamxett harbours. The fort was small and held a garrison of only 60 knights and a few hundred men. Mustafa Pasha was confident that it would fall in less than a week.

Dragut Reis, the wily old corsair who had always been the scourge of the Mediterranean sea lanes, was now, like la Valette, an old man. The 80-year-old ex-pirate was in the employ of Sultan Suleyman and arrived in Malta a few weeks into the siege to advise Mustafa and Piali. He was unhappy with their decision to concentrate first on the taking of St Elmo, but preparations were too far advanced to change plans. Dragut tirelessly went around the Turkish positions, inspiring his men and helping to set up batteries on Dragut Point and Ricasoli Point to increase the pressure on the tiny garrison. It was while setting up one such battery on Mt Sceberras that he was struck in the head by a splinter of rock thrown up by an enemy cannonball and retired, mortally wounded, to his tent.

Dragut's fears over the wisdom of besieging St Elmo were proved right. Despite continuous bombardment and repeated mass assaults on its walls, Fort St Elmo held out for over four weeks, and cost the lives of no less than 8000 Turkish soldiers before it was finally taken; not one of the Christian defenders survived. On receiving the news that the fort had been captured, old Dragut smiled, and died. Looking across at the looming bulk of Fort St Angelo from the smoke and rubble of St Elmo, Mustafa Pasha is said to have muttered, 'Allah! If so small a son has cost us so dear, what price shall we have to pay for so large a father?'

Hoping to intimidate the already demoralised defenders of Fort St Angelo, Mustafa Pasha ordered that several of the leading Knights should be beheaded and their heads fixed on stakes looking across towards Birgu. The Turks then nailed the decapitated bodies to makeshift wooden crucifixes and sent them floating across the harbour towards St Angelo. La Valette's response was immediate and equally cruel. All Turkish prisoners were executed and decapitated. The Knights then used their heads as cannonballs and fired them back across the harbour to St Elmo.

Then began the final Turkish assault on the strongholds of Birgu and Isla. Piali's fleet moved from Marsaxlokk to Marsamxett harbour to unload heavy artillery, and several ships were dragged across the neck of the Sceberras peninsula – the entrance to Grand Harbour was still commanded by the guns of Fort St Angelo – to aid the ground forces with fire from the sea. Through the heat of summer, the Turks launched no less than 10 massed assaults on the walls of Birgu and Isla, but each time they were beaten back. On 18 August, when a large section of wall was brought down and it looked as if the Turkish troops were on the verge of fighting their way into the town, Grand Master la Valette himself joined his Knights in the breach. The day was saved.

Turkish morale was drained by the long, hot summer, their increasing casualties, and the impending possibility of having to spend the entire winter on Malta (the Mediterranean sailing season traditionally ended with the storms of late September). The ferocity of their attacks decreased. Then on 7 September the long-promised relief force from Sicily finally arrived. Twenty-eight ships carrying some 8000 men landed at Mellieħa Bay and took command of the high ground around Naxxar as the Turks scrambled to embark their troops and guns at Marsamxett.

Seeing the unexpectedly small size of the relief force, Mustafa Pasha ordered some of his troops to land again at St Paul's Bay, while the rest marched towards Naxxar from Marsamxett. But the tired and demoralised Turkish soldiers were in no mood to fight these fresh and ferocious knights and men-at-arms, and they turned and ran for the galleys now anchored in St Paul's Bay. Thousands were hacked to pieces in the shallow waters of the bay as they tried to escape. That night the banner of the Order of St John flew once again over the battered ruins of St Elmo, and in their churches the knights and the people of Malta gave thanks for the end of the siege.

The part played in the Great Siege by the ordinary people of Malta is often overlooked, but their courage and resilience was a deciding factor in the Turkish defeat. The defence force was made up of some 5000 or 6000 Maltese soldiers, and local women and children contributed by repairing walls, bringing food and ammunition to the soldiers, and tending the wounded. Although their names do not appear in the official accounts, local heroes like Toni Bajada – who has streets named after him in Valletta, St Paul's Bay and Naxxar – live on in Maltese legend. The date of the end of the siege, 8 September, is still celebrated in Malta as the Victory Day public holiday.

After the Siege

The Knights of Malta, previously neglected, were now hailed as the saviours of Europe. Money and honours were heaped on them by grateful monarchs, and the construction of the new city of Valletta – named after the hero of the siege – and its enormous fortifications began. Although sporadic raids continued, Malta was never again seriously threatened by the Turks. Suleyman the Magnificent died in 1566, and much of the Turkish fleet was destroyed by a magazine explosion in the Istanbul dockyards. What remained of Ottoman naval power was crushed at the Battle of Lepanto in 1571, a victory in which the galleys of the Order of St John played an important (and enthusiastic) part.

The period following the Great Siege was one of building – not only of massive new fortifications and watchtowers, but of churches and palaces and auberges. The military engineer Francesco Laparelli was sent to Malta by the Pope to design the new defences of Valletta, and Italian artists arrived to decorate its churches, chapels and palazzos. An influx of new knights, eager to join the now prestigious Order, swelled the coffers of the treasury.

The pious Grand Master Jean de la Cassière (1572-81) oversaw the construction of the Sacra Infermeria – the Order's new hospital – and the magnificent new Cathedral of St John, which replaced the old Conventual Church of St Lawrence in Birgu (renamed Vittoriosa, or Victorious, after the siege). His successor Hugues Loubeux de Verdalle (1581-95) was more inclined to enjoy the privileges rather than the responsibilities of power, and built himself the grandiose Verdala Palace near Rabat (see the Central Malta chapter).

Alof de Wignacourt (1601-22) initiated many worthy projects, including the construction of an aqueduct to bring water to Valletta from the hills near Mdina. In contrast, the decadent Antoine de Paule (1623-36) built the San Anton Palace as a summer retreat for hedonistic parties, an unchivalrous tendency which was to increase in the ensuing century. Grand Master Antonio Manoel de Vilhena (1722-36) adorned Malta with many magnificent buildings, including the Manoel Theatre, Fort Manoel and the Palazzo Vilhena (in Mdina), but the

long reign of the haughty Emanuel Pinto de Fonseca (1741-73), who considered himself on a level with the crowned heads of Europe, epitomised the change that had come over the Order. One glance at the portrait of Pinto in the Museum of St John's Co-Cathedral in Valletta will reveal how far the Order had strayed from its vows of poverty, chastity and obedience.

With the Turkish threat removed, the Knights occupied themselves less with militarism and monasticism, and more with piracy, commerce, drinking and duelling. Although the Order continued to embellish Valletta, the Knights sank into corrupt and ostentatious ways.

Napoleon in Malta

In the aftermath of the French Revolution, Grand Master Emmanuel de Rohan (1775-97) provided money for Louis XVI's doomed attempt to escape from Paris. By the late 18th century around three-quarters of the Order's income came from the knights of the French langue, so when the revolutionary authorities confiscated all of the Order's properties and estates in France, the Order was left in dire financial straits.

In 1798 Napoleon Bonaparte arrived in Malta aboard his flagship *L'Orient* at the head of the French Navy, on his way to Egypt to counter the British influence in the Mediterranean. He demanded that he be allowed to water his ships, but the knights refused. The French landed and captured the island with hardly a fight – many of the knights were in league with the French, and the Maltese were in no mood for a battle. On 11 June 1798 the Order surrendered to Napoleon – although the French knights were allowed to remain, the German Grand Master Ferdinand von Hompesch (1797-98) and the rest of the Order were given three days to gather what belongings they could and leave.

Napoleon stayed on in Malta for only six days (in the Palazzo de Parisio in Valletta), but when he left *L'Orient* was weighed down with silver, gold, paintings and tapestries looted from the Order's churches, auberges and infirmary. (Most of this treasure went to the bottom of the sea a few months later when the British Navy under Admiral Nelson destroyed the French fleet at the Battle of the Nile.) The French also abolished the Maltese aristocracy, defaced coats of arms, desecrated churches and closed down monasteries.

Napoleon left behind a garrison of 4000 men, but they were taken unawares by a spontaneous uprising of the Maltese people (see boxed text 'The Mdina Uprising' in the Central Malta chapter) and had to retreat within the walls of Valletta. A Maltese deputation sought help from the British, and a naval blockade was enforced under the command of Captain Alexander Ball, who was sympathetic to the islanders' aspirations. The French garrison finally capitulated in September 1800, but having taken Malta the British government were unsure what to do with it.

The Treaty of Amiens (March 1802) provided for the return of Malta to the Order of St John (then taking refuge in Russia and Naples), but the Maltese did not want them back and sent a delegation to London to petition the British to stay. Their pleas fell on deaf ears, and arrangements had been made for the return of the Knights when war between Britain and France broke out again in May 1803. Faced with the blockade of European ports against British trade, the British government soon changed its mind regarding the potential usefulness of Malta. Even Admiral Nelson, who had previously dismissed the islands, wrote: 'I now declare that I consider Malta as a most important outwork ... I hope we shall never give it up'.

While the latter stages of the Napoleonic Wars wore on, Malta rapidly became a prosperous entrepot, and with the Treaty of Paris in 1814 it was formally recognised as a Crown Colony of the British Empire, with Lieutenant-General Sir Thomas Maitland as its first governor and commander-in-chief.

Crown Colony

The end of the Napoleonic Wars brought an economic slump to Malta as trade fell off and little was done in the way of investment in the island. But its fortunes revived during the Crimean War (1853-56) when it was developed by the Royal Navy as a major naval base and supply station, and with the opening of the Suez Canal in 1869 Malta became one of the chief coaling ports on the imperial steamship route between Britain and India.

The early 19th century also saw the beginnings of Maltese political development. In 1835 a Council of Government made up of prominent local citizens was appointed to advise the governor, and a free press was established. The constitution of 1849 allowed for eight elected representatives to partake in the government of Malta, but it was not until 1887 that the elected members constituted a majority.

In the second half of the 19th century vast sums were spent on improving Malta's defences and dockyard facilities as the island became a linchpin in the imperial chain of command. The Victoria Lines (see boxed text in the North-West Malta chapter) and several large dry docks were built during this period. Commercial facilities were also improved to cater for the busy trade route to India and the Far East. In 1883 a railway was built between Valletta and Mdina (it was closed down in 1931). Between 1800 and 1900 the population of Malta doubled to 200,000.

During WWI Malta served as a military hospital – it was known as the 'Nurse of the Mediterranean' – providing 25,000 beds for casualties from the disastrous Gallipoli campaign in Turkey. But prices and taxes rose during the war and the economy slumped. During protest riots in 1919 four Maltese citizens were shot dead by panicking British soldiers and several more were injured.

The British government replied to the unrest by giving the Maltese a greater say in the running of Malta. The 1921 constitution created a diarchic system of government, with a Maltese assembly presiding over local affairs, and a British imperial government controlling foreign policy and defence. The 1921 elections saw Joseph Howard of the Unione Politica (which later merged to become the Nationalist Party) take his place as the first prime minister of Malta.

[continued on page 21]

Knights of St John

Knights of St John

JULIET COOMBE

NEIL WILSON

NEIL WILSON

Origins

The Sovereign and Military Order of the Knights Hospitaller of St John of Jerusalem – also known variously as the Knights of St John, the Knights of Rhodes, the Knights of Malta, and the Knights Hospitallers – had its origins in the Christian Crusades of the 11th and 12th centuries.

A hospital and guesthouse for poor pilgrims in Jerusalem was founded by some Italian merchants from Amalfi in 1070. The hospital, operated by monks who followed the Augustinian rule, won the protection of the papacy in 1113 and was raised to the status of an independent religious order known as the Hospitallers. The Order set up more hospitals along the pilgrimage route from Italy to the Holy Land, and knights who had been healed of their wounds showed their gratitude by granting funds and property to the growing Order.

Other knights offered their services as soldiers to provide protection for pilgrims, and thus the Order's dual role of healing the sick and waging war on the enemies of Christ began to evolve. Knights of the Order kept the road to Jerusalem free of bandits. To kill an infidel was to win glory for Christ, and to die in battle in defence of the faith was to become a martyr in heaven.

When the armies of Islam recaptured the Holy Land in 1291, the Order sought refuge first in the Kingdom of Cyprus. In 1309 they acquired the island of Rhodes, planning to stay close to the Middle East in the hope of reconquering Jerusalem. But here they remained for over 200 years, building fortresses, auberges and a hospital, and evolving from a land-based army into the most formidable naval fighting force the medieval world had ever seen.

Organisation

The Knights of St John were European noblemen who lived the lives of monks and soldiers. The objective of the Order was 'the service of the poor, and the defence of the Catholic faith'. The Order was financed by the revenue of properties and estates spread throughout Europe, which were either owned by members of the Order, or had been gifted to it.

There were three basic divisions within the Order. The Military Knights were the elite of the Order, and formed the core of its military fighting force. They were drawn from the younger male members of Europe's aristocratic families – in other words, those who were not the principal heirs – and had to prove noble descent. After a year as a Novice, a knight then spent three years in the galleys and two years in service in the Convent (the name given to the Knights' headquarters) before becoming eligible for higher ranks.

The Chaplains did not need to prove noble descent, and were more monk than soldier, though they were still expected to serve in the galleys and to fight in times of need. Their main duties were in the hospital and in the Order's churches and chapels. Sergeants-at-Arms were likewise not restricted by birth, and served mainly as soldiers and nurses. The Order was ruled over by the Supreme Council, headed by the Grand Master, who was elected by his peers from among the highest ranks of the Knights of Justice.

The Knights' traditional attire was a hooded monk's habit, made of black camel-hair with a white Maltese cross emblazoned on the breast. The distinctive eight-pointed cross is thought to have evolved from the symbol of the Italian city of Amalfi. It did not assume its present form until the 16th century, when the eight points were said to represent the eight virtues which the Knights strove to uphold: to live in truth; to have faith; to repent of sins; to give proof of humility; to love justice; to be merciful; to be sincere and whole-hearted; and to endure persecution.

The Order comprised eight nationalities or langues (literally 'tongues' or languages) – Italy, France, Provence, Auvergne, Castile, Aragon, Germany and England. (The English langue was dissolved by King Henry VIII in 1540 following his breach with the Roman Catholic Church.) Each langue was led by a *pilier* (literally 'pillar'), and its members lived and dined together in an *auberge* (hostel), which operated a bit like an Oxford college or an American fraternity house. Each langue was assigned to a particular task or part of the city walls during battle (hence the Poste de France, the Poste d'Aragon, etc, on the walls of Vittoriosa), and each pilier had a specific duty – for example, the pilier of the Italian langue was always the admiral of the galley fleet.

The Order's properties and estates in Europe were managed by a network of commanderies and priories, often headed by older Knights who had retired from active service in the Mediterranean. Although the Knights were bound by vows of individual poverty, the Order as a whole was immensely wealthy. A Knight was required to bequeath four-fifths of his personal wealth to the Order; the remaining fifth – known as the *quint* – could be disposed of as he chose.

Hospitals

The hospitals created by the Order – first in Jerusalem and the Holy Land, then in Rhodes and finally in Malta – were often at the leading edge of the development of medical and nursing science. Ironically, although the Knights had sworn to bring death and destruction to the 'infidel' Muslims, many of their medical skills and treatments were gleaned from the study of Arabic medicine.

The Sacra Infermeria in Valletta (built in the 1570s) had 600 beds – the Great Ward alone could hold 350 patients – and was famous throughout Europe. It was obliged to provide care for the sick of any race or creed – slaves included – though non-Catholics were put in a separate ward. Patients were nursed by the members of the Order – even the Grand Master tended the sick at least once a week – and treated by physicians, surgeons and pharmacists. The hospital's plate and cutlery was made of solid silver – 'to increase the decorum of the Hospital and the cleanliness of the sick' – and basic rules of hygiene were observed.

The hospital was overseen by the Grand Hospitaller, a post traditionally filled by the pilier of the French langue. The Order's surgeons performed many advanced operations including trepanation, bladder stone removal and cataract removal as well as more commonplace amputations and wound treatments. From 1676 onwards the study of anatomy and human dissection was taken up.

After Malta

Following the loss of their French estates and their expulsion from Malta by Napoleon in 1798, the Knights sought refuge first in Russia, where they were welcomed by Tsar Paul I, and later in Italy. After several years of uncertainty, they finally made their headquarters in the Palazzo di Malta (the former Embassy of the Hospitallers) in Rome.

In the late 19th and 20th centuries the Order rebuilt itself as a religious and charitable organisation. Now known as the Sovereign Military Order of Malta, it is an internationally recognised sovereign entity that mints its own coins and prints its own postage stamps. In effect, it's a state without a territory, although its properties in Rome enjoy extra territorial status. It concerns itself largely with providing hospitals, medical supplies and humanitarian aid in regions stricken by poverty, war and natural disasters.

The Order now has diplomatic relations with 83 countries, has legations in several countries (including France, Germany, Belgium and Switzerland) and has been a permanent observer at the UN since 1994. The Order has an embassy in Malta (housed in the Cavalier of St John in Triq L-Ordinanza in Valletta), and since 1991 it has re-occupied its old home in the upper part of Fort St Angelo in Vittoriosa. Since 1988 the Grand Master has been Fra' Andrew Bertie, a Scot.

Further details of the Order's history and its present-day activities can be found on its official Web site at www.smominfo.org.

Right: Phillipe Villiers de L'Isle-Adam was Malta's first Grand Master.

Grand Masters of the Order in Malta 1530-1798

Year	Name	Nationality
1530-34	Phillipe Villiers de L'Isle-Adam	France
1534-35	Pietro del Ponte	Italy
1535-36	Didier de Saint-Jaille	France
1536-53	Juan de Homedes	Aragon
1553-57	Claude de la Sengle	France
1557-68	Jean Parisot de la Valette	Provence
1568-72	Pietro del Monte San Savino	Italy
1572-82	Jean l'Eveque de la Caissière	Auvergne
1582-95	Hugues Loubeux de Verdalle	Provence
1595-1601	Martino Garzes	Aragon
1601-22	Alof de Wignacourt	France
1622-23	Louis Mendez de Vasconcelos	Portugal
1623-36	Antoine de Paule	Provence
1636-57	Jean-Paul de Lascaris-Castellar	Provence
1657-60	Martin de Redin	Aragon
1660	Annet de Clermont-Gessan	Auvergne
1660-63	Rafael Cotoner	Aragon
1663-80	Nicolas Cotoner	Aragon
1680-90	Gregorio Carafa	Italy
1690-97	Adrien de Wignacourt	France
1697-1720	Ramon Perellos y Roccaful	Aragon
1720-22	Marco Antonio Zondadari	Italy
1722-36	Antonio Manoel de Vilhena	Portugal
1736-41	Ramon Despuig	Aragon
1741-73	Manuel Pinto de Fonseca	Castille, Leon, Portugal
1773-75	Francisco Ximenes de Texada	Aragon
1775-97	Emmanuel Marie de Rohan-Polduc	France
1797-98	Ferdinand von Hompesch	Germany

ANN JEFFREE

Left: For a nominal rent of two Maltese falcons a year, the Knights took control of Malta.

[continued from page 16]

The inter-war years were marked by economic depression and political turmoil (the constitution was revoked in 1930 and again in 1933) and by growing tensions with Italy. Emigration became an increasingly attractive option, and many Maltese moved to Britain, Canada, the USA and Australia, especially the latter. (Emigration to Canada and Australia increased after WWII, and today Australia has one of the largest Maltese communities in the world.)

In 1930s Malta, Italian was the language of law and of polite conversation among the upper classes – Malti was the everyday language of the common people, and an increasing number could also speak English. Mussolini made the ridiculous claim that Malti was merely a dialect of Italian, and that the Maltese Islands rightly belonged within his new Roman Empire. In 1934 Britain decreed that Malti would be the language of the law courts, and that henceforth Malti and English would be Malta's official languages.

Fortress Malta

The outbreak of WWII found Britain undecided as to the strategic importance of Malta. The army and air force felt that the islands could not be adequately defended against bombing attacks from Sicily and should be evacuated. However, Winston Churchill (then First Lord of the Admiralty) insisted that possession of Malta was vital to Britain's control of supply lines through the bottleneck of the central Mediterranean. As a result of this indecision Malta was unprepared when Mussolini entered the war on 10 June 1940. The very next day Italian bombers attacked Grand Harbour.

The only aircraft available on the islands on 11 June were three Gloster Gladiator biplanes – quickly nicknamed *Faith*, *Hope* and *Charity* – whose pilots fought with such skill and tenacity that Italian pilots estimated the strength of the Maltese squadron to be in the region of 25 aircraft! (What remains of *Faith* can be seen in Malta's National War Museum, described in the Valletta & Floriana chapter.) The Gladiators battled on alone for three weeks before squadrons of modern Hurricane fighters arrived to bolster the islands' air defences.

Malta effectively became a fortified aircraft carrier, a base for bombing attacks on enemy shipping and harbours in Sicily and North Africa. It also harboured submarines which preyed on Italian and German supply ships. These operations played a vital part in reducing the supplies of fuel and materiel to the Panzer divisions of Rommel's Afrika Korps, which were then sweeping eastwards through Libya towards British-held

The British Legacy

For 150 years, from 1814 to 1964, Malta was part of the British Empire. The legacy of British rule takes many forms, most noticeably the fact that almost everyone speaks English as well as Malti. But there are many others – the Maltese drive on the left, and many of the vehicles on the road are vintage British models from the 1950s, '60s and '70s; the local football teams have typically British names like United, Hotspur, Wanderers and Rovers; cafes serve sausage, egg and chips and pots of tea; and beer is sold in pints and half-pints. Traditional items of British street furniture – red telephone boxes, red pillar boxes, and blue lamps outside police stations – persist in Malta, though they have largely disappeared from British towns. And conversations in Malti are liberally sprinkled with the English expression 'Awright?'

NEIL WILSON

Egypt. Malta's importance was clear to Hitler too, and crack squadrons of Stuka dive-bombers were stationed in Sicily with the objective of pounding the island into submission.

Malta's greatest ordeal came in 1942, when the island came close to starvation and surrender. It suffered 154 days and nights of continuous bombing – in April alone some 6700 tonnes of bombs were dropped on Grand Harbour and the surrounding area. By comparison, at the height of London's Blitz there were 57 days of continuous bombing. On 15 April 1942 King George VI awarded the George Cross – Britain's highest award for civilian bravery – to the entire population of Malta. The citation from the king read: 'To honour her brave people I award the George Cross to the island fortress of Malta to bear witness to a heroism and devotion that will long be famous in history'.

Just as Malta's importance to the Allies lay in disrupting enemy supply lines, so its major weakness was the difficulty of getting supplies to the island. At the height of the siege in the summer of 1942 the governor made an inventory of remaining food and fuel and informed London that if more supplies did not get through before the end of August then Malta would be forced to surrender. A massive relief convoy, known as Operation Pedestal and consisting of 14 supply ships escorted by three aircraft carriers, two battleships, seven cruisers and 24 destroyers, was despatched to run the gauntlet of enemy bombers and submarines. It suffered massive attacks, and only five supply ships made it into Grand Harbour – the crippled oil tanker *Ohio,* with its precious cargo of fuel, limped in lashed between two warships on 15 August. This date, the Feast of the Assumption of the Virgin Mary, led to the Maltese christening the relief ships 'The Santa Marija Convoy'.

In the words of Winston Churchill, 'Revictualled and replenished with ammunition and essential stores, the strength of Malta revived', and it was able to continue its vital task of disrupting enemy supply lines. The aircraft and submarines based in Malta succeeded in destroying or damaging German convoys to North Africa to the extent that Rommel's Afrika Korps was low on fuel and ammunition during the crucial Battle of El Alamein in October 1942, a situation that contributed to a famous Allied victory and the beginning of the end of the German presence in North Africa.

In July 1943 Malta served as the operational headquarters and air support base for Operation Husky, the Allied invasion of Sicily. By coincidence, the date on which the Italian Navy finally surrendered to the Allies – 8 September – was the same as that on which the Great Siege had ended 378 years previously. As the captured enemy warships gathered in Marsaxlokk Bay, Admiral Cunningham, Commander-in-Chief of Britain's Mediterranean Fleet, cabled the Admiralty in London: 'Be pleased to inform their Lordships that the Italian battle fleet now lies at anchor under the guns of the fortress of Malta'.

Independent Republic

After 1943 Malta's role in the war rapidly diminished. WWII left the islands with 40,000 homes destroyed and the population on the brink of starvation. In 1947 the wartorn island was given a measure of self-government, and a £30 million war-damage fund to help rebuilding and restoration. But the economic slump that followed Britain's reductions in defence spending and the loss of jobs in the naval dockyard led to calls either for closer integration with Britain, or for Malta to go it alone. On 21 September 1964, with Prime Minister Dr George Borg Olivier at the helm, Malta gained its independence. It remained within the British Commonwealth, with Queen Elizabeth as the head of state represented in Malta by a Governor-General.

Borg Olivier's successor as prime minister in 1971 was the Labour Party's Dominic (Dom) Mintoff, whose name was rarely out of the news headlines in the 1970s. Mintoff was a fiery and controversial politician who was not afraid to speak his mind. During his prime ministership (1971-84) Malta became a republic (in 1974, replacing the

Queen as head of state with a president appointed by parliament). In 1979 links with Britain were reduced further when Mintoff expelled the British armed services and signed agreements with Libya, the Soviet Union and North Korea.

In 1987 the Nationalist Party assumed power under the prime ministership of Dr Eddie Fenech Adami, and won a second term with a landslide victory in 1992, when one of the party's main platforms was Malta's application to join the EC. However, the 1996 general election saw the Labour Party, led by Dr Alfred Sant, narrowly regain power with a one-seat majority. One of its main policies was to suspend the country's application for full EC membership. However, in 1998, during a debate on development of the Cottonera waterfront into a marina for private yachts, Dom Mintoff, then 82 years old but still capable of causing controversy, crossed the floor of the house to vote with the Opposition. A snap general election in September 1998 was effectively a vote of confidence in the Labour government. Labour lost, and Fenech Adami's Nationalist Party was returned to power. The future of the Cottonera remains uncertain, but Malta's EC application is now back on track.

GEOGRAPHY

The Maltese Islands cover a total area of only 316 sq km – less than the Isle of Wight in the UK or Martha's Vineyard in the USA. There are three inhabited islands – Malta, Gozo and Comino – and two small uninhabited islets, Cominotto and Filfla. They lie in the central Mediterranean Sea, 93km south of Sicily, 290km east of Tunisia and 290km north of Libya.

The highest point in the Maltese Islands is Ta'Żuta (253m) on the south-west coast of Malta. This high plateau is bounded on the south-west by sea-cliffs, and drops away gradually towards rolling plains in the south and east. North-western Malta is characterised by a series of flat-topped north-east and south-west ridges – the Victoria Lines escarpment, the Wardija Ridge, the Bajda Ridge, the Mellieħa Ridge and the Marfa Ridge – separated by broad valleys. The landscape of Gozo consists of flat-topped hills and terraced hillsides, with high sea-cliffs in the south and west. The highest point is Ta'Dbieġi (190m) to the south of Għarb.

The soil is generally thin and rocky, although some valleys are terraced and farmed intensively. There are few trees and, for most of the year, little greenery to soften the stony, sun-bleached landscape. The only notable exception is Buskett Gardens, a lush valley of pine trees and orange groves protected by the imposing Dingli sea-cliffs of the south coast. There is virtually no surface water and there are no permanent creeks or rivers. The water table is the main source of fresh water, but it is supplemented by several large desalination plants.

GEOLOGY

Geologically speaking, the Maltese Islands are lumps of the Mediterranean sea-bed which have been warped upward until they are poking above sea level. The warping was caused by the collision between the African tectonic plate to the south and the European plate to the north. This collision is ongoing and is also responsible for the volcanoes of Etna and Vesuvius, and for the earthquakes which occasionally strike southern Italy and Malta (see boxed text 'The 1693 Earthquake' in the Gozo & Comino chapter).

The rocks that make up Malta are between seven million and 30 million years old, and are layered one on top of the other. From the bottom up, there are four main layers – the Lower Coralline Limestone, the Globigerina Limestone, the Blue Clay, and the Upper Coralline Limestone. The limestones are rich in fossils, especially at the junction between the Lower Coralline Limestone and the Globigerina Limestone, where there is a huge concentration of fossil scallop shells and sand dollars (flat, disc-shaped relatives of sea urchins).

The Upper and Lower Coralline Limestones are hard and resistant to weathering, and form the great sea-cliffs of south-west Malta and Ta'Ċenċ, and the crags that ring the flat tops of Gozo's hills. The golden-coloured Globigerina Limestone is softer, and underlies much of central and eastern Malta. The sticky Blue Clay is rich in nutrients, and is responsible for the more fertile soils of Gozo – you can see it in the cliffs west of ir-Ramla.

Local quarrymen refer to the easily worked Globigerina Limestone as *franka;* the harder-wearing coralline limestones are called *zonqor.* Both were widely used in the building of the islands' massive fortifications.

CLIMATE

Malta has a typically Mediterranean climate, with mild winters and hot, dry summers. The total annual rainfall is low, at around 580mm, and it falls mainly between October and February. Very little, if any, rain falls in mid-summer when daytime temperatures can reach more than 35°C – uncomfortably hot. Winters are not at all unpleasant, with an average of six hours of sunshine daily in January and daytime temperatures around 15°C.

Winds are a feature of Malta's weather (see boxed text 'The Maltese Compass' in the South-East Malta chapter). The stiff sea breeze is cooling in summer, but in winter the north-easterly *grigal* can whip up the waves that pound across the harbour walls and occasionally disrupt the ferry service to Gozo. In spring and autumn the south-easterly *xlokk* (scirocco) sometimes blows in from North Africa, bringing humid and occasionally foggy conditions.

Sea temperatures around the islands range from 14.5°C in mid-winter, to a balmy 25°C in August and September.

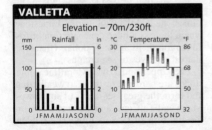

ECOLOGY & ENVIRONMENT

The combined pressures of population, land use and development, as well as pollution and the lack of protection of natural areas, have had a significant environmental impact on the islands. There is only one waste treatment plant in Malta, and the majority of the island's sewage is discharged raw into the sea. There is also a severe shortage of fresh water – the only natural supply comes from ground water, which is increasingly contaminated with nitrate runoff from farmland. This has been eased slightly by the construction of several large desalination plants.

Air pollution is caused by the high concentration of cars, lorries and buses – many of them old – in the congested roads around Grand Harbour, and by discharges from coal-fired power stations and factories. With such a small land area, disposal of rubbish in landfill sites is also increasingly problematic. In 1991 the Maltese government passed an Environmental Protection Act which designated development zones and identified areas of ecological importance, but many difficult problems lie ahead.

FLORA & FAUNA

Malta has little in the way of natural vegetation. Much of the island is cultivated, and where it is not the land is often bare and rocky. The only extensive area of woodland is at Buskett Gardens (see the Central Malta chapter), which is dominated by Aleppo pines. The rough limestone slopes of the hill-tops and sea-cliffs support a typical Mediterranean flora of stunted olive, oleander and tamarisk trees, with growths of thyme, euphorbia, rosemary and brambles. Samphire, sea campion, spurge and saltwort can be found on the rocks beside the sea, and the rare parasitic plant *Cynomorium coccineus* is found at Dwejra on Gozo (see boxed text 'Fungus Rock' in the Gozo & Comino chapter).

The sparse vegetation supports very little in the way of land-based wildlife – just a handful of rats, mice, hedgehogs, weasels and shrews. Rabbits have been hunted almost to extinction. Geckoes and lizards are

Malta's Marine Life

Malta's location in the narrows between Sicily and North Africa, far away from the pollution of major cities and silt-bearing rivers, means that its marine life is richer than in many other parts of the Med.

Loggerhead Turtle

Invertebrates such as brightly coloured bryozoans, cup corals, sea anemones, sponges, starfish and sea urchins encrust the underwater cliffs and caves around the shores of Malta and Gozo. The countless nooks and crannies in the limestone provide shelter for crabs, lobsters, common octopus *(Octopus vulgaris)* and white-spotted octopus *(O. macropus)*. By night, cuttlefish *(Sepia officinalis)* graze the algal beds below the cliffs.

Most divers who visit Malta hope to catch sight of a seahorse. The maned seahorse *(Hippocampus ramulosus)* is fairly common around the Maltese coast, preferring shallow, brackish water. They grow up to 15cm in length, and feed on plankton and tiny shrimps. They mate for life, and display an unusual inversion of common male and female reproductive roles. Using her tube-like ovipositor, the female deposits her eggs in a brood pouch in the male's abdomen where they are fertilised. Here the eggs develop and finally hatch before the male 'gives birth' by releasing the live brood into open water.

Migratory shoals of sardine, sprat, bluefin tuna, bonito, mackerel and dolphin fish *(Coryphaena hippurus)* – known in Malti as *lampuka,* and a local delicacy – pass through the offshore waters in late summer and autumn. Swordfish *(Xiphias gladias)* are fairly common all year round. Sea bream, sea bass, groper, red mullet, wrasse, dogfish and stingray frequent the shallower waters closer to shore, where moray and conger eels hide among the rocks and venture out at night to feed on octopus and fish.

The seas around Malta are known among shark-watchers as one of the 'sharkiest' spots in the Med. In April 1987 a great white shark *(Carcharodon carcharias)* measuring around 5.3m in length was caught by local fisherman Alfredo Cutajar off Filfla. It was claimed to be a world record at 7.13m in overall length, but later investigations brought the accuracy of the original measurements into doubt. Photographs of the shark – including some of Alfredo with his head in the (dead!) shark's mouth – can be bought in souvenir shops at Wied iż-Żurrieq.

Other shark species known to haunt Maltese waters include the blue, thresher and mako. However, bathers and divers should not be unduly alarmed. Shark sightings in inshore waters are extremely rare. Indeed, the great white is considered to be an endangered species, and the decrease in its numbers is thought to have resulted from dwindling stocks of tuna, their main food source.

The loggerhead turtle *(Caretta caretta)* is another endangered species that is occasionally sighted in Maltese waters, but the lack of secluded sandy beaches means that they do not nest in the Maltese Islands. The common dolphin *(Delphinus delfis)* – known as *denfil* in Malti – and the bottlenose dolphin *(Tursiops truncatus)* are fairly common in Maltese waters, and are occasionally seen from cruise boats and dive boats.

The marine life of the Maltese Islands is under increasing pressure from divers, fishermen and pollution, but as yet there are no marine conservation areas. Marine Life Care Group Malta (☎ 373611, fax 341595, ✉ mlcg@waldonet.net.mt) is a non-profit organisation dedicated to preserving the marine environment. Check the Web site at www.waldonet.net.mt/mlcg for more information.

fairly common – the dark green and red lizard *Lacerta filfolensis* is found only on the islet of Filfla – and there are three species of snake, none of them poisonous.

There are barely a dozen resident bird species, including sparrows, rock doves, linnets, corn buntings, herring gulls and the blue rock thrush – Malta's national bird, which appears on the 25c coin – but more than 150 species have been recorded as migrants and winter visitors.

The seas around Malta and Gozo are clean and clear, and support a rich and diverse marine fauna which attracts scuba-divers from all over Europe.

GOVERNMENT & POLITICS

Malta is an independent, nonaligned, democratic republic. The single-chamber House of Representatives has 65 members, elected by proportional representation using the single transferable vote system. Executive power lies with the prime minister and the cabinet, the latter chosen from the majority party in the House of Representatives, which sits in the Great Hall of the Knights in the Grand Master's Palace in Valletta.

The president is the head of state and is elected by the House of Representatives for a five-year period. The president has executive authority but must act on the cabinet's advice and the position is therefore largely ceremonial. The current president of Malta, inaugurated in 1999, is Professor Guido de Marco. The prime minister and the leader of the opposition are both appointed by the president. The cabinet is appointed by the president on the prime minister's advice. All appointees must be members of parliament.

There are two major political parties: the socialism-inclined Partit Tal-Ħaddiema, or Malta Labour Party (MLP), and the more economically liberal Partit Nazzjonalista, or Nationalist Party (PN). In the parliamentary elections of 1998 the Nationalist Party took 51.81% of the vote and gained 35 seats, while the Labour Party got 48.97% of the vote and 30 seats. The Nationalist leader Dr Eddie Fenech-Adami is the current prime minister of Malta. The next parliamentary elections must be held by 2003.

Malta is a member of the UN, the Commonwealth, the Council of Europe and the Organisation for Security and Co-operation in Europe. Political debate rages over Malta's application to join the EC, made in 1990 by PN leader Eddie Fenech-Adami, but withdrawn by Prime Minister Alfred Sant during the short-lived MLP government of 1996-98. The bid was renewed following the PN's re-election in September 1998, and Malta is currently among the leading group of applicants.

ECONOMY

The Maltese enjoy a good standard of living, low inflation (around 2% to 3%) and low unemployment (around 5%). The government's economic strategy is to concentrate on the development of the tourism industry, manufacturing, and financial services.

Tourism in particular is rapidly growing in importance. From a total of 20,000 visitors a year in 1960, the islands now attract around 1.2 million visitors a year, mostly from Britain, Germany and Italy. Tourism accounts for around 40% of Malta's national earnings and employs in the region of 30,000 people. The current strategy is to drive Malta's tourist industry upmarket, away from the old-fashioned cheap-n-cheerful package holiday image, and to develop niche markets such as conference travel, cultural and educational tours, and cruise liners. This tendency is epitomised by the new Portomaso apartment and marina complex near Paċeville, and the controversial plan to develop the old Cottonera waterfront in Vittoriosa as a marina for 'superyachts'.

Manufacturing of high quality goods is the other main sector of Malta's economy, particularly electronics, clothing, footwear and textiles. The state-owned Malta Drydocks and Malta Shipbuilding yards employ around 6000 workers, and the Malta Freeport Container Terminal in Marsaxlokk Bay, opened in 1991, has made Malta a major transshipment and distribution centre for the Mediterranean. The government is also introducing measures to develop Malta as an international financial centre. Despite all these positive trends, there's still a sizable budget deficit to be dealt with.

Malta is one of the world's largest flag nations in shipping, with more than 3000 vessels taking advantage of Malta's cheaper registration fees and less rigid inspection procedures. However, Maltese-registered ships had the world's worst safety record for the year 1998-99 with six serious maritime accidents, including the tanker *Erika* which broke up in heavy seas off the French coast in December 1999, spilling 10,000 tonnes of fuel oil into the sea.

POPULATION & PEOPLE

Malta's population is around 378,000, with most people living in the satellite towns around Valletta, Sliema and the Grand Harbour. Of the total, 29,000 live on Gozo, while Comino has a mere handful of farmers, six or seven in winter, and a couple of hundred tourists in summer. Around 85% of the population live in urban areas, and only 15% in rural. More than 95% of the population is Maltese-born.

Malta is one of the most densely populated countries in the world, with an average population density of 1200 persons per square kilometre. The comparable figure for the Netherlands is around 430.

EDUCATION

Schooling is compulsory between the ages of five and 16, and is provided free in state and church schools (church schools are subsidised by the government). Primary education covers the five to 12 age group; after two years in secondary school, some pupils go on to trade schools or craft centres, others to senior secondary, leading to sixth form or technical college. Despite spending more on education than it does on health, Malta has an illiteracy rate of 10%.

The University of Malta, founded as a Jesuit college in 1592, is the oldest university in the Commonwealth outside the UK. A university education is free to Maltese citizens, and students receive an annual stipend. Courses on offer include medicine, law, architecture, engineering, education, arts and sciences, theology and diplomatic

studies, and in 1997 there were 7500 students enrolled. Other educational institutions include a Nursing School, a School of Art and an Academy of Dramatic Art. The International Maritime Law Institute is based in Malta.

ARTS
Crafts

Malta is noted for its fine crafts – particularly its handmade lace, hand-woven fabrics and silver filigree. Lace-making probably arrived with the Knights in the 16th century. It was traditionally the role of village women – particularly on the island of Gozo – and, although the craft has developed into a healthy industry, it is still possible to find women sitting on their doorsteps making lace tablecloths.

The art of producing silver filigree was probably introduced to the island in the 17th century via Sicily, which was then strongly influenced by Spain. Malta's silversmiths still produce beautiful filigree by traditional methods, but in large quantities to meet tourist demand.

Other handicrafts include weaving, knitting and glass-blowing; the latter is an especially healthy small industry which produces glassware exported throughout the world.

Literature

Pietro Caxaro's *Cantilena*, an epic poem composed in the mid-15th century, is the earliest known literary work in the Maltese language, but Italian remained the language of literature in Malta until the late 19th century. Important writers of this period include Ġan Anton Vassallo (1817-67) and Gużè Muscat Azzopardi (1853-1927). *Inez Farruġ* by Anton Manwel Caruana (1838-1907), published in 1889, is considered to be the first literary novel written in Malti.

Probably the best known and best loved of Maltese writers is Carmelo Psaila (1871-1961). Under his pen name of Dun Karm he became Malta's national poet, movingly chronicling the island's sufferings in WWII. Anton Buttiġieġ (1912-1983) was another important poet, who captured the essence of

Edward de Bono

lateral thinking *n.* a way of solving problems by rejecting traditional methods and employing unorthodox and apparently illogical means

(Collins English Dictionary)

Type 'Edward de Bono' into an Internet search engine and you will retrieve a list of over 4300 Web pages. Do the same with 'lateral thinking' and the number is almost 10,000.

Dr Edward de Bono (b. 1933) is a world authority on cognitive science and the study of thinking and creativity. A pioneer in the teaching of creative thinking, he was born in Malta and educated at St Edward's College, Malta, and the University of Malta, where he qualified in medicine. He later gained an honours degree in psychology and physiology at Oxford University and holds post-graduate degrees from Oxford, Cambridge and Malta universities.

Inventor of the widely used technique of 'lateral thinking', Dr de Bono's principal achievement has been to remove the mystique from creativity, and to develop tools and methods for teaching, enhancing and using creative thinking. His book *The Mechanism of Mind*, published in 1969, took the novel viewpoint that the human brain was a self-organising information system and suggested that creativity was quite simply a necessary behaviour in any such system. The Nobel Prize-winning physicist Murray Gell-Mann praised the book as being 10 years ahead of its time in tackling the sub-ject of non-linear systems – a forerunner of chaos theory.

De Bono believes that the traditional emphasis on analysis, critical thinking and argument is im-portant, but not sufficient. He seeks to put an equal emphasis on constructive and creative think-ing, and to promulgate these techniques in educational and business settings around the world. To this end he has written 57 books – notably *Lateral Thinking, Po: Beyond Yes and No, Six Thinking Hats* and *I Am Right, You Are Wrong* – which have been translated into 34 languages, and pro-duced two television series as well as speaking and lecturing around the world. There is a De Bono Institute in Melbourne which serves as a world centre for creative thinking, and a De Bono Foun-dation in Dublin.

Dr de Bono's methods are taught and used in a vast range of environments, from primary school classrooms to the boardrooms of the world's biggest corporations. De Bono himself was invited to give the keynote address to Microsoft's first ever marketing meeting in Seattle.

In 1995 he was awarded the National Order of Merit by the president of Malta, the country's highest civilian award. In 1996 the International Astronomical Union named a planet Edebono in his honour. Edward de Bono now lives in Venice and runs international seminars on thinking, creativity and education.

❄❄

the Maltese landscape and man's relation with nature in his lyric poetry and tightly written vignettes.

Among modern writers, the playwright and novelist Francis Ebejer (1925-1993), who wrote in both Malti and English, stands out. His novels deal with the tensions be-tween tradition and modernity. A collection of short stories, *For Rozina A Husband,* is available in English. Oliver Friġġieri (b. 1947), Professor of Maltese at the Univer-sity of Malta, is Malta's best-known and most prolific living novelist.

Architecture

Malta's architectural heritage is dominated by two influences – the Knights of St John and the Roman Catholic Church. Together they created a distinctive variation of the baroque style of architecture that swept across Europe between the end of the 16th century and the 18th century.

The greatest Maltese architect of the 16th century was Gerolamo Cassar (1520-86). He was born in the fishing village of Birgu 10 years before the Knights of St John ar-rived from Rhodes, and worked as an assistant to Francesco Laparelli, the military engineer who designed the fortifications of Valletta. He studied architecture in Rome, and was responsible for the design of many of Malta's finest buildings including the Grand Master's Palace, the facade of St John's Co-Cathedral, and many of the Knights' auberges.

The prolific Tommaso Dingli (1591-1666) created many of Malta's parish churches. His masterpiece is the Church of Santa Marija in Attard, which was designed when he was still only 22 years of age. Lorenzo Gafa (1630-1704) designed many of the island's finest examples of Maltese baroque, including the cathedrals of Mdina and Gozo.

Other important architects working in the Maltese baroque style were Giovanni Barbara (Palazzo de Vilhena, Mdina, 1730), Giuseppe Bonnici (the Old Customs House, Valletta, 1747) and Domenico Cachia (the Auberge de Castile et Leon, Valletta, 1744).

Painting

As in architecture, Maltese art was much influenced by neighbouring Italy. Many Italian artists were invited to Malta (most famously Caravaggio – see the boxed text 'Caravaggio in Malta'), and most Maltese artists went to study in Italy.

The greatest Maltese painter of the 17th century was Mattia Preti (1613-99; see boxed text 'Il Cavalier Calabrese'), who painted the vault frescoes in St John's Co-Cathedral as well as many altarpieces for parish churches and for the cathedral at Mdina. Although he was born in Calabria in Italy, he lived and worked in Malta for 30 years. Some of his finest works can be seen in the Museum of Fine Arts in Valletta.

Giuseppe Cali (1846-1930) was a portraitist and religious artist who painted altarpieces for parish churches and also created the murals in the Mosta Dome.

Exhibitions by contemporary Maltese artists are regularly held in the Museum of Fine Arts in Valletta. Names to look out for include Anthony Calleja (b. 1955) and Pawlu Grech (b. 1938).

Sculpture

Antonio Sciortino (1879-1947) was the leading Maltese sculptor of the 20th century, creating lively and thrusting compositions like the *Arab Horses* in the National Museum of Fine Arts in Valletta. Vincent Apap (b. 1938) created many of the sculptures that adorn Malta's public spaces, notably the *Trition Fountain* in the centre of the City Gate bus terminal between Valletta and Floriana.

Il Cavalier Calabrese

Mattia Preti (1613-99) was a painter from Calabria who lived and worked in Malta for 30 years. In 1661 he was commissioned by Grand Master Rafael Cotoner to decorate the vault of St John's Co-Cathedral in Valletta. The 18 vivid scenes depicting events in the life of St John the Baptist – from Zachary in the Temple to the beheading of St John – took five years to complete. Preti also designed the ornately carved decoration on the walls and pillars of the cathedral – a rich confection of gilded leaves, scrolls, flowers, Maltese crosses and coats of arms – and painted several of the altarpieces in the side chapels. Some of his best work can be seen in Valletta's National Museum of Fine Arts. Preti was eventually accepted into the Order of St John, and came to be known as *Il Cavalier Calabrese* – the Calabrian Knight.

JULIET COOMBE

Though best known as a painter, Mattia Preti also supervised the carved decorations lining the vaults of St John's Co-Cathedral.

Caravaggio in Malta

Michelangelo Merisi (1571-1610), better known by the name of his home town, Caravaggio, was a revolutionary Italian painter whose naturalistic representation of religious subjects replaced the traditional symbolism of 16th-century art. In particular, he introduced the bold use of shadow and selective lighting to dramatise his subjects.

He made his name in Rome with a series of controversial paintings, but also earned a reputation as a wild man, and numerous brawls and encounters with the law culminated in Caravaggio murdering a man during an argument over a tennis game. He fled Rome and went into hiding in Naples for several months. Then, towards the end of 1607, he moved to Malta.

In Malta, Caravaggio was welcomed as a famous artist and was commissioned to produce several works for the Knights of St John, including the famous *Beheading of St John the Baptist*, now on display in the oratory of the cathedral in Valletta. In July 1608 he was himself admitted into the Order as a Knight of Justice. But only two months later he was arrested for an unspecified crime – it may be that news arrived of the murder he had committed – and he was promptly imprisoned in Fort St Angelo.

He escaped to Sicily, but was expelled from the Order, and spent the next two years on the run. He created some of his finest paintings during this period, before dying of exhaustion and fever before the age of 38.

SOCIETY & CONDUCT

Malta is a fairly conservative country, with traditions and attitudes similar to those of southern Italy. Although its influence is waning, the Roman Catholic Church still plays an important part in everyday life. Baptisms, weddings and funerals are still celebrated in church (weddings in the parish where the bride was born), and the most important event in the calendar is the annual parish *festa*. Divorce and abortion are illegal; however, the possibility of divorce being legalised is a widely discussed issue.

Dos and Don'ts

Don't go into a church wearing shorts or a short skirt, or with bare shoulders. Although topless sunbathing is, strictly speaking, illegal on public beaches, it does happen. If you want to strip off, do so well away from any local people who might take offence. Smoking is prohibited on public transport.

Treatment of Animals

Bird-shooting is still a very popular pastime in Malta, and one of the more unpleasant aspects of the islands for many foreign visitors. The shooters will take a pot-shot at almost anything that flies – from a sparrow to a swift – though the main prey are turtle doves and wildfowl. Shooters' hides can be seen in the quieter corners of the countryside, and the crack of shotguns is a common accompaniment to an evening walk.

Bird-netting is also very popular – the rickety little towers of stones and metal poles you see in the Maltese countryside are for supporting the drop-nets and for holding cages containing decoy birds. Greenfinches are a popular prey, and you can often see them being bought and sold at the markets in Valletta. In all, it has been estimated that around half a million birds are shot or trapped in Malta each year.

Laws were introduced in 1980 designating a close season for shooting and trapping (22 May to 31 August), protecting many bird species (especially migrants) and making shooting and trapping illegal in certain protected areas. They include the Għadira Nature Reserve at Mellieħa Bay, Filfla island, Buskett Gardens, the Ta'Qali area and Gozo's Ta'Ċenċ cliffs. However, these laws are regularly flouted and poorly policed.

RELIGION

Under the constitution, Roman Catholic Christianity is the official state religion and must be taught in state schools, but the Maltese constitution guarantees freedom of worship. Around 98% of the population are members of the Roman Catholic Church.

Malta and Gozo are separate dioceses – the Bishop of Malta sits at St John's Co-Cathedral in Valletta, and the Bishop of Gozo at the Cathedral of the Assumption in Victoria.

LANGUAGE

The native language of Malta is called Malti. Some linguists attribute its origins to the Phoenician occupation of Malta in the first millennium BC, but most consider it to be related to the Arabic dialects of western North Africa. The language has an Arabic grammar and construction, but is laced with Sicilian, Italian, Spanish, French and English loan-words. Malti is the only Semitic language that is written in a Latin alphabet.

Malti is the language of the law courts, but both Malti and English are considered official languages. English is taught to schoolchildren from an early age, and almost everyone on the islands speaks it well. Many also speak Italian, helped by the fact that Malta receives Italian TV. French and German are also spoken, though less widely.

See the Language chapter at the back of the book for pronunciation guidelines and useful words and phrases.

Facts for the Visitor

HIGHLIGHTS

Malta may be small, but there is plenty of interest crammed into this diminutive island nation.

Valletta The magnificent fortified city built by the Knights of St John in the 16th century is home to the Grand Master's Palace and the beautiful and ornate Co-Cathedral of St John.

Vittoriosa Older than Valletta, this finger of land with Fort St Angelo at its tip was the first home of the Knights when they arrived in 1530. With neighbouring Senglea, it bravely defied the Turks in the Great Siege of 1565.

Megalithic Temples The oldest freestanding stone structures on Earth, Malta's prehistoric temples pre-date Stonehenge and the Pyramids of Egypt by 1000 years.

Mdina The Citta Notabile, or Noble City, was the capital of Malta before the building of Valletta. Its silent streets still exude an air of aristocratic elegance and seclusion.

Churches Malta has around 365 churches, and many of them are masterpieces of baroque architecture. Each parish church is associated with a *festa*, or feast day, which is enthusiastically celebrated with fireworks, brass bands and processions.

Il-Kastell The Citadel of Gozo is like Mdina in miniature, with its own cathedral, museums of archaeology, folklore and natural history.

Dwejra This area of spectacular coastal scenery on Gozo's west coast has superb swimming, snorkelling, diving and coastal walking.

SUGGESTED ITINERARIES

Malta's small size means that you can squeeze a lot of sightseeing into a short time if you want to. But it's more fun to take it easy – leave yourself time to absorb the sense of history that seeps from the stones of Valletta and Vittoriosa, and to appreciate the slower pace of rural life on the neighbouring island of Gozo.

Two or three days
On the first day see St John's Co-Cathedral, the Grand Master's Palace and the Museum of Archaeology in Valletta, and spend some time wandering the streets and walking around the

vast fortifications. On the second day, explore Vittoriosa and Senglea, and visit Tarxien Temples and the Hypogeum (if open). If you have a third day, spend the morning at Hagar Qim and Mnajdra temples and the Blue Grotto, and the afternoon in Mdina.

One week
As above, plus a boat trip to Comino, a day or two in Gozo seeing Victoria, Ġgantija and Dwejra, and a day on the beach.

Two weeks
A week on Malta, seeing the sights described above, and a whole week chilling out on Gozo.

One month
Enough time to see all the sights, as well as solve the 'Riddle of the Ruts' (see boxed text in the Central Malta chapter).

PLANNING
When to Go

Malta is a year-round holiday destination. The peak season is July to September, when many resort hotels are booked solid. However, July and August can be uncomfortably hot. Weather-wise, the most pleasant time to visit is in spring and autumn, though the pleasant weather can sometimes be interrupted by the enervating *xlokk*, a hot and humid wind.

April to June, and September and October are the best months, though September still counts as high season in many hotels. In November and December you can expect daytime temperatures of 12°C to 18°C and a fair amount of sunshine between spells of heavy rain showers. January and February are the coldest months, when a strong north-east wind makes conditions more unpleasant.

The main season for *festi* (village festivals – see Public Holidays & Special Events) is June to September, but if you want to catch a *festa* out of season, there's the Feast of St Paul's Shipwreck in Valletta in February, and the Feast of the Immaculate Conception in Cospicua in December. Two of the liveliest and most popular events on the islands, marked by public holidays, are the Karnival

The aerial view of Malta reveals a landscape of flat-topped hills, high sea cliffs and terraced hillsides.

"Am I cute or what?"

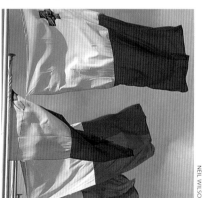

The Maltese flag has a long and chequered history.

Sharing a sunny spot, Argotti Gardens, Floriana

Who needs a sunlamp when you live in Malta?

Fancy some snails for dinner?

The well-preserved temple at Ħaġar Qim

Church of St Publius, Floriana, floodlit at dusk

Christmas in Malta

The festive season is celebrated with style in Malta. The strong Catholic tradition of the islands means that the religious aspect of Christmas is still very strong and the parish church, decorated with colourful lights, is the focus of the festivities. Candle-lit carol services are held in the days leading up to Christmas, and midnight mass on Christmas Eve is the highpoint of the proceedings.

Every town and village has its crib (called *presepju* in Malti, and often signposted), showing the nativity scene. The tradition of the crib or nativity scene dates back to the 5th or 6th century, as shown by surviving sketches in the Catacombs of St Agatha in Rabat (see Central Malta – Mdina & Rabat). Villages compete to construct the most impressive nativity scenes, complete with motorised mechanical figures, elaborate lighting and even waterfalls. Some travel agents offer guided tours of the best cribs.

The commercial aspect of Christmas is fully celebrated too, with street lights and decorations, window displays, band club concerts and a frenzy of evening shopping in the streets of Valletta in the week or two before Christmas Day. It's a good time to visit. The weather in December is pleasantly mild and not too wet, the islands are quiet and at their greenest, and red poinsettia flowers – a traditional Christmas sight – brighten many a garden and windowsill.

Week in early March and the L-Imnarja festival on 28-29 June.

The Christmas and New Year period is a mini-high season in the midst of winter, when many Maltese emigrants return home to visit friends and family, and European tourists come looking for a spot of winter sunshine. Otherwise you can find some very cheap flight and accommodation deals from November to March.

If you are interested in Malta's prehistoric temples, you might want to plan your trip to coincide with the winter solstice (21 December) – it has been argued that the orientation of the temples is related to the position of sunrise at the winter solstice.

Maps

There is a wide selection of maps of the Maltese Islands to choose from. A general one that is good value and hard-wearing is the *Malta FlexiMap* (£4.99) from Insight Maps. It shows Malta and Gozo at 1:50,000 scale, and has street maps of Valletta,

Sliema & St Julian's, Buġibba, Mdina and Victoria, with useful town and street indexes. For motorists, the 1:30,000 *Malta & Gozo* map (£6.95), published by Freytag & Berndt, accurately depicts major and minor roads and roundabouts – vital for navigation in Malta – and also includes a 1:12,000 town plan covering Valletta, Floriana, Sliema and St Julian's.

The most useful maps for walkers are the 1:25,000 topographic maps published by the Maltese government's Works Division in 1984, even though they are out of date in some respects. There are three sheets – Gozo, Malta West and Malta East – and they are sometimes available from the Aquilina bookshop in Valletta. If not, you can purchase them at the Works Division in Block A, Beltissebh, Floriana, at Lm6 for the full set. These maps can also be obtained from Stanfords Travel Bookshop (☎ 020-7836 1321 for mail order) at 12-14 Longacre, Covent Garden, in London, but here they will cost you £8.50 per sheet.

The mAZe by Frans A Attard is a street atlas covering every town and village in Malta and Gozo; it costs Lm4.95 from bookshops in Malta. Although the text is in English, street names are given in Malti only.

What to Bring

Maltese shops have been catering to tourists for decades – anything you've forgotten can probably be bought in Malta. Clothes in particular are very cheap.

In summer you'll need lightweight cotton clothes to beat the heat and ward off the strong sunshine – there's no point in lugging rain-gear around at this time of year. Don't forget to bring a hat and plenty of sunscreen. If you plan to visit churches you'll need to wear long trousers or a long skirt, and something to cover your shoulders with, as too much bare flesh is generally frowned upon.

In spring and autumn a light jersey or fleece should be added, and for winter it's worth bringing a lightweight raincoat and/or umbrella. Although winter evenings can sometimes be chilly, when the sun is out it can still be T-shirt weather, even in the middle of December.

Walkers planning to wander into untracked countryside should bring good stout walking boots – the bare limestone is rough and the vegetation often thorny.

TOURIST OFFICES
Local Tourist Offices

The head office of the Malta Tourism Authority (formerly the National Tourism Organisation – Malta) is for postal and telephone inquiries only. The contact details are 280 Triq ir-Repubblika, Valletta CMR02 (☎ 224444/5 or 225048/9, fax 220401, ✆ info@visitmalta.com). For more information, you can also look up the Web site www.visitmalta.com.

There are local tourist information offices at 1 City Arcade, Valletta (☎ 237747), Malta International Airport (☎ 249600), Mġarr Harbour, Gozo (☎ 553343) and in the Banca Giuratale, Victoria, Gozo (☎ 558106 or 557407).

Tourist Offices Abroad

The Malta Tourist Authority has many overseas offices, including the following:

France (☎ 01 48 00 03 79, fax 01 48 00 04 41, Minitel 3615 MALTE, ✆ france@visitemalte .com) Office du Tourisme de Malte, 9 Cité Trevise, 75009 Paris
Germany (☎ 069-285890 or 284060, fax 285479, ✆ info@urlaubmalta.de) Fremdenverkehrsamt Malta, Schillerstrasse 30-40, D-60313 Frankfurt-am-Main
Italy (☎ 02-86 73 76 or 87 63 95, fax 87 46 87, ✆ info@malta.it) Ente per il Turismo di Malta, Via M Gonzaga 7, 20123 Milan
Netherlands (☎ 020-620 72 23, fax 620 72 33, ✆ office.nl@visitmalta.com) Verkeersbureau Malta, Singel 540, 4th Floor, 1017 AZ Amsterdam
Russia (☎/fax 095-232 6413, ✆ office.ru@ visitmalta.com) Malta Tourist Office, Korovy Val ulitsa 7/219, 117049 Moscow
UK (☎ 020-7292 4900, fax 7734 1880, ✆ maltauk@aol.com) Malta Tourist Office, 36-38 Piccadilly, London, W1V 0PP
USA (☎ 212-695 9520, fax 695 8229, ✆ office.us@visitmalta.com) Malta Tourist Office, Empire State Building, 350 Fifth Ave, Suite 4412, New York NY 10118

There are also representative offices in the following countries:

Australia (☎ 02-9321 9514, fax 9290 3641) World Aviation Systems, 403 George St, Sydney NSW 2000
Ireland (☎ 01-405 8200, fax 473 2962, ✆ office.ie@tourism.org.mt) J Walter Thomson Communications, 1 Christchurch Hall, High St, Dublin 8

VISAS & DOCUMENTS
Passport

All visitors to Malta need a valid passport, except for nationals of Austria, Belgium, France, Germany, Greece, Italy, Luxembourg, Netherlands, Portugal, Spain and Switzerland, for whom a valid national ID card will suffice for stays of up to three months.

Visas

Visas are not needed for visits of up to three months by nationals of most Commonwealth countries (including UK, Australia, New

Zealand, Canada and South Africa, but excluding India and Pakistan), most European countries, the USA, Japan, Libya, Morocco and Tunisia.

If you wish to stay for more than three months you should apply for an extension at the Immigration Office in the Police Headquarters in Beltissebh in Floriana before your three months are up. You will need four recent passport photographs and proof that you have enough money to support yourself and not be a burden on the state. Extensions are usually granted without a problem. Applications for temporary residence should also be made at Police HQ.

Travel Insurance

A travel insurance policy to cover theft, loss and medical problems is a good idea. A wide variety of policies are available, so check the small print. Some policies specifically exclude 'dangerous activities', which can include scuba-diving – a very popular attraction in Malta.

You may prefer a policy which pays doctors or hospitals directly rather than you having to pay on the spot and claim later. If you have to claim later make sure you keep all documentation. Some policies ask you to call back (reverse charges) to a centre in your home country where an immediate assessment of your problem is made.

Check that the policy covers ambulances or an emergency flight home.

Student Cards

A valid ISIC card is worth bringing along. The NSTS travel agency (see Valletta – Information) issues a booklet listing shops, restaurants, transport and other establishments in Malta offering discounts of 15% to 40%. Entry to state-run museums is free to students.

Copies

All important documents (passport data page and visa page, credit cards, travel insurance policy, air/bus/train tickets, driving licence etc) should be photocopied before you leave home. Leave one copy with someone at home and keep another with you, separate from the originals.

EMBASSIES & CONSULATES
Your Own Embassy

It's important to realise what your own embassy – the embassy of the country of which you are a citizen – can and can't do to help you if you get into trouble.

Generally speaking, it won't be much help in emergencies if the trouble you're in is remotely your own fault. Remember that you are bound by the laws of the country you are in. Your embassy will not be sympathetic if you end up in jail after committing a crime locally, even if such actions are legal in your own country.

In genuine emergencies you might get some assistance, but only if other channels have been exhausted. For example, if you need to get home urgently, a free ticket home is exceedingly unlikely – the embassy would expect you to have insurance. If you have all your money and documents stolen, it might assist with getting a new passport, but a loan for onward travel is out of the question.

Some embassies used to keep letters for travellers or have a small reading room with home newspapers, but these days the mail-holding service has usually been stopped and even newspapers tend to be out of date.

Maltese Embassies & Consulates

Diplomatic representation abroad includes:

Australia
  High Commission: (☎ 02-6295 1586, fax 6239 6084) 261 La Perouse St, Canberra ACT 2603
Canada
  Consulate General: (☎ 709-722 2744, fax 722 3208, ✉ pocil@nfld.com) Suite 1, Puglisevich Building, 611 Torbay Road, St John's, Newfoundland. Also, consulates in Montreal, Toronto and Vancouver.
Egypt
  Embassy: (☎ 02-375 4451 or 350 0655, fax 375 4452, ✉ maltaemb@idsc.gov.eg) 25 Road 12, Maadi, Cairo
France
  Embassy: (☎ 01 56 59 75 90, fax 01 45 62 00 36) 92 Avenue des Champs Elysees, 75008 Paris
Germany
  Embassy: (☎ 0228-36 30 17/18, fax 36 30 19, ✉ maemba@blatzheim.com) 1 Viktoriastrasse, 53173 Bonn

Ireland
  Honorary Consul: (☎ 01-280 1081, fax 280 8867) Traverslea, Glenageary, Co Dublin
Italy
  Embassy: (☎ 06-687 99 90/47, fax 689 26 87) 12 Lungotevere Marzio, 00186 Rome
Russia
  Embassy: (☎ 095-237 1939 or 230 2524, fax 237 2158, ☻ maltamsk@glasnet.ru) Korovy Val 7, Kv. 219, 117049 Moscow
Spain
  Embassy: (☎ 91-373 21 34 or 373 36 79, fax 373 73 82) San Martin de Porres 20 1B, 28035 Madrid
Tunisia
  Embassy: (☎ 01-74 89 74, fax 74 86 44) 11 Avenue de la Republique, 2070 La Marsa, Tunis
UK
  High Commission: (☎ 020-7292 4800, fax 7734 1831) Malta House, 26/38 Piccadilly, London W1V 0PQ
USA
  Embassy: (☎ 202-462 3611/2, fax 387 5470, ☻ malta-embassy@compuserve.com) 2017 Connecticut Avenue NW, Washington DC 20008. Also, consulates in Boston, Detroit, Houston, Independence, Los Angeles, New York, Pittsburgh, St Paul and San Francisco.

Embassies & Consulates in Malta

Countries with embassies in Malta include:

Australia
  Embassy: (☎ 338201) Villa Fiorentina, Ta'Xbiex Terrace, Ta'Xbiex
Canada
  Consulate: (☎ 233121/6) 103 Triq L-Arċisqof, Valletta
France
  Embassy: (☎ 335856) Villa Seminia, 12 Triq Sir Temi Zammit, Ta'Xbiex
Germany
  Embassy: (☎ 336520/31) Il-Piazzetta, Entrance B, 1st Floor, Triq it-Torri, Sliema
Italy
  Embassy: (☎ 233157/8/9) 5 Triq Vilhena, Floriana
Japan
  Consulate: (☎ 236703 or 231407) 19 Pjazza Luigi Preziosi, Floriana
Libya
  Embassy: (☎ 486347/8 or 441874) Dar Jamahirya, Notabile Road, Balzan
Tunisia
  Embassy: (☎ 345866 or 332182) 144/2 Triq it-Torri, Sliema

UK
  High Commission: (☎ 233134/5/6) 7 Triq Sant'Anna, Floriana
USA
  Embassy: (☎ 235960/1/2) 3rd Floor, Development House, Triq Sant'Anna, Floriana

CUSTOMS

Items for personal use are not subject to duty. The duty free allowance per person is: 1L of spirits, 1L of wine, 200 cigarettes or 100 cigarillos or 50 cigars or 250g of tobacco, 60ml of perfume and 250ml of eau de toilette. Duty will be charged on any gifts over Lm50 that are intended for local residents.

Meat and poultry (cooked or not), and plants and plant produce (including soil), must not be brought into the country, so forget about that Christmas turkey or the present of a pot plant. Speaking of pot plants, being caught trying to bring any kind of illegal drugs into the country will land you in jail. Possession of even small amounts of cannabis for personal use is punishable by a prison sentence.

MONEY
Currency

The Maltese lira, plural liri (Lm) is divided into 100 cents (c). There are 1c, 2c, 5c, 10c, 25c, 50c and Lm1 coins, and Lm2, Lm5, Lm10 and Lm20 notes. The currency is often referred to as the pound, and a £ symbol is also sometimes used.

Exchange Rates

Banks almost always offer better rates than hotels or restaurants. The maximum amount of Maltese currency that you can take into/out of Malta is Lm50/25. Try not to have too many liri when you leave – it is difficult to change Maltese liri outside Malta.

country	unit		lira
Australia	A$1	=	Lm0.26
Canada	C$1	=	Lm0.29
euro	€1	=	Lm0.40
France	1FF	=	Lm0.06
Germany	DM1	=	Lm0.21
Italy	L1000	=	Lm0.21
Japan	¥100	=	Lm0.41

New Zealand	NZ$1	=	Lm0.21
UK	UK£1	=	Lm0.69
USA	US$1	=	Lm0.43

Exchanging Money

There is a 24-hour exchange bureau at the airport available to passengers only. Travellers arriving by ferry should note that there are no exchange facilities at the ferry terminal.

Cash Cash can be changed at hotels, banks, bureaux de change and some tourist shops. There are also 24-hour exchange machines at banks in the main tourist towns, including Valletta, Sliema and Buġibba, where you can feed in foreign banknotes and get Maltese currency back automatically. Most major European currencies and US dollars are widely accepted.

Travellers Cheques & Eurocheques All the main brands of travellers cheques can be easily exchanged at hotels, banks and bureaux de change. You'll find that pounds sterling, Deutschmarks and US dollars are the favoured denominations. Banks give better rates than hotels, but they often levy a charge of 20c to 25c per transaction. Remember that you will need your passport when cashing travellers cheques. Eurocheques up to the value of Lm70 a day can be cashed at banks and hotels.

ATMs There are ATMs in all the main towns in Malta where you can withdraw Maltese cash using a credit card and PIN. However, this usually incurs a 'handling charge' of around 1.5% of the amount withdrawn, with a minimum charge of £1.50, and you'll be paying interest on the cash advance until you pay off your credit card bill.

Credit Cards Visa, MasterCard and American Express credit and charge cards are widely accepted in hotels, restaurants, shops, travel agencies and car hire agencies.

International Transfers You can have money wired to you in Malta via Western Union. Call ☎ 0800 773773 in Malta to find the nearest office.

Security

You are much less likely to suffer from theft in Malta than in mainland Europe. Still, it's wise to take commonsense precautions. Divide your money and keep it in two or three separate places on your person. A money belt worn inside your trousers or a neck pouch under your shirt are good ideas.

Costs

By European standards, Malta is good value, although prices are increasing slowly. If you can budget on around Lm10 per day, you'll get pleasant hostel accommodation, a simple restaurant meal, a decent street-side snack and enough cold drinks to keep you going. If you cook your own meals your costs will be even lower. On Lm15 to Lm20 a day you can start to live it up in a hotel with a swimming pool and enjoy meals at better restaurants, especially in the low season.

The following table shows some typical high season costs:

Hostel	Lm4 per person
Budget hotel	Lm8 per person
Mid-range hotel	Lm15 per person
Top end hotel	Lm25 per person
Burger, fries & drink	Lm1.80
Nice restaurant	Lm6 a head
Gourmet restaurant	Lm12 a head
Loaf of bread	11c
Bottle of local beer	30c (in bar)
Bottle of local wine	Lm1.30 (in shop)
Bottle of quality wine	Lm8 (in restaurant)
1L petrol	32c
Bus journey	15c
Boat trip to Comino	Lm11
Car hire	Lm8 a day
Local phone call	10c
Local newspaper	15c
UK newspaper	65c

Tipping & Bargaining

Tipping etiquette generally follows normal practice in mainland Europe. In restaurants where no service charge is included in the bill, waiting staff expect a 10% tip. Baggage porters should get 50c, car park attendants 20c, and chamber maids in top end hotels about Lm1 a week. Taxi drivers don't expect a tip, but make sure you agree on a fare before getting into the cab.

Bargaining for handicrafts at stalls or markets is essential, but most shops have fixed prices. Hotels and car hire agencies will often be prepared to bargain in the off season between October and mid-June – stays/rentals of a week or more will often get a 10% discount.

POST & COMMUNICATIONS
Post
Malta has a reliable postal service. Post office branches are found in most towns and villages. A poste restante service is available at the main post office in Pjazza Castile, Valletta, but you have to write in advance to the Postmaster, c/o General Post Office, Valletta, Malta, requesting to use this service.

Local postage costs 6c; postcards or letters sent airmail to Europe cost 16c, to the USA 22c and to Australia 27c.

Telephone
Public telephones are widely available in the street and at Maltacom offices – coin phones are yellow, card phones are silver. You can buy phonecards at the offices of Maltacom (the country's phone company), post offices and stationery shops for Lm2, Lm3 or Lm5. The main Maltacom office is at Mercury House, Triq San Ġorġ, Paċeville (open 24 hours). Other offices are at Triq Nofs in-Nhar, Valletta (open from 7 am to 6 pm), and Triq Bisazza, Sliema (open 8 am to 11 pm).

Local calls cost 10c. International calls are discounted by around 20% between 6 pm and midnight and all day Saturday and Sunday (off-peak rate), and by up to 36% between midnight and 8 am (night rate). A three-minute call to the USA costs Lm1.50 (standard rate), Lm1.20 (off-peak) and 96c (night).

The international direct dialling code is ☎ 00. To call Malta from abroad, dial the international access code, ☎ 356 (the country code for Malta) and the number. There are no area codes in Malta.

Malta uses the GSM900 mobile phone network which is compatible with the rest of Europe, Australia and New Zealand, but not with the USA and Canada's GSM1900. If you have a GSM phone, check with your service provider about using it in Malta, and beware of calls being routed internationally (very expensive for a 'local' call). You can rent a mobile phone from Vodaphone (☎ 482820), William J. England Ltd (☎ 244562) and Powerwave Ltd (☎ 345566) for around Lm5 a day or Lm20 a week.

Fax and telex services are available at Maltacom offices.

Email & Internet Access
Malta is a fairly well-wired destination. At the time of writing there were around half a dozen Internet cafes in Malta and one in Gozo, and more will no doubt spring up in the near future. Rates vary, but typical charges for Internet access are around Lm1.50 an hour.

If you intend to use Malta's cybercafes to keep in touch with your email, you should remember to carry three pieces of information with you to enable you to access your Internet mail account. They are your incoming (POP or IMAP) mail server name, your account name and your password. Your ISP or network supervisor will be able to give you these.

Armed with this information, you should be able to access your Internet mail account from any net-connected machine in the world, provided it runs some kind of email software (remember that Netscape and Internet Explorer both have mail modules). It pays to become familiar with the process for doing this before you leave home. You can also pick up POP3 mail by using Web sites such as www.mailstart.com and www.webbox.com.

Another option for collecting mail via cybercafes is to open a free eKno Web-based email account online at www.ekno.lonelyplanet.com. You can then access your mail from anywhere in the world from any net-connected machine running a standard Web browser.

INTERNET RESOURCES

The World Wide Web is a rich resource for travellers. You can research your trip, hunt down bargain air fares, book hotels, check on weather conditions or chat with locals and other travellers about the best places to visit (or avoid!).

There's no better place to start your Web explorations than the Lonely Planet Web site (www.lonelyplanet.com). Here you'll find succinct summaries on travelling to most places on earth, postcards from other travellers and the Thorn Tree bulletin board, where you can ask questions before you go or dispense advice when you get back. You can also find travel news and updates to many of our most popular guidebooks, and the subWWWay section links you to the most useful travel resources elsewhere on the Web.

The Malta Tourist Authority has a useful Web site at www.visitmalta.com (www .tourism.org.mt is the same site), which includes an annual calendar of events, usually updated at the beginning of the year.

The most useful site is SearchMalta (www.searchmalta.com), which has a searchable directory of links to Malta-related Web sites. There's also Gozo.com (www.gozo.com), which has Gozo-specific news and travel information.

BOOKS

Most books are published in different editions by different publishers in different countries. As a result, a book might be a hardcover rarity in one country while it's readily available in paperback in another. Fortunately, bookshops and libraries search by title or author, so your local bookshop or library is best placed to advise you on the availability of the following recommendations.

Some of the books listed below are easily obtained from bookshops in Malta, but might be hard to find elsewhere.

Lonely Planet

If you are planning to include Malta as part of a bigger European trip, you might want to take along Lonely Planet's *Mediterranean Europe* guide, which includes brief coverage of Malta along with 16 other countries around the shores of the Med.

Guidebooks

There are two guidebooks to scuba-diving in Maltese waters – *Maltese Islands Diving Guide* by Ned Middleton, and *The Dive Sites of Malta, Gozo & Comino* by Lawson & Leslie Wood. The latter is the better (and cheaper) of the two.

Landscapes of Malta, Gozo & Comino has details of 70 walks of varying length around the islands, while *Malta: A Guide to the Fortifications* by the British architect Quentin Hughes is the classic guide to the defences of Valletta, Floriana and the Three Cities, as well as the forts that dot the coastline.

History & Politics

For an inexpensive and readable introduction to the full sweep of Maltese history, try *The Story of Malta* by Brian Blouet. *Malta: An Archaeological Guide* by Dr David Trump describes the main prehistoric sites in Malta; it is widely available in bookshops and souvenir shops. *Secrets of the Stone Age* by Richard Rudgely includes a chapter on Malta's megalithic temples.

The history of the Knights of St John is told in a range of titles, including *Malta of the Knights* by Elizabeth Schermerhorn (first published in 1929), *The Knights of Malta* by Henry Sire, *Knights of Malta* by Claire Elaine Engel and *The Monks of War* by Desmond Seward.

The Great Siege by Ernle Bradford is a well-written and entertaining account of the Turkish siege of 1565. *Siege Malta: 1940-43*, also by Bradford, details the islands' ordeal during WWII. *Malta: A Thorn in Rommel's Side* by Laddie Lucas is another WWII account, written from first-hand experience by a fighter pilot based in Malta. *Malta Convoy* by Peter Shankland & Anthony Hunter describes the famous Operation Pedestal that succeeded in re-supplying Malta at its lowest point in 1942.

Britain & Malta: The Story of an Era by Joseph Attard is a historical account of British involvement in Malta from 1800 until the 1970s seen from a Maltese point of view.

Fiction

For Rozina ... A Husband, by Maltese writer Francis Ebejer, is a collection of short stories in English that attempt to capture the essence of Maltese village life.

The Kappillan of Malta by Nicholas Monsarrat is the classic English-language novel about Malta. Written in the early 1970s when the author was living in San Lawrenz, Gozo, it describes the experiences of the humble parish priest Dun Salvatore during WWII, interlaced with a potted history of Malta.

Nicholas Rinaldi's novel *The Jukebox Queen of Malta*, published in 1999, uses WWII Malta as the setting for a love story, this time between an American soldier and a girl called Melita. The book has been compared to *Captain Corelli's Mandolin* with its juxtaposition of island romance, local history and the senseless violence of war.

The British novelist Anthony Burgess was a tax exile in Malta for a brief spell at the end of the 1960s. He lived in a house in Lija, which became the fictional home of the 81-year-old protagonist in his masterly novel *Earthly Powers*.

General

The Malta Buses by Michael Cassar & Joseph Bonnici is an illustrated history of the island's celebrated public transport. *The Food & Cookery of Malta* by Anne & Helen Caruana Galizia is the definitive guide to Maltese cuisine, packed with recipes and information on local ingredients.

FILMS

Many films have been shot in Malta using the facilities of the Mediterranean Film Studios near Fort Rinella. The studio's vast filming tanks have been used to shoot the water scenes in movies such as *The Spy Who Loved Me, Never Say Never Again, Raise the Titanic* and *White Squall*. Fort St Elmo in Valletta was used as the Turkish prison setting for the classic *Midnight Express*. Ridley Scott's *Gladiator* – the late Oliver Reed's final performance – was filmed in Malta.

The 1953 British war film *The Malta Story*, starring Alec Guinness and Jack Hawkins, dramatises the events leading up to the island's award of the George Cross in 1942.

NEWSPAPERS & MAGAZINES

Local English-language daily newspapers include the long-established *Times of Malta*, with a mix of local, European and world news, and the newer *Malta Independent*, which has good coverage of domestic social issues. The weeklies are *Malta Today*, which includes a useful supplement with listings of TV, cinema and events for the coming week, and the *Malta Business Weekly*, which covers local financial and business matters.

British, French, German and Italian newspapers can be bought in the main tourist towns, usually on the evening of the day of publication.

RADIO & TV

There are more than a dozen local radio stations broadcasting mostly in Malti but occasionally in English. The BBC World Service can be found on the following short-wave frequencies (all MHz): 17.640, 15.575, 12.095, 9.760, 9.680, 9.410, 7.325 and 6.195. BBC Radio News in English is broadcast every hour from 7.30 am to 5.30 pm on Island Radio (101.8 MHz FM). The Voice of America is on 9.760, 6.040, 1.197 and 0.792 MHz SW.

There are two state-run TV stations and half a dozen small commercial channels broadcasting in Malti. All of the main Italian TV stations can also be received in Malta. Satellite and cable TV are widely available in hotels and bars.

PHOTOGRAPHY & VIDEO
Film & Equipment

Film, camcorder cassettes and camera equipment are easily obtained at dozens of photographic shops in all the main towns in Malta. Print film is also available from souvenir shops and hotels in the main tourist areas. Prices for 36-exposure print and slide films are around Lm2.90, excluding processing.

Many photo shops offer one-hour print processing, but at a hefty price. Kodak Express (☎ 570187) at the Primera Hotel in Buġibba charges Lm8.10 for one-hour processing and printing of a 36-exposure film, including a replacement film.

Foto Vision (☎ 221610), 10 Triq it-Teżorerija, Valletta, does E6 colour slide processing as well as prints – it costs Lm3.35 for a 36-exposure film (mounted slides). There are other branches of Foto Vision in Pjazza Paola in Paola, and at 53a Islets Promenade in Buġibba.

For B&W film and processing, try The Foto Grafer (☎ 661380) in Triq San Tumas, Għira.

Technical Tips

For the best results, shoot your pictures early and late in the day – before 10 am and after 4 pm. The blazing sun of a Maltese summer will give a flat and washed-out look to pics taken in the middle of the day. If you want to capture that 'tropical turquoise' look of the water in Comino's Blue Lagoon, you will need to use a polarizing filter.

Remember to keep film in a cool place – don't leave it lying around where it will get baked in the sun, like on the dashboard of your car.

Photographing People

Local people are generally pretty cool about having their picture taken, as long as you ask them first.

TIME

Malta is two hours ahead of GMT/UTC from the last Sunday in March to the last Sunday in October, and one hour ahead the rest of the year.

ELECTRICITY

Malta's electricity supply is 240V/50Hz and the plugs have three flat pins as in the UK. Continental European appliances, which have plugs with two round pins, will need an adaptor. North American appliances running on 110V will also need a transformer, best purchased before you leave home.

WEIGHTS & MEASURES

Like the rest of Europe, Malta uses the metric system. However, the British legacy persists in the use of pint glasses in some pubs.

LAUNDRY

There are coin-operated laundrettes in the main tourist areas of Sliema and Buġibba, but they are expensive at around Lm2.50 for a load. Most of the larger hotels and apartment complexes have a laundry room for guests, where you can use a washing machine, tumble dryer and iron either free of charge or for a small fee.

TOILETS

Malta is well-equipped with public toilets, often at the entrance to a public garden or near the village square. They are usually clean and in good order; if there is an attendant, it is good manners to leave a tip of a few cents in a dish by the door.

HEALTH

Travel health depends on your predeparture preparations, your daily health care while travelling and how you handle any medical problem that does develop.

Predeparture Planning

Make sure that you have adequate health insurance. See Travel Insurance under Visas & Documents earlier in this chapter for details. There are no unusual health risks in Malta and no inoculations are required. Citizens of Australia and the UK are entitled to free health care through reciprocal agreements with the health authorities.

Make sure you're healthy before you travel. If you're going on a long trip check that your teeth are OK. If you wear glasses take a spare pair and your prescription.

If you require a particular medication take an adequate supply, as it may not be available locally. Take part of the packaging showing the generic name rather than the brand, which will make getting replacements easier. It's a good idea to have a legible prescription or letter from your doctor to show that you legally use the medication to avoid any problems.

Basic Rules

Care in what you eat and drink is the most important health rule. Stomach upsets are the most likely travel health problem – between 30% and 50% of travellers experience stomach problems on a two-week trip – but the majority of these are relatively minor. Unfortunately food poisoning can sometimes be a problem so it's important not to become complacent.

Water Malta's tap water is safe to drink but heavily chlorinated, so stick to the bottled variety if you don't like the taste. Any water in the countryside, whether from a stream or a spring, is best left alone.

Medical Problems & Treatment

Heat Exhaustion In the fierce heat of a Maltese summer, dehydration and salt deficiency can cause heat exhaustion. Take time to acclimatise to high temperatures, drink sufficient liquids and do not do anything too physically demanding. Salt deficiency is characterised by fatigue, lethargy, headaches, giddiness and muscle cramps; salt tablets may help, but adding extra salt to your food is better.

Heatstroke This serious, occasionally fatal, condition can occur if the body's heat-regulating mechanism breaks down and the body temperature rises to dangerous levels. Long, continuous periods of exposure to high temperatures and insufficient fluids can leave you vulnerable to heatstroke.

The symptoms are feeling unwell, not sweating very much (or at all) and a high body temperature (39°C to 41°C or 102°F to 106°F). Where sweating has ceased, the skin becomes flushed and red. Severe, throbbing headaches and lack of coordination will also occur, and the sufferer may be confused or aggressive. Eventually the victim will become delirious or convulse. Hospitalisation is essential, but in the interim get victims out of the sun, remove their clothing, cover them with a wet sheet or towel and then fan continually. Give fluids if they are conscious.

Jet Lag Jet lag is experienced when a person travels by air across more than three time zones (each time zone usually represents a one-hour time difference). It occurs because many of the functions of the human body (such as temperature, pulse rate and emptying of the bladder and bowels) are regulated by internal 24-hour cycles. When we travel long distances rapidly, our bodies take time to adjust to the 'new time' of our destination, and we may experience fatigue, disorientation, insomnia, anxiety, impaired concentration and loss of appetite. These effects will usually be gone within three days of arrival, but to minimise the impact of jet lag:

• Rest for a couple of days prior to departure.
• Try to select flight schedules that minimise sleep deprivation; arriving late in the day means you can go to sleep soon after you arrive. For very long flights, try to organise a stopover.
• Avoid excessive eating (which bloats the stomach) and alcohol (which causes dehydration) during the flight. Instead, drink plenty of non-carbonated, nonalcoholic drinks such as fruit juice or water.
• Avoid smoking.
• Make yourself comfortable by wearing loose-fitting clothes and perhaps bringing an eye mask and ear plugs to help you sleep.
• Try to sleep at the appropriate time for the time zone you are travelling to.

Motion Sickness Eating lightly before and during a trip will reduce the chances of motion sickness. If you are prone to motion sickness try to find a place that minimises movement – near the wing on aircraft, close to midships on boats, near the centre on buses. Fresh air usually helps; reading and cigarette smoke don't. Commercial motion-sickness preparations, which can cause drowsiness, have to be taken before the trip commences. Ginger (available in capsule form) and peppermint (including mint-flavoured sweets) are natural preventatives.

Sunburn Malta lies farther south than northern Tunisia and Algeria – you can get sunburnt surprisingly quickly, even through cloud. Use a sunscreen, a hat, and a barrier cream for your nose and lips. Calamine lotion or a commercial after-sun preparation are good for mild sunburn. Protect your eyes with good quality sunglasses.

Diarrhoea Simple things like a change of water, food or climate can all cause a mild bout of diarrhoea, but a few rushed toilet trips with no other symptoms is not indicative of a major problem.

Dehydration is the main danger with any diarrhoea, particularly in children or the elderly as dehydration can occur quite quickly. Under all circumstances *fluid replacement* (at least equal to the volume being lost) is the most important thing to remember. Weak black tea with a little sugar, soda water, or soft drinks allowed to go flat and diluted 50% with clean water are all good. With severe diarrhoea a rehydrating solution is preferable to replace minerals and salts lost. Commercially available oral rehydration salts (ORS) are very useful; add them to boiled or bottled water. In an emergency you can make up a solution of six teaspoons of sugar and a half teaspoon of salt to a litre of boiled or bottled water. You need to drink at least the same volume of fluid that you are losing in bowel movements and vomiting. Urine is the best guide to the adequacy of replacement – if you have small amounts of concentrated urine, you need to drink more. Keep drinking small amounts often. Stick to a bland diet as you recover.

Gut-paralysing drugs such as loperamide or diphenoxylate can be used to bring relief from the symptoms, although they do not actually cure the problem. Only use these drugs if you do not have access to toilets (eg, if you *must* travel). Note that these drugs are not recommended for children under 12 years.

Fungal Infections Fungal infections occur more commonly in hot weather and are usually found on the scalp, between the toes (athlete's foot) or fingers, in the groin and on the body (ringworm). You get ringworm (which is a fungal infection, not a worm) from infected animals or other people. Moisture encourages these infections.

To prevent fungal infections wear loose, comfortable clothes, avoid artificial fibres, wash frequently and dry yourself carefully. If you do get an infection, wash the infected area at least daily with a disinfectant or medicated soap and water, and rinse and dry well. Apply an antifungal cream or powder like tolnaftate. Try to expose the infected area to air or sunlight as much as possible and wash all towels and underwear in hot water, change them often and let them dry in the sun.

HIV & AIDS Infection with the human immunodeficiency virus (HIV) may lead to acquired immune deficiency syndrome (AIDS), which is a fatal disease. Any exposure to blood, blood products or body fluids may put the individual at risk. The disease is often transmitted through sexual contact or dirty needles – vaccinations, acupuncture, tattooing and body piercing can be potentially as dangerous as intravenous drug use.

Sexually Transmitted Diseases HIV/AIDS and hepatitis B can be transmitted through sexual contact. Other STDs include gonorrhoea, herpes and syphilis; sores, blisters or rashes around the genitals and discharges or pain when urinating are common symptoms. In some STDs, such as wart virus or chlamydia, symptoms may be less marked or not observed at all, especially in women. Chlamydia infection can cause infertility in men and women before any symptoms have been noticed. Syphilis symptoms eventually disappear completely, but the disease continues and can cause severe problems in later years. While abstinence from sexual contact is the only 100% effective prevention, using condoms is also effective. The treatment of gonorrhoea and syphilis is with antibiotics. The different sexually transmitted diseases each require specific antibiotics. There is no cure for herpes or AIDS.

Gynaecological Problems Antibiotic use, synthetic underwear, sweating and contraceptive pills can lead to fungal vaginal infections, especially when travelling in hot climates. Fungal infections are characterised by a rash, itch and discharge and can be treated with a vinegar or lemon-juice douche, or with yogurt. Nystatin, miconazole or clotrimazole pessaries or vaginal cream are the usual treatment. Maintaining good personal hygiene and wearing loose-fitting clothes and cotton underwear may help prevent these infections.

Sexually transmitted diseases are a major cause of vaginal problems. Symptoms include a smelly discharge, painful intercourse and sometimes a burning sensation when urinating. Medical attention should be sought and male sexual partners must also be treated. For more details see the section on Sexually Transmitted Diseases earlier. Besides abstinence, the best thing is to practise safer sex using condoms.

Insect Bites & Stings Bee and wasp stings are usually painful rather than dangerous. However, in people who are allergic to them severe breathing difficulties may occur and require urgent medical attention. Calamine lotion or a sting relief spray will give relief and ice packs will reduce the pain and swelling. Mosquitoes can be a nuisance in Malta in the warmer months – bring mosquito repellent and a mosquito killer.

WOMEN TRAVELLERS
Attitudes Towards Women

Malta remains a conservative society by western standards, and women are still expected to be wives and mothers; however, an increasing number of women are now joining the workforce. Young males have adopted the Mediterranean macho style, but they are not usually aggressive.

Malta presents no unusual dangers for women travelling alone. Normal caution should be observed, but problems are unlikely. If you are alone, Paċeville – the nightclub zone at St Julian's – is hectic but not particularly unsafe. However, be aware that walking alone at night in Gżira (south of Sliema) is not recommended as it is the centre for prostitution.

GAY & LESBIAN TRAVELLERS

Homosexual sex was legalised in Malta in 1973. The age of consent for both males and females is 18. Attitudes towards homosexuality in Malta are much the same as in most of southern Europe. Younger people and women are likely to be more tolerant than older people and straight men.

Although Malta is not a very 'out' destination, there are several openly gay and lesbian bars, including the Lady Godiva Bar in Triq Wilga, Paċeville (male and female) and the Tom Bar, at the top of Telgħa Tal-Kurċifiss in Floriana. Malta held its first Gay Pride festival in 1996, organised by the Pride of Malta Organisation (☎ 250780). The Gay Malta Web site at www.geocities .com/WestHollywood/Village/3619 contains some useful information.

DISABLED TRAVELLERS

Maltese government policy is to improve access for people with disabilities, but many of Malta's historic places – notably the steep, stepped streets of Valletta – remain difficult, if not impossible, to negotiate in a wheelchair. Several sites are accessible, however, including the Malta Experience and the Museum of Archaeology in Valletta and the prehistoric temples at Tarxien and Ħaġar Qim. A good number of the more expensive hotels have wheelchair access, and some have rooms specially designed for disabled guests. The Malta Tourist Authority can provide a list of hotels that are equipped for wheelchair users.

Organisations

The National Commission for Persons with Disabilities (☎ 487789), Triq il-Kbira San Ġużepp, Santa Venera, can provide information on facilities and access for disabled travellers in Malta. The Association for the Physically Handicapped (☎ 693863) at the Rehabilitation Centre on Corradino Hill, Paola, is also a useful contact.

SENIOR TRAVELLERS

Malta has always been a popular destination for older travellers, especially British pensioners looking for a relatively inexpensive place to enjoy some winter sun. Many tour operators specialise in holidays targeted at the over-50s age-group – see Organised Tours in the Getting There & Away chapter.

In Malta, people over 65 are entitled to free admission to all government-owned museums.

TRAVEL WITH CHILDREN

Malta is a good destination for a family holiday. Children are made welcome everywhere, and there are plenty of activities to keep them occupied. Pharmacies are well stocked with baby products such as formula, bottles, pacifiers and nappies (diapers).

Kids might enjoy the Malta Experience (see Walking Tour 2 in the Valletta & Floriana chapter), or a boat trip on the harbour (see Activities in the Sliema chapter). In summer, you can hire snorkelling gear, canoes, dinghies etc at most tourist resorts. A sandy beach with safe paddling and swimming for kids can be found at Mellieħa Bay.

The Splash & Fun Park (☎ 342724), with its water slides and playground, is at Baħar iċ-Ċagħaq (see the North-West Malta chapter). Popeye Village at Anchor Bay (also see the North-West Malta chapter) is always popular with younger children, even if they've never heard of Popeye. Another option for older kids (who are not easily frightened) is a visit to the Mdina Dungeons, which are fitted out with spooky sound effects and gory torture scenes (see the Mdina section in the Central Malta chapter).

More expensive distractions include Captain Morgan's glass-bottomed boat trips from Sliema and Buġibba, and helicopter sightseeing flights (see Getting Around – Organised Tours).

Lonely Planet's *Travel with Children* by Maureen Wheeler is also packed with useful advice.

DANGERS & ANNOYANCES
Road Conditions & Driving

Much of the road network in Malta is badly in need of repair, which means that driving is often an uncomfortably bumpy experience. Rules of the road are rarely observed, which adds to the stress of driving in unfamiliar territory, especially during rush hour conditions around Sliema and St Julian's.

There is something of a macho, devil-may-care culture among young male drivers, and the accident rate is correspondingly high. This attitude extends to the buses too, and as a passenger there will be times when you might suspect that a kid has stolen his father's bus and is taking you on a joyride.

Taxi Drivers

Taxi drivers often try to rip off travellers – always agree on a fare before getting into a taxi. On arrival at the airport, ignore any taxi drivers who tell you that the bus stop is a 20-minute walk away, or that the bus won't be along for another hour – they're just touting for business.

Walking

If you go walking in the countryside, beware of the national obsession with shooting and trapping birds – the little stone shacks that pepper the clifftops are shooters' hides. You will hear the popping of shotguns before you see the shooters. The close season for shooting is 22 May to 31 August.

Theft

Crime against visitors is a rarity in Malta, but in past years there have been increasing reports of thieves breaking into cars parked in quiet areas like Marfa and Delimara Point. The only real defence is to leave the car unlocked and not leave anything of value in it.

EMERGENCIES

Dial ☎ 196 for an ambulance. St Luke's Hospital (☎ 241251) in Gwardamanga (on the promontory north-west of the Valletta defences) is Malta's main general hospital. Gozo General Hospital (☎ 561600), also known as the Craig Hospital, is the main medical facility on Gozo. Both have 24-hour emergency services. General first aid can be administered at local polyclinics.

Pharmacies are generally open 8.30 am to 12.30 pm and 4 to 7 pm Monday to Friday, and mornings only on Saturday. Duty pharmacists that stay open late and over the weekend are listed in the weekend newspapers.

Some useful telephone numbers include:

Police	☎ 191
Ambulance	☎ 196
Fire	☎ 199
Rescue Helicopter	☎ 244371
Rescue Patrol Boat	☎ 238797
Directory Inquiries	☎ 190
Overseas Operator	☎ 194
Time check	☎ 195
Government Information Line	☎ 153

LEGAL MATTERS

The police (*pulizija* in Malti) wear black uniforms with chequered caps not unlike their British equivalents. The cool shades are not compulsory but seem to be standard. All towns and most villages have their own police station, the smaller ones manned by a single officer and often marked by a traditional British-style blue lamp.

For an emergency requiring help from the police, call ☎ 191. Police headquarters (☎ 224001/9) is in Beltissebħ in Floriana. Gozo's main police station (☎ 562046/8) is in Triq ir-Repubblika in Victoria.

If you are arrested or detained by the police you have the right to be informed, in a language that you understand, of the reasons for your arrest or detention, and if the police do not release you they must bring you before a court within 48 hours. You also have the right to inform your consulate and to speak to a lawyer.

BUSINESS HOURS
Banks

Banks are open from 8.30 am to 12.30 or 12.45 pm Monday to Friday (some banks also open in the afternoon) and 8.30 am to noon on Saturday between 1 October and 14 June. The summer hours are the same (although few banks are open in the afternoon) except for Saturday, when they close at 11.30 am. There are 24-hour foreign exchange facilities at Malta international airport all year round.

Museums

The standard opening hours for all government museums (including the prehistoric temples of Tarxien, Ħaġar Qim, Mnajdra and Ġgantija) are: 8.15 am to 5 pm Monday to Saturday, and 8.15 am to 4 pm Sunday, from 1 October to 15 June; and 7.45 am to 2 pm daily from 16 June to 30 September (closed on public holidays). For inquiries call the Museums Department (☎ 230711).

Offices

Offices are open from 8 am to 1 pm and 2.30 or 3 to 5.30 pm Monday to Friday, and 8.30 am to 1 pm on Saturday from 1 October to 30 June; they open from 7.30 am to 1.30 pm Monday to Saturday from July to September.

Pharmacies

Pharmacies are generally open from 8.30 am to 12.30 pm and 4 to 7 pm Monday to Friday, and mornings only on Saturday. Duty pharmacists that open late and on Sunday or public holidays are listed in local newspapers.

Shops

Shops are generally open between 9 am and 1 pm, and again between 3.30 or 4 and 7 pm. In tourist areas in summer they will usually be open all day.

PUBLIC HOLIDAYS & SPECIAL EVENTS
Public Holidays

Malta observes 14 national public holidays:

New Year's Day	1 January
St Paul's Shipwreck	10 February
St Joseph's Day	19 March
Good Friday	
Freedom Day	31 March
Labour Day	1 May
Commemoration of 1919 independence riots	7 June
Feast of Sts Peter and Paul (L-Imnarja Festival)	29 June
Feast of the Assumption	15 August
Victory Day	8 September
Independence Day	21 September
Feast of the Immaculate Conception	8 December
Republic Day	13 December
Christmas Day	25 December

Special Events

Festi (feast days) are important events in Maltese family and village life. During the past 200 years they have developed from simple village feast days into extravagant five-day spectacles, lasting from Wednesday to Sunday. Every village has a *festa*, usually to celebrate the feast day of its patron saint. Most of them are in summer, and for days in advance the island reverberates to the sound of exploding fireworks announcing the forthcoming celebration.

The main fireworks display is usually on Saturday night, accompanied by one or more local brass bands. On the Sunday, pontifical high mass is celebrated at 9.15 am and 7 pm. Then the statue of the patron saint is paraded through the streets accompanied by brass bands, fireworks, petards and church bells. People then repair to the bars to drink, chat and sample savoury snacks or sweets such as *qubbajt* (nougat) sold from mobile kiosks that make the rounds of the festi.

If a festa is held while you are visiting, go along. A list of Maltese festi is provided in the special section 'Churches & Feast Days' later in this chapter. The Malta Tourist Authority also publishes an annual calendar of special events.

February/March

Malta Marathon Road race from Mdina to Sliema with large international field.

Karnival A week of colourful celebrations preceding Lent, with a traditional procession of floats with fancy dress and grotesque masks. It's celebrated throughout the islands, but the main procession is in Valletta.

April

Tour of Malta International cycling race

June

L-Imnarja Harvest festival with an agricultural show and traditional horse races; festivities are centred on Rabat. See boxed text 'The Festival of L-Imnarja' in the Central Malta chapter.

July

International Trade Fair Held at the Exhibition Grounds in Naxxar.

Malta Jazz Festival An increasingly popular event, with outdoor performances held beneath the bastions of Valletta. Held on the third weekend in July.

Farsons Food & Beer Festival Held on the weekend following the Jazz Festival.

September

Malta International Air Show Exhibition of visiting aircraft and aerial displays.

ACTIVITIES
Snorkelling

One of the most popular activities in Malta is diving (see later in this section). But if you don't fancy scuba-diving, you can still sample the delights of the underwater world by donning mask, snorkel and fins and exploring the rocks and bays around Malta's coastline. The only qualification necessary is the ability to swim. You can rent equipment from hotels, lidos and water-sports centres in all the tourist areas for a couple of pounds a day.

Top snorkelling spots include the Blue Lagoon and around the crags and caves east of Santa Marija Bay on Comino; the cave-riddled coastline at Dwejra; and along the salt-pan rocks west of Xwieni Bay near Marsalforn on Gozo.

Windsurfing

Windsurfing is a popular sport enjoyed throughout the year in Malta. Equipment hire and instruction are available at all the main tourist resorts. Mellieħa Bay and St Paul's Bay are popular venues.

There are two major international competitions held in Maltese waters each year: the Sicily to Malta Windsurfing Race in May, and the International Open-Class Boardsailing Championships in September.

Sailing

Malta is a major yachting centre, with a large marina at Msida, a smaller one at Gozo's Mġarr harbour and another under construction as part of Paċeville's Portomaso development. Many yacht owners cruise the Med in summer, and winter their vessels in Malta.

A full program of races and regattas is held between April and November each year – for details of events and opportunities for crewing, contact the Royal Malta

Yacht Club (☎ 333109 or 318417/8) on Manoel Island, or check its Web site at www.rmyc.org.

Qualified sailors are able to hire a yacht by the day or the week from one of several charter companies. Try Captain Morgan Yacht Charter (☎ 343373), Web site www.yachtcharter.com.mt, or S&D Yachts (☎ 320577, 331515 or 339908), Web site www.sdyachts.com. High/low season rates for a six-berth Oceanis 320 sailing yacht begin at Lm750/575 a week, or Lm110/98 a day including tax. You'll need an RYA Coastal Skipper qualification; otherwise, you'll find a professional skipper costs another Lm25 a day.

If a yacht seems like a little too much to handle, sailing dinghies can be rented by the hour at most tourist resorts for around Lm4 an hour.

Walking

There is some good walking to be enjoyed on the winding back roads and clifftop paths of Malta and Gozo, although fences, dogs and bird-shooters can occasionally prove to be a nuisance. Distances are small, and you can easily cover much of the islands on foot. A circuit of Gozo is a good objective for a multi-day hike.

Running

There are several major running events held each year in Malta, including triathlons and half-marathons, culminating in the Malta Marathon and Half-Marathon in late February or early March. Maltese athlete John Buhagiar won the event on 27 February 2000. For details and entry requirements try contacting the Malta Marathon Organising Committee (☎ 432402, @ maltamarathon@ orbit.net.mt), PO Box 9, Hamrun, or you can find more information at the Web site www.maltamarathon.com.mt.

Bird-Watching

Although there are barely a dozen species of birds that are permanent residents on Malta, the islands sustain important breeding colonies of sea-birds, including storm petrels and Cory's shearwaters. Malta also

ANN JEFFREE

Malta Marathon local hero, John Buhagiar

lies on an important migration route between Africa and Europe, and in spring and autumn vast numbers of migrating birds can be seen. A New Guide to the Birds of Malta by Joe Sultana and Charles Gauci (published by the Malta Ornithological Society, 1982) describes more than 350 species that have been recorded in the Maltese Islands.

BirdLife Malta (☎ 347646, @ blm@orbit .net.mt) organises a camp at Buskett Gardens each September to observe and record the annual migration of birds of prey.

Horse Riding

Horses have long played an important part in Maltese life, and you can often see proud owners out exercising their favourite trotting horses. The quieter back roads offer enjoyable riding – hire of a horse and instruction can be organised through most major hotels.

Riding schools in Malta include the Darmanin Riding Establishment (☎ 238507) in Marsa, Pandy's Riding School (☎ 342506) in St Andrews and Golden Bay Horse Riding (☎ 573360) at Għajn Tuffieħa.

[continued on page 56]

NEIL WILSON

JULIET COOMBE

MALTA'S CHURCHES

JULIET COOMBE

The Maltese claim to be one of the oldest Christian peoples in the world, having been converted by St Paul after his shipwreck on the island in AD 60.

There are 64 parishes and 313 churches in Malta, and 15 parishes and 46 churches in Gozo. These range from full cathedrals down to tiny wayside chapels, and were built between the 15th and 20th centuries. The main period of church-building in Malta took place after the arrival of the Knights of St John, in the 16th, 17th and 18th centuries. The oldest surviving churches in Malta are the tiny medieval chapels at H-al Millieri near Żurrieq. These date from the mid-15th century, and are in Maltese vernacular style.

The 16th century saw the Renaissance style imported from Italy by the Knights, followed by the more elaborate forms of Maltese baroque which evolved throughout the 17th century and culminated in the Cathedral of St Paul in Mdina. The 19th and 20th centuries saw the addition of several large churches in the neogothic style, including St Paul's Anglican Cathedral in Valletta (1839-41) and the Church of Our Lady of Lourdes in Mġarr, Gozo (1924-75). Two huge rotundas were also built by public subscription: the Church of St Mary at Mosta (1833-60) and the Church of St John the Baptist (1951-71) at Xewkija in Gozo.

Title Page: A papier mache festa figurine adorns a float (Photographer: Veronica Carbutt).

Facing Page:
Top Left: Church of St Nicholas with Christmas lights, Siġġiewi

Bottom Left: Ceiling paintings on the barrel vaults in St John's Co-Cathedral show 18 episodes in the life of St John the Baptist.

Right: The interior of St John's Co-Cathedral in Valletta is the perfect place to admire Mattia Preti's baroque style.

JULIET COOMBE

The following list includes 10 of the most impressive examples of church architecture in the Maltese Islands.

Co-Cathedral of St John, Valletta
(1573-77; Gerolamo Cassar, interior by Mattia Preti)
The austere Renaissance facade of St John's – the Conventual Church of the Order of St John from 1577 to 1798 – conceals a richly ornamental interior. The tombs of Grand Masters Nicolas Cotoner and Ramon Perellos in the Chapel of Aragon are floridly baroque.

Church of St Paul's Shipwreck, Valletta
(c. 1580; Gerolamo Cassar, remodelled by Lorenzo Gafa in 1629)
Don't be fooled by the largely 19th-century facade on Triq San Pawl – this is one of Valletta's oldest churches. The wooden statue of St Paul was carved by Melchiorre Gafa in 1657, and is paraded through the streets on the festa day (10 February).

Church of St Mary, Attard
(1613-16; Tommaso Dingli)
This is one of the finest examples of Renaissance-style architecture in Malta, built on a Latin cross plan with an elegant and restrained facade adorned with statues of the saints.

NEIL WILSON

Left: The Renaissance-style Parish Church of St Mary is in Attard in Central Malta.

Church of St Lawrence, Vittoriosa
(1681-97; Lorenzo Gafa)
St Lawrence occupies the site of a small church built by Count Roger in 1090. It was enlarged and taken over by the Knights as their original conventual church in Malta in 1530, and it houses relics brought from Rhodes, a silver processional cross, and a fine altarpiece by Mattia Preti showing the martyrdom of St Lawrence. The dome was rebuilt after being damaged by a bomb in 1942.

Church of St Nicholas, Siġġiewi
(1675-93; Lorenzo Gafa)
This church is dedicated to St Nicholas of Myra, better known to the Western world as Santa Claus, and has one of the most richly ornamental baroque interiors on the island. The huge dome and the neoclassical facade were added in the 19th century.

Cathedral of St Paul, Mdina
(1697-1702; Lorenzo Gafa)
Designed by Gafa at the height of his career, this is probably the finest example of the Maltese baroque style (rather more restrained and less florid than the baroque of Italy). The cathedral occupies the site of a Norman church built in the 1090s, and there may have been a church here since the 4th century.

Cathedral of the Assumption, Victoria, Gozo
(1697-1711; Lorenzo Gafa)
Gozo's cathedral is another fine example of Maltese baroque designed by Gafa. Lack of funds meant the dome was never built, but an 18th-century trompe-l'oeil painting looks convincing on the inside. The cathedral occupies the site of an older Norman church, and possibly of a Roman temple.

Right: St John's Co-Cathedral boasts an elaborately carved side chapel roof.

JULIET COOMBE

Church of St Helen, Birkirkara
(1727-45; Domenico Cachia)
Birkirkara's parish church is probably the most ornate of Malta's churches, a late flowering of baroque exuberance. On the strength of his performance here, Cachia was given the job of designing the facade of the Auberge of Castile in Valletta.

Church of Sts Peter & Paul, Nadur, Gozo
(1760-80; Giuseppe Bonnici)
The extravagance of Bonnici's original design has been tempered by a more sober 19th-century facade, but the beautiful and ornate marble interior is pure baroque. The twin statues of its patron saints have given it the nickname iż-Żewġ (the pair, or the twins), and its festa (29 June) is one of the liveliest on the islands.

Church of St John the Baptist, Xewkija, Gozo
(1951-71; Joseph D'Amato)
This huge rotunda was built with money and labour donated by the parishioners of Xewkija. It is the biggest church in the Maltese Islands, and can seat up to 4000 people.

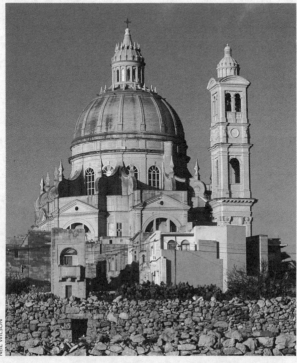

NEIL WILSON

Left: The Parish Church of St John the Baptist in Xewkija was built by the people, for the people.

FEAST DAYS

JULIET COOMBE

The *festa* (plural *festi*, feast day) is an important event in Maltese village life. Every village celebrates the feast day of its patron saint. Most of them are held from June to September. The church is decorated with coloured lights and its treasures and relics are cleaned and polished and placed proudly on display. Festivities begin five days before the main feast day, and include band club concerts and fireworks. The climax of the festa is the procession, during which a statue of the parish church's patron saint is carried through the streets.

The timing of church services and events during a festa is usually as follows: on the eve of the feast day, Vespers and Mass are at 6 pm, followed by band club concerts at 7 pm; on the feast day itself, High Mass is at 9.15 am, and the procession begins at 7 pm.

Good Friday pageants are held in several towns and villages. Life-size statues depicting scenes from the passion and death of Jesus Christ are carried shoulder high in procession along the main streets of the town, accompanied by men and women dressed as biblical characters.

Early in the morning of Easter Sunday there are processions bearing the statue of the Risen Christ. Particularly interesting are those held at the three harbour towns of Vittoriosa, Senglea and Cospicua, where the statue bearers actually run with the statue. It is customary for children to have their *figolla* (an almond-based Easter cake), blessed by the Risen Christ during these processions.

NEIL WILSON

Right: Services at churches such as the Basilica of Ta'Pinu in Gharb, Gozo, are an integral part of festa celebrations.

Feast Days

Date	Festa	Town
1st Sunday in February	St Agatha	Rabat
10 February	St Paul's Shipwreck	Valletta
10 February	St Paul's Shipwreck	St Paul's Bay
2nd Sunday in March	St Gregory	Kerċem, Gozo
date varies	Good Friday	(various parishes)
date varies	Easter Sunday	(various parishes)
3rd Sunday after Easter	St Publius	Floriana
3rd Sunday after Easter	St Augustine	Valletta
last Sunday in May	St Joseph	Kirkop
last Sunday in May	St Paul	Munxar, Gozo
5th Sunday after Easter	The Annunciation	Tarxien
1 June	Corpus Christi	Valletta
4 June or nearest Sunday	Our Lady of Fatima	Gwardamanġa
1st Sunday in June	Corpus Christi	Għasri, Gozo
1st Sunday in June	St Joseph	Għaxaq
2nd Sunday in June	Our Lady of Liesse	Valletta
2nd Sunday in June	St Anthony	Mġarr, Gozo
2nd Sunday in June	St Philip	Żebbuġ
1st Sunday after Pentecost	Holy Trinity	Marsa
2nd or 3rd Sunday in June	Sacred Heart of Jesus	Fontana, Gozo
3rd Sunday in June	Our Lady of the Lily	Mqabba
3rd Sunday in June	St Catherine	Żejtun
last Sunday in June	Corpus Christi	Rabat
29 June or Sunday before	Our Lady of the Sacred Heart	Burmarrad
last Sunday in June	St George	Qormi
last Sunday in June	St John the Baptist	Xewkija, Gozo
last Sunday in June	St Nicholas	Siġġiewi
29 June	St Peter & St Paul	Mdina
29 June	Sts Peter & Paul	Nadur, Gozo
1st Sunday in July	Christ Redeemer	Senglea
1st Sunday in July	Immaculate Conception	Ħamrun
1st Sunday in July	Our Lady of Lourdes	Qrendi
1st Sunday in July	Our Lady of Mt Carmel	Fleur-de-Lys
1st Sunday in July	St Andrew	Luqa
1st Sunday in July	St Elizabeth	Għarb, Gozo
1st Sunday in July	St Joseph The Worker	Birkirkara
1st Sunday in July	St Paul	Rabat
2nd Sunday in July	Annunciation	Balzan
2nd Sunday in July	Our Lady of Mt Carmel	Fgura
2nd Sunday in July	Our Lady of Mt Carmel	Gżira
2nd Sunday in July	Our Lady of Perpetual Help	Kerċem, Gozo
2nd Sunday in July	Our Lady of the Sacred Heart	Sliema
2nd Sunday in July	St Joseph	Kalkara
3rd Sunday in July	Our Lady of Mt Carmel	Valletta
3rd Sunday in July	Our Lady of Mt Carmel	Birkirkara
3rd Sunday in July	St George	Victoria, Gozo
3rd Sunday in July	St Sebastian	Qormi
16 July or Sunday after	St Joseph	Msida
4th Sunday in July	Our Lady of Mt Carmel	Żurrieq
4th Sunday in July	Our Lady of Mt Carmel	Mdina
4th Sunday in July	St Margaret	Sannat, Gozo
26 July or Sunday after	St Anna	Marsaskala
last Sunday in July	Christ the King	Paola

Feast Days

Date	Festa	Town
last Sunday in July	Our Lady of Mt Carmel	Balluta
last Sunday in July	Our Lady of Sorrows	St Paul's Bay
last Sunday in July	St Lawrence	San Lawrenz, Gozo
last Sunday in July	St Venera	Santa Venera
1st Sunday in August	Our Lady of Lourdes	San Ġwann
1st Sunday in August	Our Lady of Pompei	Marsaxlokk
1st Sunday in August	St Joseph	Qala, Gozo
1st Sunday in August	St Peter	Birżebbuġa
4 August or Sunday before	St Dominic	Valletta
6 August	Transfiguration of Our Lord	Lija
7 August or Sunday after	St Gaetan	Ħamrun
10 August or nearest Sunday	St Lawrence	Vittoriosa
15 August	The Assumption of Our Lady	Mqabba
15 August	The Assumption of Our Lady	Qrendi
15 August	The Assumption of Our Lady	Mosta
15 August	The Assumption of Our Lady	Attard
15 August	The Assumption of Our Lady	Għaxaq
15 August	The Assumption of Our Lady	Gudja
15 August	The Assumption of Our Lady	Victoria, Gozo
15 August or Sunday after	Our Lady of Lourdes	Paola
18 August or nearest Sunday	St Helen	Birkirkara
18 August or Sunday after	Our Lady Star of the Sea	Sliema
20 August or nearest Sunday	Holy Mary	Mġarr (Malta)
20 August or nearest Sunday	Holy Mary	Dingli
20 August or nearest Sunday	Holy Mary	Żebbuġ, Gozo
24 August or Sunday after	St Bartholomew	Għarghur
last Sunday in August	Maria Regina	Marsa
last Sunday in August	Our Lady of Loreto	Għajnsielem, Gozo
last Sunday in August	St Dominic	Vittoriosa
last Sunday in August	St Joseph	Manikata
last Sunday in August	St Julian	St Julian's
last Sunday in August	St Paul	Safi
1st Sunday in September	Our Lady of Mt Carmel	Xlendi, Gozo
1st Sunday in September	Our Lady of The Cintura	Rabat
1st Sunday in September	Our Lady of The Cintura	Gudja
1st Sunday in September	St Catherine	Żurrieq
1st Sunday in September	St Gregory	Sliema
8 September	Our Lady of Victories	various parishes
8 September	The Nativity of Our Lady	Xagħra, Gozo
8 September	The Nativity of Our Lady	Senglea
8 September	The Nativity of Our Lady	Mellieħa
8 September	The Nativity of Our Lady	Naxxar
8 September or Sunday after	Our Lady of Graces	Żabbar
8 September or Sunday after	Our Lady of Graces	Victoria, Gozo
3rd Sunday in September	St Leonard	Kirkop
4th Sunday in September	St Francis	Marsa
1st Sunday in October	Our Lady of The Rosary	Gudja
3rd Sunday in October	Our Lady of Health	Rabat
2nd Sunday in November	St Coronatus	Nadur, Gozo
3rd Sunday in November	St Fortunatus	Żebbuġ, Gozo
8 December	Immaculate Conception	Cospicua
8 December	Immaculate Conception	Qala, Gozo
8 December	Immaculate Conception	Victoria, Gozo

[continued from page 48]

Diving
Malta and Gozo offer some of the finest scuba-diving in the Mediterranean, and indeed in the whole of Europe. For details see the boxed text 'Diving in Malta'.

COURSES
Malta is one of the few places where people wanting to learn or improve their English can combine a language course with a Mediterranean holiday. There are dozens of English language schools in Malta, ranging from one-person operations to the Berlitz Language Centre, and catering to around 40,000 students a year from over 50 countries.

Full details of vacation and business courses can be obtained from the Malta Tourist Authority, or you could try contacting the Federation of English Language Teaching Organisations Malta (FELTOM; fax 230330, @ feltom@maltanet.net), Foundation for International Studies, Old University Buildings, Triq San Pawl, Valletta VLT 07.

WORK
It is difficult for foreigners to work legally in Malta. Casual (illegal) work waiting tables or washing dishes in bars and discos can sometimes be found.

ACCOMMODATION
There is a wide range of accommodation available in the Maltese Islands, though much of it is in fairly uniform resort hotels and apartments. The government is attempting to drive Malta's tourist industry upmarket, and almost all the new hotels and developments are at the luxury end of the spectrum. However, there are still plenty of good budget options.

Camping
There are no official camp sites on Malta, and wild camping is not allowed. Travellers sometimes sleep out on the quieter beaches, particularly on Gozo, but strictly speaking this is illegal.

Hostels
The National Student Travel Service (NSTS; ☎ 244983, @ nsts@nsts.org) is the official HI affiliate in Malta. It can arrange dormitory accommodation in hostels in Sliema, Lija and Buġibba on Malta and Għajnsielem on Gozo.

There is an organisation called the Malta Youth Hostels Association (☎ 693957, @ myha@keyworld.net), 17 Triq Tal-Borg, Paola PLA 06, Malta, but it is not affiliated to HI. It offers shelter to Malta's homeless people, and accepts travellers only as volunteers, offering free accommodation in return for working in the hostels. For further information about this organisation, contact the MYHA by email, or phone or call at the Paola address between 4 and 5 pm Monday to Friday.

University Accommodation
Accommodation in the University Residence at Lija (see The Three Villages in the Central Malta chapter) can be arranged through NSTS (see Hostels earlier in this section).

Hotels & Guesthouses
Hotels in Malta range from crumbling but characterful old townhouses in Valletta to modern, gilt and chrome palaces of five-star luxury overlooking a private marina. The vast majority are bland, faceless tourist hotels, block-booked by package tour companies in summer, and either closed or eerily quiet in winter. Typical high season rates are Lm8 to Lm15 per person, but they rise to Lm20 to Lm40 for the four- and five-star places.

However, there are a few places that have real character, like the Castille Hotel in Valletta, which is housed in an old mansion; the Xara Palace in Mdina; and the L-Imġarr and Ta'Ċenċ on Gozo, but the latter three hotels are among the most expensive in the islands.

Guesthouses are usually family-run, with six to 10 rooms, and are often good value at around Lm5 to Lm7 per person. Toilets are mostly shared, but breakfast is normally included in the price.

Diving in Malta

Why Malta?

The Maltese Islands offer some of the best scuba-diving in Europe, and have many advantages for beginners, including a pleasant climate; warm, clear water; a wide range of interesting dive sites, many of them accessible from the shore; and a large number of dive schools with qualified, professional instructors. Most schools offer courses that lead to qualifications issued by one or more of the internationally recognised diving bodies – the Professional Association of Diving Instructors (PADI), the British Sub-Aqua Club (BSAC) and the Confederation Mondiale des Activites Subaquatiques (CMAS).

For information about diving in Malta, check out the Dive Malta Web site at www.divemalta.com. For general information about diving and dive qualifications, you can also try www.padi.com, www.bsac.co.uk or www.cmas.org.

Requirements

If you want to learn to dive in Malta, there are a few things required of you, not least of which is the ability to swim. You will also have to pass a simple medical examination to make sure you are fit to dive – this will be organised by the dive school, and costs about Lm3. The minimum age is 12 years, and those under 18 must have written parental consent.

Courses and Qualifications

Most schools offer a 'taster course' or 'beginner's dive', which begins with one or two hours of shore-based instruction on the workings of scuba equipment and safety procedures. You will then be introduced to breathing underwater in a pool or shallow bay, and will end up doing a 30-minute dive in the sea. A beginner's course should cost no more than Lm15 including the compulsory medical examination.

A so-called 'resort course' gives you shore-based instruction plus four to six open water dives accompanied by an instructor, and costs around Lm40 to Lm70. These courses do NOT result in an official qualification.

A course that will give you an entry-level diving qualification (CMAS One-Star Diver, PADI Open Water Diver, BSAC Ocean Diver) should take four or five days and cost around Lm125.

Diving Schools

There are over 30 dive school operators in Malta. The majority are members of the Professional Diving Schools Association (PDSA; 1 Msida Court, 61 ix-Xatt Ta-Msida, Msida, @ pdsa@digigate.net), an organisation that is dedicated to promoting high standards of safety and professionalism. The following dive schools all offer PADI, BSAC or CMAS approved courses.

Aquaventure (☎ 522141, fax 521053, @ aquaventure@maltanet.net) Mellieħa Bay Hotel, Mellieħa Bay

Calypso Diving Centre (☎ 562000, fax 562020, @ caldive@digigate.net) Calypso Hotel, Marsalforn, Gozo

Divecare (☎ 339240, fax 341729, @ divecare@digigate.net) St Julian's Aqua Sports Club, Triq Ġorġ Borg Olivier, St Julian's

Dive Deep Blue (☎ 583495 or 250280, fax 583495, @ deepblue@digigate.net) 100 Triq Annanija, Buġibba

Dive Med (☎ 690909, fax 666536, @ divemed@mail.link.net.mt) 237 Triq Żabbar, Paola

Diveshack (☎ 320594, fax 345670, @ info@diveshackscuba.com) ix-Xatt Ta-Qui-si-sana, Qui-si-sana, Sliema

Dive Systems (☎ 319123, fax 342040, @ divesys@digigate.net) ix-Xatt Ta-Qui-Si-Sana, Sliema

Divewise (☎ 336441, fax 310708) Dragonara Complex, St Julian's

Dwejra Divers (☎ 553525, fax 552056, @ dwejra@global.net.mt) Inland Sea, Dwejra, Gozo

Diving in Malta

Frankie's Gozo Diving Centre (☎ 551315, fax 560356, ✉ frankie@digigate.net) Triq Mġarr, Xewkija, Gozo

Gozo Aqua Sports (☎ 563037, fax 559938, ✉ gailbuge@keyworld.net) Green Valley, Triq Rabat, Marsalforn, Gozo

Maltaqua (☎ 571873 or 572558, fax 580064, ✉ maltaqua@pobox.com) Triq Mosta, Buġibba

Meldives (☎ 577223 or 573116, fax 577223, meldives@digigate.net) Seabank Complex, Triq Marfa, Mellieħa Bay

Moby Dives (☎ 551616, fax 554606, ✉ moby@digigate.net) Triq il-Gostra, Xlendi Bay, Gozo

Northeast Diving Services Ltd (☎ 311889, fax 340511, ✉ nds@digigate.net) Pebbles Lido, Qui-si-sana, Sliema

Octopus Garden (☎/fax 582586, ✉ sharkman@orbit.net.mt) New Dolmen Hotel, Buġibba

Paradise Diving & Watersports (☎ 573981, fax 573115, ✉ paradive@global.net.mt) Paradise Bay Hotel, Ċirkewwa

Scubatech Diving Centre (☎ 580617, fax 455916, ✉ scubatech@usa.net) Triq L-Alka, St Paul's Bay

Sport Diving (☎ 829292, fax 829418, ✉ sportdiv@digigate.net) Triq il-Qaliet, Marsaskala

St Andrews Divers Cove (☎ 551301, fax 561548, ✉ standrew@digigate.net) Triq San Ximun, Xlendi, Gozo

Strand Diving Services (☎ 574502, fax 577480, ✉ strand@digigate.net) Triq Ramon Perellos, St Paul's Bay

Subway Scuba Diving School (☎ 580611, fax 573654, ✉ info@subwayscuba.com) 39 Xemxija Hill, St Paul's Bay

Suncrest Diving Centre (☎ 577101, fax 575478) Suncrest Hotel, Qawra

Tony's Dive Services (☎ 529821/9 or 315611, fax 529826) Comino Hotel, Comino

Considerations for Responsible Diving

The popularity of diving is placing immense pressure on many sites – over 40,000 divers a year visit the Maltese Islands. Please consider the following tips when diving and help preserve the ecology and beauty of Malta's underwater world:

- Avoid touching living marine organisms with your body or dragging equipment across the rocks.

- Be conscious of your fins. Even without contact the surge from heavy fin strokes can damage delicate organisms.

- Practise and maintain proper buoyancy control. Make sure you are correctly weighted and that your weight belt is positioned so that you stay horizontal. If you have not dived for a while, have a practice dive in a pool before taking to the sea. Be aware that buoyancy can change over the period of an extended trip: initially you may breathe harder and need more weight; a few days later you may breathe more easily and need less weight.

- Take great care in underwater caves. Spend as little time within them as possible as your air bubbles may be caught within the roof, leaving previously submerged organisms high and dry. Taking turns to inspect the interior of a small cave will lessen the chances of damaging contact.

- Resist the temptation to collect or buy shells or other remains of marine organisms. Aside from the ecological damage, taking home marine souvenirs depletes the beauty of a site and spoils the enjoyment of others. The same goes for marine archaeological sites (mainly shipwrecks). Respect their integrity; some sites are protected from looting by law.

- Ensure that you take home all your rubbish and any litter you may find as well. Plastics in particular are a serious threat to marine life. Turtles can mistake plastic for jellyfish and eat it.

- Resist the temptation to feed fish. You may disturb their normal eating habits, encourage aggressive behaviour or feed them food that is detrimental to their health.

Rental Accommodation

There are hundreds of self-catering apartments with little to choose between them. Most have a private bathroom, a balcony and a kitchen area with fridge, sink and two-ring electric cooker. Though lacking a little in charm, they are often very good value at under Lm10 per person, even in high season.

If you are looking for something with a little local colour, then get in touch with a tour operator or agency that specialises in Gozo farmhouses. Dozens of these old, square-set farm buildings have been converted into self-catering accommodation, often with a private swimming pool at the back. The Malta Tourist Authority can provide a list of tour operators that specialise in offering Gozo farmhouse holidays. Alternatively check out the Farmhouses pages on the Web site www.gozo.com.

High & Low Seasons

The cost of accommodation in Malta can vary considerably with the time of year, and low season rates are often a bargain. Low season is almost always 1 November to 31 March. High season generally refers to the period 1 April to 31 October, but some hotels have a 'shoulder' or 'mid' season covering April, May and October, with high season prices restricted to July, August and September. Many hotels count the Christmas and New Year period as high season too. The high and low season prices quoted in this book are generally the maximum and minimum rates for each establishment.

FOOD

Malta is not known as a destination for gourmets, but the food is both good and cheap. The most obvious influence is Sicilian, and most of the cheaper restaurants serve pasta and pizza. English standards (eg, grilled chops, sausages and mash, and roast with three veg) are also commonly available, particularly in the tourist areas. Vegetarians are well catered for, with many restaurants offering vegetarian dishes as main courses.

The Fenkata

A *fenkata* is a big, communal meal of rabbit, usually eaten in the countryside. It supposedly originated as a gesture of rebellion against the occupying Knights, who hunted rabbits and denied them to the local population. The most important fenkata is associated with the L-Imnarja harvest festival at the end of June, when hundreds of people gather at Buskett Gardens to eat rabbit, drink wine, sing folk songs and dance the night away. Fenkata is also eaten on special occasions, when a group of family and friends will take over a country restaurant for an afternoon and evening of food, drink and celebration.

✶✶✶✶✶✶✶✶✶✶✶✶✶✶✶✶✶✶✶

Snacks

The traditional Maltese snack is the *pastizza*, a small parcel of flaky pastry filled with either ricotta cheese or mushy peas. A couple of pastizzi make for a tasty – if somewhat high-fat – breakfast or afternoon filler.

Another traditional snack, much loved by Maltese children, is *ħobż biż-żejt,* slices of bread rubbed with ripe tomatoes and olive oil until they are pink and delicious. Freshly baked Maltese bread is delightful. It is made in a similar manner to American sourdough bread, using a scrap of yesterday's dough to leaven today's loaves. *Ftira* is bread baked in a flat disc and stuffed with a mixture of tomatoes, olives, capers and anchovies.

You will either love or hate *ġbejniet,* the small, hard, white cheese traditionally made from unpasteurised sheep's or goat's milk. They are dried in baskets and often steeped in olive oil flavoured with salt and crushed black peppercorns.

One of Malta's favourite sweetmeats is *mqaret,* diamond-shaped pastries stuffed with chopped, spiced dates and deep-fried. *Qubbajt* is Maltese nougat, flavoured with almonds or hazelnuts and traditionally sold on festa days.

Main Dishes

Here is a selection of the most popular and widely available Maltese dishes.

Soppa tal-armla The so-called 'widow's soup' is traditionally made only with ingredients that are either green or white. Basically a vegetable soup, it contains cauliflower, spinach, endive, and peas, poured over a poached egg, a *ġbejniet* and a lump of ricotta cheese.

Minestra Minestra is a thick soup of tomatoes, beans, pasta and vegetables, similar to Italian minestrone.

Timpana A rich pie filled with macaroni, cheese, egg, minced beef, tomato, garlic and onion, timpana is a Sicilian dish not dissimilar to Greek *pastitsio*.

Aljotta This is a delicious fish soup made with tomato, rice and lots and lots of garlic.

Ravjuletti This is a Maltese variety of ravioli (pasta pouches filled with ricotta, parmesan and parsley).

Braġioli These are prepared by wrapping a thin slice of beef around a stuffing of breadcrumbs, chopped bacon, hard-boiled egg and parsley, then braising these 'beef olives' in a red wine sauce.

Fenek Fenek – rabbit – is *the* favourite Maltese dish, whether fried in olive oil, roasted, stewed or baked in a pie.

Torta Tal-Lampuki The local fish speciality is *torta tal-lampuki,* or *lampuki* pie. Lampuka *(Coryphaena hippurus)* – plural *lampuki* – is known in English as dolphin fish, dorado or mahi-mahi. It's a large, swift carnivorous fish with a high, domed forehead (hence the name dolphin) and powerful

Lampuki, also known as mahi-mahi

tapered body. When freshly caught, it is beautifully coloured in shimmering blue and gold, but the colours quickly fade after death.

The lampuka is a migratory fish, and is caught in Maltese waters only during the period from August to November. It is delicious simply fried in olive oil, but the traditional way to prepare it is to bake it in a pie with tomatoes, onions, black olives, spinach, sultanas and walnuts.

Self-Catering

There are plenty of supermarkets, minimarkets, delicatessens and fresh produce markets where you can buy food to prepare yourself or to take on a picnic. You can also buy fresh fruit and veg and other produce from the farmers' vans that can be found in most villages from dawn till lunchtime.

DRINKS
Nonalcoholic Drinks

Good Italian coffee – espresso and cappuccino – is widely available in cafes and bars, and in the main tourist areas you will also find a cup of good strong British tea, heavy on the milk and sugar.

Cold soft drinks are available everywhere. Kinnie – you'll see its advertising signs all over the place in Malta – is the brand name of a local soft drink flavoured with bitter oranges and aromatic herbs. It makes a change from cola and lemonade, and slips down nicely when mixed with rum or vodka.

Alcoholic Drinks

Maltese bars serve up every kind of drink you could ask for, from pints of British beer to shots of Galliano liqueur. The good locally made beers, Cisk Lager and Hop Leaf Ale, are about half the price of imported brews.

The main local wine producers are Marsovin and Delicata, which both make wine from local grapes and also produce more expensive 'special reserve' wines – merlot, cabernet sauvignon, chardonnay and sauvignon blanc – using imported grapes from Italy and France.

The cheaper reds, like La Vallette, are a bit rough around the edges, but Green Label

Dry is a very drinkable white, and costs only Lm1.30 a bottle from a shop, or Lm2.40 if bought in a restaurant. Half bottles are widely available.

ENTERTAINMENT

Malta is not noted as a nightlife destination, but there's plenty of buzz in the tourist bars in summer, and Paċeville's pubs and clubs go off on weekends all year round. There are casinos in Buġibba and near Paċeville, and cinemas in Paċeville, Marsaskala, Fġura, Ħamrun and Victoria.

The venerable Manoel Theatre in Valletta stages a varied program of drama, ballet, opera and concerts from October until May, and puts on a traditional pantomime for the Christmas season. The Astra and Aurora theatres in Victoria have a more limited repertoire. Local brass bands perform during festas and on public holidays.

SPECTATOR SPORTS
Football (Soccer)

The Maltese are great football fans, and follow the fortunes of local sides and international teams with equal fervour. The local football season runs from September till May, and there is a Maltese Premier League with 10 teams. League and international matches are held at the National Stadium at Ta'Qali between Mosta and Rabat. Results are reported in the local newspapers. More information can be obtained from the Football Association (☎ 222697).

Water Polo

As the heat of summer increases, football gives way to water polo, with its season lasting from July till September. The fans who were shouting on the terraces now yell from the poolsides. Games are hard fought and physical, and it's worth trying to take in a match during your stay in Malta. The important clashes are held at the National Water Polo Stadium at Zonqor Point in Marsaskala. Further information is available from the Amateur Swimming Association (☎ 236033).

Horse Racing

Horse racing is one of the Maltese Islands' most popular spectator sports, with race meetings held at the Marsa Racecourse every Sunday from the months of October to May. Races are mostly trotting – where the jockey rides a light two-wheeled gig drawn by the horse – rather than flat, and the betting is frantic.

SHOPPING

Traditional handicrafts include lace, silver filigree, blown glass and pottery, and are available throughout the country. Hand-knitted clothing is produced in the villages and can be quite cheap, but remember to shop around before you make a purchase – the Malta Crafts Centre in Pjazza San Ġwann in Valletta or the Ta'Qali Crafts Centre are good places to start. The best bargains are to be found on Gozo.

Getting There & Away

AIR
Airports & Airlines

All flights arrive and depart from Malta International Airport (☎ 249600, 697800) at Luqa, which is 5km south of Valletta. There is a heliport on Gozo (☎ 557905) with a helicopter link to Luqa (see the Getting Around chapter).

Malta is well connected to Europe, North Africa and the Middle East, with daily direct flights from London, Frankfurt, Rome, Zürich, Catania (Sicily) and Tripoli (Libya), and several direct flights a week from Milan, Paris, Geneva, Vienna, Moscow, Tunis, Cairo and Dubai.

The Maltese national airline is Air Malta (☎ 662211). Air Malta's overseas sales agents include:

Australia (☎ 02-9241 2011, fax 9290 3306) World Aviation Systems, 403 George St, Sydney, NSW 2000
Austria (☎ 01-586 5909, fax 586 5905) Opernring 1/R/5/513-5, Vienna A-1010
Canada (☎ 416-604 4112, fax 604 3452) Trans-Med Aviation Inc, General Sales Agents, 3323 Dundas St West, Toronto, Ontario M6P 2A6
Egypt (☎ 02-578 2692) Air Malta Office, Nile Hilton Commercial Centre, Executive Suite, 34 Tahir Square, Cairo
France (☎ 1-44 86 08 40, fax 44 86 08 41), 9 Boulevard de la Madeleine, Paris 75001
Germany (☎ 69-9203 521, fax 9203 551) Rossmarkt 11, Frankfurt 60311
Italy (☎ 06-488 3106, fax 487 2175) Via Barberini 29, Rome 00187
Libya (☎ 21-335 0578, fax 335 0580) Tower No 5, Floor 13, Dhat el Emad Complex, Tripoli
Russia (☎ 502-937 5950, fax 937 5951) Aviareps, Sadovaya, Chernogryazskaya ulitsa 13-3, Moscow
Switzerland (☎ 01-816 3012, fax 816 3017) 2-723 Terminal B (Departures Level), Zürich Airport, Zürich CH-8058
Tunisia (☎ 01-703229 or 703489, fax 703867) Complexe Ariana, Bureau A215, Ariana, Tunis 2080

> ## Warning
>
> The information in this chapter is particularly vulnerable to change: Prices for international travel are volatile, routes are introduced and cancelled, schedules change, special deals come and go, and rules and visa requirements are amended. Airlines and governments seem to take a perverse pleasure in making price structures and regulations as complicated as possible. You should check directly with the airline or a travel agent to make sure you understand how a fare (and ticket you may buy) works. In addition, the travel industry is highly competitive and there are many lurks and perks.
>
> The upshot of this is that you should get opinions, quotes and advice from as many airlines and travel agents as possible before you part with your hard-earned cash. The details given in this chapter should be regarded as pointers and are not a substitute for your own careful, up-to-date research.

United Arab Emirates (☎ 04-295 0456 or 203 3787, fax 225 973) City Tower 2, Office No. 1904, Sheikh Zayed Rd, Dubai
UK (☎ 020-7292 4949 or 0845-607 3710, fax 020-7734 1836) Malta House, 26/38 Piccadilly, London W1V 9PA
USA (☎ 212-983 8504 or 800-756 2582, fax 212-983 8508) World Aviation Systems, 205 East 42nd St, Suite 1908, New York, NY 10017

Airlines with offices in Malta include:

Aeroflot	☎ 243581/2 or 232641
Alitalia	☎ 234454
Austrian Airlines	☎ 243444/5
Balkan Bulgarian Airlines	☎ 339808
British Airways	☎ 242233/6 or 237333
CSA Airlines	☎ 333407/8
Egyptair	☎ 322256/7
Emirates	☎ 251384
JAT-Jugoslav Airlines	☎ 332888
Lufthansa	☎ 249341/2/3
Swissair	☎ 249336/3
Transavia	☎ 220940
Tuninter	☎ 320732

Air Travel Glossary

Cancellation Penalties If you have to cancel or change a discounted ticket, there are often heavy penalties involved; insurance can sometimes be taken out against these penalties. Some airlines impose penalties on regular tickets as well, particularly against 'no-show' passengers.

Courier Fares Businesses often need to send urgent documents or freight securely and quickly. Courier companies hire people to accompany the package through customs and, in return, offer a discount ticket which is sometimes a phenomenal bargain. However, you may have to surrender all your baggage allowance and take only carry-on luggage.

Full Fares Airlines traditionally offer 1st class (coded F), business class (coded J) and economy class (coded Y) tickets. These days there are so many promotional and discounted fares available that few passengers pay full economy fare.

Lost Tickets If you lose your airline ticket an airline will usually treat it like a travellers cheque and, after inquiries, issue you with another one. Legally, however, an airline is entitled to treat it like cash and if you lose it then it's gone forever. Take good care of your tickets.

Onward Tickets An entry requirement for many countries is that you have a ticket out of the country. If you're unsure of your next move, the easiest solution is to buy the cheapest onward ticket to a neighbouring country or a ticket from a reliable airline which can later be refunded if you do not use it.

Open-Jaw Tickets These are return tickets where you fly out to one place but return from another. If available, this can save you backtracking to your arrival point.

Overbooking Since every flight has some passengers who fail to show up, airlines often book more passengers than they have seats. Usually excess passengers make up for the no-shows, but occasionally somebody gets 'bumped' onto the next available flight. Guess who it is most likely to be? The passengers who check in late.

Promotional Fares These are officially discounted fares, available from travel agencies or direct from the airline.

Reconfirmation If you don't reconfirm your flight at least 72 hours prior to departure, the airline may delete your name from the passenger list. Ring to find out if your airline requires reconfirmation.

Restrictions Discounted tickets often have various restrictions on them – such as needing to be paid for in advance and incurring a penalty to be altered. Others are restrictions on the minimum and maximum period you must be away.

Round-the-World Tickets RTW tickets give you a limited period (usually a year) in which to circumnavigate the globe. You can go anywhere the carrying airlines go, as long as you don't backtrack. The number of stopovers or total number of separate flights is decided before you set off and they usually cost a bit more than a basic return flight.

Transferred Tickets Airline tickets cannot be transferred from one person to another. Travellers sometimes try to sell the return half of their ticket, but officials can ask you to prove that you are the person named on the ticket. On an international flight tickets are compared with passports.

Travel Periods Ticket prices vary with the time of year. There is a low (off-peak) season and a high (peak) season, and often a low-shoulder season and a high-shoulder season as well. Usually the fare depends on your outward flight – if you depart in the high season and return in the low season, you pay the high season fare.

Buying Tickets

An air ticket alone can gouge a great slice out of anyone's budget, but you can reduce the cost by finding discounted fares. Stiff competition has resulted in widespread discounting – good news for travellers! The only people likely to be paying full fare these days are travellers flying in 1st or business class. Passengers flying in economy can usually manage some sort of discount. But unless you buy carefully and flexibly, it is still possible to end up paying exorbitant amounts for a journey.

For long term travel there are plenty of discount tickets which are valid for 12 months, allowing multiple stopovers with open dates. For short term travel cheaper fares are available by travelling mid-week, staying away at least one Saturday night or taking advantage of short-lived promotional offers.

When you're looking for bargain air fares, go to a travel agent rather than directly to the airline. From time to time, airlines do have promotional fares and special offers but generally they only sell fares at the official listed price. One exception to this rule is the expanding number of 'no-frills' carriers operating in the United States and north-west Europe, which mostly sell direct to travellers. Unlike the 'full service' airlines, no-frills carriers often make one-way tickets available at around half the return fare, meaning that it is easy to put together a return ticket when you fly to one place but leave from another.

The other exception is booking on the Internet. Many airlines, full-service and no-frills, offer some excellent fares to Web surfers. They may sell seats by auction or simply cut prices to reflect the reduced cost of electronic selling. Many travel agents around the world have Web sites, which can make the Internet a quick and easy way to compare prices, a good idea before you start negotiating with your favourite travel agency. Online ticket sales work well if you are doing a simple one-way or return trip on specified dates. However, online superfast fare generators are no substitute for a travel agent who knows all about special deals, has strategies for avoiding layovers and can offer advice on everything from which airline has the best vegetarian food to the best travel insurance to bundle with your ticket.

The days when some travel agents would routinely fleece travellers by running off with their money are, happily, almost over. Paying by credit card generally offers protection, as most card issuers provide refunds if you can prove you didn't get what you paid for. Similar protection can be obtained by simply buying a ticket from a bonded agent, such as one covered by the Air Transport Operators License (ATOL) scheme in the UK. Agents who only accept cash should hand over the tickets straight away and not tell you to 'come back tomorrow'. After you've made a booking or paid your deposit, call the airline and confirm that the booking was made. It's generally not advisable to send money (even cheques) through the post unless the agent is very well established – some travellers have reported being ripped off by fly-by-night mail-order ticket agents.

You may decide to pay more than the rock-bottom fare by opting for the safety of a better known travel agent. Firms such as STA Travel, which has offices worldwide, Council Travel in the USA and usit CAMPUS (formerly Campus Travel) in the UK are not going to disappear overnight and they do offer good prices to most destinations.

If you purchase a ticket and later want to make changes to your route or get a refund, you need to contact the original travel agent. Airlines only issue refunds to the purchaser of a ticket – usually the travel agent who bought the ticket on your behalf. Many travellers change their routes halfway through their trips, so think carefully before you buy a ticket that is not easily refunded.

Student and Youth Fares Full-time students and people under 26 have access to better deals than other travellers. The better deals may not always be cheaper fares but can include more flexibility to change flights and/or routes. You have to show a document proving your date of birth or a valid International Student Identity Card (ISIC) when buying your ticket

A glimpse of green in the Upper Barrakka Gardens, Valletta

Vedette detail, Senglea

Malta's brightly painted buses are a tourist attraction in themselves … so are their jolly drivers.

Glass Factory, Manoel Island

Valletta's bombed-out Opera House was the victim of an air raid.

During the Great Siege, decapitated heads were used as cannonballs at Fort St Angelo, Vittoriosa.

Christmas lights in Triq ir-Repubblika, Valletta

Queen Victoria, Misrah Repubblika, Valletta

The British influence is everywhere: locals chat outside a UK-style phone booth, Valletta.

and boarding the plane. There are plenty of places around the world where nonstudents can get fake student cards, but if you get caught using a fake card you could have your ticket confiscated.

Courier Flights Courier flights can be a great bargain if you're lucky enough to find one. Air freight companies expedite delivery of urgent items by sending them with you as your baggage allowance. You are permitted to bring along a carry-on bag, but that's all. In return, you get a steeply discounted ticket.

There are other restrictions: courier tickets are sold for a fixed date and it can be difficult to make schedule changes. If you buy a return ticket, your schedule will be even more rigid. Before you fly you need to clarify what restrictions apply to your ticket, and don't expect a refund once you've paid.

Booking a courier ticket takes some effort. They are not readily available and arrangements have to be made a month or more in advance. You won't find courier flights on all routes either – just on the major air routes.

Courier flights are occasionally advertised in the newspapers, or you could contact air freight companies listed in the phone book. You may even have to go to the air freight company to get an answer – the companies aren't always keen to give out information over the phone. Travel Unlimited (PO Box 1058, Allston, MA 02134, USA) is a monthly travel newsletter from the USA that publishes many courier flight deals from destinations worldwide. A 12 month subscription to the newsletter costs US$25, or US$35 for residents outside the US. Another possibility (at least for US residents) is to join the International Association of Air Travel Couriers (IAATC). The membership fee of $45 gets members a bimonthly update of air courier offerings, access to a fax-on-demand service with daily updates of last minute specials and the bimonthly newsletter *The Shoestring Traveler*. For more information, contact IAATC (☎ 561-582 8320) or visit its Web site at www.courier.org. However, be aware that joining this organisation does not guarantee that you'll get a courier flight.

Travellers with Special Needs

Most international airlines can cater for people with special needs – travellers with disabilities, people with young children and even children travelling alone.

Special dietary preferences (vegetarian, kosher etc) can be catered for with advance notice. If you are travelling in a wheelchair, most international airports can provide an escort from check-in desk to plane where needed, and ramps, lifts, toilets and phones are generally available.

Airlines usually carry babies up to two years of age for 10% of the adult fare, although a few may carry them free of charge. Reputable international airlines usually provide nappies (diapers), tissues, talcum and all the other paraphernalia needed to keep babies clean, dry and half-happy. For children between the ages of two and 12, the fare on international flights is usually 50% of the regular fare or 67% of a discounted fare.

The UK & Ireland

Airline ticket discounters are known as bucket shops in the UK. Despite the somewhat disreputable name, there is nothing under-the-counter about them. Discount air travel is big business in London. Advertisements for many travel agents appear in the travel pages of the weekend broadsheets, such as the Independent on Saturday and the Sunday Times. Look out for free magazines, such as *TNT*, which are widely available in London – start by looking outside the main railway and underground stations.

For students or travellers under 26, popular travel agencies in the UK include STA Travel (☎ 020-7361 6161), which has an office at 86 Old Brompton Rd, London SW7 3LQ, and other offices in London and Manchester. You can also visit its Web site at www.statravel.co.uk. Usit CAMPUS (☎ 020-7730 3402), at 52 Grosvenor Gardens, London SW1WOAG, has branches throughout the UK. The Web address is www.usitcampus.com. Both of these agencies sell tickets to all travellers but cater especially to young people and students. Other recommended bucket shops include: Trailfinders (☎ 020-7938 3939), 194 Kensington High St, London W8 7RG; Bridge the World (☎ 020-7734 7447), 4 Regent Place, London W1R 5FB; and Flightbookers (☎ 020-7757 2000), 177-178 Tottenham Court Rd, London W1P 9LF.

For travel to Malta, charter flights are usually much cheaper than scheduled flights, especially if you do not qualify for the under-26 and student discounts. Typical prices for London-Malta flight-only deals in 2000 ranged from £129 return in November to £229 in July and August. However, winter prices as low as £109 return from Glasgow to Malta can be found. Try phoning around travel agencies, or check out Web sites like www.bargainholidays.com or www.lastminute.com.

Continental Europe
Malta is well connected to many European cities, with daily flights to Frankfurt, Rome, Zürich and Catania (Sicily), and several direct flights a week from Milan, Paris, Geneva, Vienna and Moscow.

France Voyages et Découvertes (☎ 01-42 61 00 01), 21 rue Cambon, is a good place to start hunting down cheap air fares in Paris. You can also try the Web sites www.travelprice.com and www.anyway.fr. In 2000, direct Air Malta flights from Paris to Malta ranged from 1690FF to 2080FF, depending on season.

Germany In Munich, a great source of travel information and equipment is the Därr Travel Shop (☎ 089-28 20 32) at Theriesenstrasse 66. In Berlin, Kilroy Travel ARTU Reisen (☎ 030-310 00 40), at Hardenbergstrasse 9, near Berlin Zoo (and with five branches around the city) is a good travel agent. In Frankfurt-am-Main, you might try SRID Reisen (☎ 069-70 30 35), Bergerstrasse 118.

Italy Really cheap air fares are hard to come by in Rome, where bucket shops don't exist. Centro Turistico Studentesco (CTS; ☎ 06 687 26 72), Corso Vittorio Emanuele II 297, is Italy's official student travel service and offers discounted air fares to students and travellers under 30 years old. The nearest airport to Malta is at Catania in Sicily, which has daily flights to Malta for around L200,000.

Netherlands In Amsterdam, some of the best fares are offered by student travel agency NBBS Reiswinkels (☎ 020-620 5071). Its fares are comparable to those of London bucket shops, and it has branches in Brussels as well.

Russia Aeroflot flies direct from Moscow to Malta several times a week.

North Africa
There are frequent flights between Malta and various North African cities, including Cairo, Tunis and Casablanca, and since the lifting of UN sanctions against Libya in 1999 Air Malta has resumed flights to Tripoli and Benghazi. One-way flights cost around US$87 from Tunis to Malta, US$218 from Cairo and US$225 from Benghazi.

Middle East
Emirates has five flights a week between Dubai and Malta, with connections to/from farther-flung destinations like Bombay, Delhi, Karachi, and Manila. Air Malta flies once or twice a week to Bahrain, Beirut, Damascus and Tel Aviv.

The USA
There are no direct scheduled flights from North America to Malta. The cheapest option is to fly into a European hub such as London, Amsterdam, Frankfurt or Rome and connect with a flight from there to Malta. Flight options across the North Atlantic, the world's busiest long-haul air corridor, are bewildering and fares can vary wildly in price, from US$99 to over US$1000. Standard fares on commercial airlines are very expensive and are probably best avoided. However, travelling on a normal scheduled flight can be more secure

and reliable, particularly for older travellers and families, who might prefer to avoid the potential inconveniences of the budget alternatives.

Discount travel agents in the United States are known as consolidators (although you won't see a sign on the door saying Consolidator). San Francisco is the ticket consolidator capital of America, although some good deals can be found in Los Angeles, New York and other big cities. Consolidators can be found through the Yellow Pages or the major daily newspapers. *The New York Times*, the *Los Angeles Times*, the *Chicago Tribune* and the *San Francisco Examiner* all produce weekly travel sections which include a number of travel agency ads.

Council Travel, America's largest student travel organisation, has around 60 offices in the USA; its head office (☎ 800-226 8624) is at 205 E 42 St, New York, NY 10017. Call headquarters for the office nearest you or you can visit the Web site at www.counciltravel.com. STA Travel (☎ 800-777 0112) has offices in Boston, Chicago, Miami, New York, Philadelphia, San Francisco and other major cities. Call the toll-free 800 number for office locations or visit its Web site at www.statravel.com.

Airhitch (☎ 212-864 2000, 800-326 2009, @ airhitch@airhitch.org) specialises in cheap stand-by fares at around 60% of the normal price. Check the Web site at www.airhitch.org.

Typical return fares on scheduled flights from New York to Rome in 2000 ranged from US$518 in March-April to US$960 in August-September (direct with Alitalia). A low season return from LA to Rome was US$725 with Alitalia via Frankfurt or with KLM via Amsterdam. In summer the best deals were US$1100 with British Airways via London and US$1130 with Lufthansa via Frankfurt.

For information about courier flights contact Now Voyager (☎ 212-431 1616), Suite 307, 74 Varrick St, New York, NY 10013. A return courier flight from New York to Rome costs about US$300 to US$400 (more from the west coast). You

may have to be a US resident and have an interview before they will take you on, and most flights depart from New York.

Charter flights are significantly cheaper than scheduled flights. STA and Council Travel are both reputable agencies specialising in cheap fares.

Canada

Canadian discount air ticket sellers are also known as consolidators and their air fares tend to be about 10% higher than those sold in the USA. The *Globe & Mail*, the *Toronto Star*, the *Montreal Gazette* and the *Vancouver Sun* carry travel agents' ads and are a good place to look for cheap fares.

Travel CUTS (☎ 888-835 2887) is Canada's national student travel agency and has offices in all major cities. Its Web address is www.travelcuts.com. For courier flights from Canada to London contact FB on Board Courier Services (☎ 514-631 7925). Airhitch (see the USA section) has stand-by fares to/from Toronto, Montreal and Vancouver.

Both Alitalia and Air Canada have direct flights from Toronto and Montreal to Rome. In 2000 scheduled return fares from Montreal to Rome ranged from US$732 in low season to US$1017 in high season; from Vancouver the corresponding fares were US$743 and US$1258.

Australia & New Zealand

For flights from Australia and New Zealand to Europe there are a lot of competing airlines and a wide variety of air fares. Round-the-world (RTW) tickets are often real bargains and since Australia is pretty much on the other side of the world from Europe, it can sometimes work out cheaper to keep going right round the world on a RTW ticket than do a U-turn on a return ticket.

Cheap flights generally go via South-East Asian capitals, involving stopovers at Kuala Lumpur, Bangkok or Singapore. If a long stopover between connections is necessary, transit accommodation is sometimes included in the price of the ticket. If it's at your own expense, it may be worth considering a more expensive ticket.

Quite a few travel offices specialise in discount air tickets. Some travel agents, particularly smaller ones, advertise cheap air fares in the travel sections of weekend newspapers, such as *The Age* in Melbourne and the *Sydney Morning Herald*.

Two well known agents for cheap fares are STA Travel and Flight Centre. STA Travel (☎ 03-9349 2411) has its main office at 224 Faraday St, Carlton, VIC 3053, and offices in all major cities and on many university campuses. Call ☎ 131 776 Australia-wide for the location of your nearest branch or visit the Web site at www.statravel.com.au. Flight Centre (call ☎ 131 600 Australia-wide) has a central office at 82 Elizabeth St, Sydney, and there are dozens of offices throughout Australia. Its Web address is www.flightcentre.com.au.

Round-the-World (RTW) and Circle Pacific fares for travel to or from New Zealand are usually the best value, often cheaper than a return ticket. Depending on which airline you choose, you may fly across Asia, with possible stopovers in India, Bangkok or Singapore, or across the USA, with possible stopovers in Honolulu, Australia or one of the Pacific Islands.

The *New Zealand Herald* has a travel section in which travel agents advertise fares. Flight Centre (☎ 09-309 6171) has a large central office in Auckland at National Bank Towers (corner Queen and Darby Sts) and many branches throughout the country. STA Travel (☎ 09-309 0458) has its main office at 10 High St, Auckland, and has other offices in Auckland as well as in Hamilton, Palmerston North, Wellington, Christchurch and Dunedin. The Web address is www.statravel.com.au.

Air Malta now code shares with Singapore Airlines, and no longer flies directly into Australia. The best fare deals from Australia to Malta are generally via Asia or the Middle East and a major European city such as Rome, Zürich, Frankfurt or London with a connection to Malta. Air Lanka, Egyptair and Singapore Airlines have low season (northern winter) return fares to European hubs that range from A$1350 to A$1800. You'll find that direct flights to Malta on mainstream carriers such as Qantas and British Airways are more expensive, with fares starting at around A$2100 during the low season.

LAND
Bus
You can travel by bus from most parts of Europe to a port in Italy and catch a ferry from there to Malta. Eurolines, in conjunction with local bus companies across Europe, is the main international carrier. Bear in mind that a discounted air fare might work out cheaper than the long bus trip once you allow for food and drink to be bought en route.

As the saying goes, all roads lead to Rome; from there you will have to continue to Malta by bus or train to one of the ferry ports in southern Italy or Sicily (see Ferry later in this chapter).

The UK Eurolines (☎ 0990-143219) runs buses twice a week from Victoria Coach Station to Rome (33 hours). Up to four services a week run in summer. The lowest youth/under-26 fares from London to Rome are £85/129 for a single/return. Full adult fares are £91/137. Fares rise in the peak summer season, but special offers in winter can see the cost drop to just £69 return. Eurolines also offers good-value explorer tickets which are valid up to six months and allow travel between a number of major European cities.

France Eurolines has offices in several French cities. In Paris it's at 28 Ave du Général de Gaulle (☎ 01-49 72 51 51).

Germany Eurolines and associated companies have stations at major cities across Germany including Hamburg, Frankfurt and Munich. In Munich, head for Deutsche Touring GmbH, Amulfstrasse 3 (Stamberger Bahnhof; ☎ 089-545 87 00).

Italy Eurolines representatives in Rome are: Lazzi Express (☎ 06 884 08 40) Via Tagliamento 27/r; and Agenzia Elios (☎ 06 44 23 39 28), Circonvallazione Nomentana

574, on the Stazione Tiburtina side. SAIS
and Segesta run buses from Rome to Sicily.
For information, contact the Piazzale
Tiburtina bus station (☎ 06 481 96 76). The
Rome to Catania bus fare is around L95,000
one-way.

Netherlands Eurolines is at Rokin 10 in
Amsterdam (☎ 020-627 51 51).

Train

Rail travel from major European cities to
southern Italy and Sicily is convenient and
comfortable, but if Malta is your only destination then you may want to rethink your
plans, as the train will prove considerably
more expensive than a charter flight. The
standard return fare from London to Rome
(30 hours) is £240, and from Rome to Catania it's another £50 return. If you require
further information, contact the British Rail
European Travel Centre at Victoria Station
in London (☎ 0990-848848).

If you are touring Europe on a Eurail,
Europass or Inter-Rail Pass, then you can
take the train to Reggio di Calabria or Catania and catch a ferry to Malta.

Car & Motorcycle

With your own vehicle, you can drive to
Italy and take a car ferry from Reggio di
Calabria, Pozzallo or Catania (Sicily) to
Malta (see Ferry later in this chapter). From
northern Europe the fastest road route is via
the Simplon Pass to Milan, from which
Italy's main highway, the Autostrada del
Sole, stretches all the way to Reggio di
Calabria. From London the distance is
around 2200km.

Drivers of cars and riders of motorbikes
will need the vehicle's registration papers,
a Green Card, a nationality plate and their
domestic licence. Contact your local auto-
mobile association for details about necessary documentation.

Anyone who is planning to take their
own vehicle with them needs to check in
advance what petrol and spare parts are
likely to be available. Lead-free is not on
sale worldwide, and neither is every little
part for your car.

SEA
Departure Tax

All passengers leaving Malta by sea are required to pay a Lm4 departure tax, which
should be added by the travel agent when
you buy your ticket.

Ferry

Malta has regular sea links in summer with
Sicily (Palermo, Pozzallo, Licata and Catania), southern Italy (Reggio di Calabria)
and northern Italy (Genoa and Livorno).
You can keep your own vehicle in Malta for
up to three months.

The shortest and fastest crossing to Malta
is Virtù Ferries' fast catamaran service between Pozzallo (in Sicily) and Valletta. The
crossing takes only 90 minutes, and the fare
is L130,000 one-way, L165,000 return (rising to L200,000 return in July and August).
The one-way/return fares for a car are
L190,000/270,000, for a motorbike L90,000/
130,000 and for a bicycle L20,000/30,000.

If you buy your ticket in Malta, the passenger fares are Lm23 one-way, Lm33 return (Lm37 in high season). Cars are
Lm35/54, motorbikes Lm17/28 and bicycles Lm4/7. A day return from Malta to
Pozzallo is Lm23. There are daily crossings
in summer, dropping to once a week in winter. The crossing to Catania (five times
weekly in mid-summer, once a week in
March and October) takes four hours, to Licata (twice weekly in July and August only)
takes two hours and 15 minutes.

Ma.Re.Si Shipping's ro-ro car ferry
makes two return trips a week between
Catania and Valletta (12 hours, passengers
Lm20/35 one-way/return, cars Lm35/55)
and one a week between Valletta and
Reggio di Calabria (14 hours, passengers
Lm25/45, cars Lm40/60).

Grandi Traghetti (part of the Grimaldi
group) run a weekly car ferry that calls at
Valletta, Palermo, Genoa, Livorno and
Tunis – check the schedule with a travel
agent. At the time of writing there were no
direct ferry services between Malta and
Tunisia, though there have been in the past
and may be again in the future. It is possible to take a bus from Pozzallo to Palermo

and catch the weekly car ferry from there to Tunis (July to September only). The crossing takes 12 hours, and the fare is around L137,000 one-way.

You should be aware that the Malta-Sicily ferries do not have exchange facilities and there are none available at the ferry terminal in Valletta. Nor is there any public transport from the ferry terminal on Pinto Wharf up to the city of Valletta – you can either catch a taxi or make the steep 15-minute climb.

Ferry schedules tend to change from year to year, and it is best to confirm the information given here, either with the ferry company or with a travel agent. In Malta, SMS (☎ 232211), 311 Triq ir-Repubblika, Valletta, has information about all of the services on offer. In the UK, Viamare Travel Ltd (☎ 020-7431 4560, fax 020-7431 5456, ✉ ferries@viamare.com), Graphic House, 2 Sumatra Rd, London NW6 1PU, is an agent for Virtù Ferries.

The following shipping lines have offices in Malta – some of them publish current timetables on their Web sites:

Grandi Traghetti (Grimaldi Group; ☎ 244373, fax 234195) O.F. Gollcher & Sons Ltd, 19 Triq San Zakarija, Valletta, has a ro-ro car ferry service calling at Valletta, Palermo, Genoa, Livorno and Tunis.
  Web site: www.grimaldi.it
Ma.Re.Si Shipping Ltd (☎ 233129, fax 248057) c/o SMS Travel & Tourism, 131 Triq il-Lvant, Valletta, has a ro-ro car ferry between Valletta and Catania and Reggio di Calabria.
  Web site: www.sms.com.mt/maresi.htm
Virtù Ferries (☎ 318854, fax 345221) 3 Triq il-Prinċipessa Eliżabetta, Ta' Xbiex, operates high-speed catamaran car and passenger ferries between Valletta and Pozzallo, Licata and Catania.
  Web site: www.virtuferries.com

Yacht

Malta's excellent harbour and its strategic location at the hub of the Mediterranean has led to its development as a major yachting centre. There are berths for over 650 yachts (up to 18m length overall) in Msida Marina near Valletta, while Mġarr Marina

in Gozo has space for 150 boats (up to 16m length overall).

If arriving in your own vessel, the authorised ports of entry are Marsamxett Harbour and Grand Harbour in Malta (all year) and Mġarr Harbour in Gozo (16 June to 30 September only). Contact Valletta Port Control on VHF Channel 16 to request customs clearance. Foreign registered yachts can purchase fuel tax-free for onward passage.

Malta's popularity with the yachting fraternity means that it is possible to make your way there as unpaid crew. Yachts tend to leave Gibraltar, southern Spain and the Balearics in April and May to head towards the popular cruising grounds of the Greek Islands and the Turkish coast. It is possible to just turn up at a marina and ask if there are any yachts looking for crew, but there are also agencies that bring together yacht owners and prospective crew for a fee (around £60 a year for membership). Check out the Crewseekers Web site at www.crewseekers.co.uk/discover.htm.

Although complete novices are occasionally taken on, it's easier to get a berth if you have some experience to offer, or even better a paper qualification like the Royal Yachting Association's Competent Crew Certificate (details on the RYA Web site at www.rya.org.uk).

ORGANISED TOURS

There are dozens of tour operators in the UK and North America who offer package holidays and organised tours to Malta. Package holidays, which include flights and accommodation, can offer some real bargains, particularly in the winter – Malta is a year-round charter destination. A comprehensive list of tour operators is available from the Malta Tourist Authority (see Tourist Offices in the Facts for the Visitor chapter for contact details).

Special Interest Holidays

There are also many tour operators catering to a wide range of special interest groups, including walking, history, archaeology, architecture and religion, and others offering holidays designed for senior travellers.

Walking
D A Study Tours (☎ 01383-882200, fax 881550, @ study@datours.co.uk) Williamton House, Low Causeway, Culross, Fife KY12 8HL
HF Holidays (☎ 020-8905 9558, fax 8205 0506, @ 101523.1274@compuserve.com) Imperial House, Edgware Rd, London NW9 5AL
Ramblers Holidays (☎ 01707-331133, fax 333276, @ ramhols@dial.pipex.com) Box 43, Welwyn Garden City, Herts AL8 6PQ

History, Culture & Archaeology
Academic Tours (☎ 800-8759171 or 718-417 8782, fax 718-417 9096) PO Box 370274, Brooklyn, NY 11237
Donna Franca Tours (☎ 800-225 6290 or 617-375 9400, fax 617 266 1062, @ leol@ donnafranca.pn.com) 470 Commonwealth Ave, Boston, MA 02215-2795
Goddess Tours to Malta (☎ 603 436 3733, fax 436 3733, @ maltatours@aol.com) PO Box 388, Portsmouth, NH 03802-0388
Legacy Tours (☎ 800-874 4445 or 617-449 8996, fax 617-449 8988, @ legacy@travelin.com) 310 First Ave, Needham, MA 02194
Martin Randall Travel Ltd (☎ 020-8742 3355, fax 8742 1066, @ info@martinrandall.co.uk) 10 Barley Mow Passage, Chiswick, London W4 4PH
OTS Foundation (☎ 941 918 9215, fax 941 918 0265, @ otsf@aol.com) PO Box 17166, Sarasota, FL 34276
Travel with the Experts Ltd (☎ 973 595 7898, fax 973 595 8389, @ tvlcxpcrt@aol.com) PO Box 7966, Haledon, NJ 07538-7966

Religious Tours
Christian Tours (☎ 01227-760133, fax 451278, @ 106147.342@compuserve.com) Lombard House, 12-17 Upper Bridge St, Canterbury, Kent CT1 2NF
Heavenly International Tours Inc (☎ 800-322 8622) 6789 North Green Bay Ave, Glendale, WI 53209
Highway Journeys (☎ 01256-895966, fax 896144) 3 Winchester St, Whitchurch, Hants RG28 7AH
Inter-Church Travel (☎ 0800-300444, fax 01303-220391) The Saga Building, Middleburg Square, Folkestone, Kent CT20 1AZ
Select International Religious Tours & Cruises (☎ 800-842 4842 or 908 412 0044, fax 908 412 0099, @ sales@select-tours.com) 116 US Highway 22 East, North Plainfield, NJ 07060
Worldwide Christian Travel (☎ 0117-973 1840, fax 973 2434) 36 Coldharbour Rd, Redland, Bristol BS6 7NA

Senior Travellers
Golden Escapes for the 50+ Traveller (☎ 800-668 9125 or 416-447 7683, fax 416-447 4824, @ roberth@goldenescapes.com) 75 The Donway West, Suite 710, Don Mills ONT M3C 2E9
Saga Holidays Ltd (☎ 01303-711111, fax 711524) Saga Building, Middleburg Square, Folkestone, Kent CT20 1AZ
Senior Citizens Tour & Travel Inc (☎ 416-322 1500, fax 322 1166) 225 Eglinton Ave West, Toronto ONT M4R 1A9

Getting Around

AIR

Malta's only internal air service is the regular helicopter link between Malta international airport and the heliport on Gozo. Operated by Malta Aircharter (MAC; ☎ 22999138 in Malta, ☎ 557905 in Gozo), a subsidiary of Air Malta, the service runs year-round with seven flights a day in winter (November to March), and departures roughly every two hours throughout the day and night in summer.

The aircraft used is the Russian-built 26-seat Mi-8, and the flight between Malta and Gozo takes only 10 to 15 minutes. The regular fare for foreign visitors is Lm17 one way, Lm25 return. Maltese citizens pay Lm8 one way and Lm16 return. Children up to 12 years of age are charged 50% of the full fare; infants aged two or under pay

10%. There's a baggage allowance of 20kg plus one small piece of hand luggage. Excess baggage is charged at 35c a kilogram.

Reservations should be made at least 24 hours in advance, through Air Malta offices or any IATA travel agent. Check-in time is half an hour before departure, or an hour if you are flying from Gozo to connect with an international flight at Malta.

BUS

On Malta, almost all bus routes originate from the City Gate Bus Terminus in Valletta and radiate to all parts of the island, which makes certain cross-country journeys (eg, Marsaxlokk to Marsaskala) a little inconvenient, as you have to travel via Valletta. There are also a few direct services (eg, from Sliema and Buġibba to Ċirkewwa

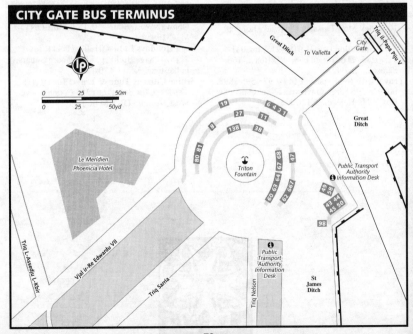

CITY GATE BUS TERMINUS

MAIN BUS ROUTES

From Valletta (except to Sliema & St John's)

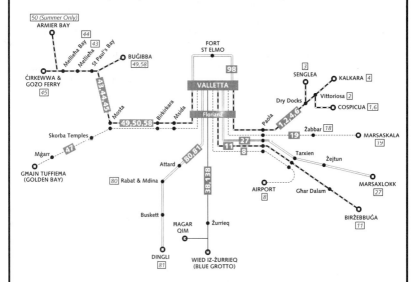

Direct Bus Routes To/From Sliema & Buġibba

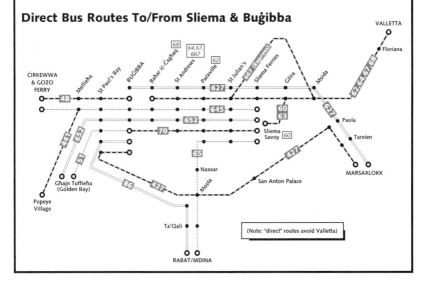

(Note: "direct" routes avoid Valletta)

and Mdina) that do not go through Valletta. Fares range from 15c to 40c depending on route and distance. Late night buses (after 11 pm) cost 50c. Pay the driver when you get on, and try to have some small change available – the driver is unlikely to give change of more than Lm1.

The buses display their route numbers, but not their destinations, in the windscreen. You can find details of routes and fares at the Public Transport Association office (☎ 250007/8/9) at City Gate Bus Terminus. A free bus map is available from bus terminals and tourist information offices. Routes of interest to travellers are shown on the Main Bus Routes map.

On Gozo, all the bus routes except the No 25 Victoria-Mġarr service are circular, starting and finishing at the Victoria Bus Terminal. The flat fare is 10c. Services are less frequent than on Malta, and are geared more to local needs than tourist requirements – buses are less frequent in the afternoon, and most stop running by early evening. Route numbers and destinations are clearly displayed on a noticeboard at the bus station in Victoria.

Bus Passes
The Public Transport Association (PTA) issues one/three/five/seven-day bus passes costing Lm1.50/4/4.50/5.50, which give unlimited travel on Malta's buses. They can be purchased from the PTA offices at City Gate Terminus, Sliema Ferry Terminus, Buġibba Terminus and at branches of the Bank of Valletta.

TAXI
Maltese taxis are white with red number plates. They all have meters, though they are rarely switched on; the government has set up a fare structure, but this is widely ignored. Details of the recommended fares are available at the taxi desk in Malta international airport, where you can pay in advance and hand a ticket to the driver. The set fare from the airport to Valletta is Lm6; to Mdina/Rabat and the Three Cities Lm7; to Sliema, St Julian's and Paċeville Lm8; to Buġibba, St Paul's Bay and

Golden Bay Lm10; to Mellieħa Lm12; and to Ċirkewwa Lm13.

For other journeys you will have to settle a fare with the driver before getting in – Maltese taxi drivers are not noted for their tourist-friendly qualities. There are taxi ranks at City Gate and outside the Grand Master's Palace in Valletta, and at bus stations and major hotels in the main tourist resorts. To order a taxi by phone, ask at your hotel reception or try one of the following services:

Belmont Garage (Gozo)	☎ 556962
Freephone Taxis	☎ 0800-773770
Sydney Garage	☎ 236641, 310177 or 099 9055
Wembley Motors	☎ 374141 or 374242

CAR & MOTORCYCLE
The Maltese love their cars. On weekends they take to the road en masse, visiting friends and family or heading for the beach or a favourite picnic site. This means that there is often serious congestion on the roads around Valletta, Sliema and St Julian's. Friday and Saturday night in Paċeville is one big traffic jam.

Road Rules
Like the British, the Maltese drive on the left. Speed limits are 65km/h on main roads and 40km/h in residential areas, but they are rarely observed. The wearing of seat belts is compulsory for the driver and front-seat passenger. Any accidents must be reported to the nearest police station (and to the rental company if the car is hired) – don't move your vehicle until the police have arrived, otherwise your insurance may be nullified.

Road signs and regulations are pretty much the same as the rest of Europe, with one important difference – in Malta no one seems to pay a blind bit of attention to any of the rules. Be prepared for drivers overtaking on the inside, ignoring traffic lights, refusing to give way at junctions, and hanging on your rear bumper if they think you're going too slowly. All rental cars have registration numbers ending in K, so tourists can be spotted easily. Vehicles coming from your right are supposed to have right of way at roundabouts, but don't count on vehicles on your left observing this rule.

You should also be aware that many of the roads are in pitiful condition, with cracks and potholes, and there are very few road markings. The 'main' road between Mdina/Rabat and Siġġiewi (on the way to Ħaġar Qim and the Blue Grotto) is particularly bad. In winter, minor roads are occasionally blocked by wash-outs or collapsed retaining walls after heavy rain. Signposting is variable – some minor sights are easy to find, while major towns remain elusive. Get yourself a good road map (see Planning in the Facts for the Visitor chapter).

Driving under the influence of alcohol did not become an offence in Malta until 1998. Now it is illegal to drive with *any* alcohol in your blood.

Petrol

The price of fuel is set by the government, and is currently 32c a litre for both leaded and unleaded petrol, and 12.5c a litre for diesel (called kerosene in Malta).

Petrol stations are generally open 7 am to 7 pm Monday to Saturday, though some close at 5.30 pm in winter. Most are closed on Sunday and public holidays.

Parking

Parking can be a bit of a nightmare in the Sliema-St Julian's and Buġibba-Qawra areas. And don't even think about taking a car into Valletta – unless you're a resident, you're not allowed to park within the city walls. Use the large underground car park next to the City Gate Bus Terminus. Local traffic police are swift and merciless in the imposition of Lm10 on-the-spot fines. Car park attendants will expect a tip of around 20c.

Rental

Car rental rates in Malta are among the lowest in Europe, and hiring a car allows you to see a lot more of the island if your time is limited. If you hire a car on Malta, you can take it over to Gozo on the ferry without a problem. However, rental rates

on Gozo are lower, and there's also the cost of a ferry ticket for the car to consider (Lm4 return).

Most of the car hire companies have representatives at the airport, but rates vary so it is worth shopping around. Make sure you know what is included in the quoted rate – many of the local agencies quote very low rates that do not include full insurance against theft and collision damage.

High season rates for a Group A vehicle (Opel Corsa, Hyundai Atos) in summer 2000 ranged from Lm84 a week (booked in the UK through an international hire company) to Lm61 a week with a local agency. Both rates include unlimited mileage, personal accident insurance, collision damage waiver and theft protection insurance. In winter in Gozo, rates can be as low as Lm6 a day.

The age limit for rental drivers is generally 21 to 70, but drivers between 21 and 25 may be asked to pay a supplement of up to Lm4 a day. You will need a valid driving licence that you have held for at least two years. Rental rates often include free delivery and collection, especially in the Valletta-Sliema-St Julian's area.

International agencies with offices in Malta include:

Avis (☎ 246640) 50 Xatt Msida, Msida
Budget (☎ 241517) Triq Zimelli, Ħamrun
Europcar (☎ 387361) Triq Naxxar, San Ġwann
Hertz (☎ 314636/7) 66 Triq Gżira, Gżira
Holiday Autos (☎ 238078) Triq Zimelli, Ħamrun
Thrifty (☎ 496588) Triq Spiteri Freemond, Qormi

There are dozens of local car hire agencies. The following have been recommended as being reliable:

Ada (☎ 691007 or 310004) 177a Triq it-Torri, Sliema
Billy's (☎ 523676) 113 Triq Ġorġ Borg Olivier, Mellieħa
Mġarr Rent-a-car (☎ 564986 or 556098) 24 Triq ix-Xatt, Mġarr, Gozo
Wembleys (☎ 370451/2) Triq San Andrija, St Andrews
Windsor Garage (☎ 346921 or 311324) 10 Triq San Franġisk, Sliema

BICYCLE

Cycling on Maltese roads can be a bit nerve-racking. The roads are often narrow and potholed, and drivers show little consideration for cyclists. Things are better on Gozo – the roads are still rough, but there's far less traffic.

For spares and repairs, try the following bike shops:

Raleigh Bikes (☎ 336750) 93a Triq it-Torri, Sliema
Shine Wheel Bicycle Centre (☎ 654791) 60 Triq San Patriziju, Birżebbuġa
The Cycle Store (☎ 432890) 135 Triq il-Kungress Ewkaristiku, Mosta
Victoria Cycle & Toy Shop (☎ 553741) Pjazza JF Kennedy, Victoria, Gozo

You can rent bikes for about Lm1.50 from the Cycle Store in Mosta and the Victoria Cycle & Toy Shop.

HITCHING

Hitchhiking is very unusual in Malta and is generally frowned upon. Hitching is never entirely safe in any country in the world, and we don't recommend it. Travellers who decide to hitch should understand that they are taking a small but potentially serious risk. People who do choose to hitch will be safer if they travel in pairs and let someone know where they are planning to go.

FERRY

The Gozo Channel Co Ltd (☎ 243964), whose head office is at Xatt it-Tbien, Sa Maison, Floriana, runs the regular ro-ro car ferry service between Malta and Gozo. The ferry that departs from the Sa Maison wharf below the Floriana fortifications is for heavy commercial vehicles only.

The ferry that shuttles back and forth between Valletta and Sliema is run by Captain Morgan Cruises (see Organised Tours). The Comino Hotel (☎ 529821) runs its own ferry service to Comino.

Ċirkewwa (Malta)-Mġarr (Gozo)

This is the main ferry service to Gozo, with crossings every 45 to 60 minutes from 6 am to 11 pm (and every two hours throughout the night in the peak summer months). The journey takes about 30 minutes, and the return fare is Lm1.75 for passengers, Lm4 for cars. There is no ticket office at the Ċirkewwa terminal – you buy your return ticket at Mġarr before boarding the ferry back to Malta.

Valletta-Sliema

The Marsamxetto Ferry (☎ 338981) crosses between Sliema and Valletta (beneath the St Salvatore Bastion at the north-west end of Triq San Ġwann). The crossing only takes about five minutes, and there are departures every hour (every half-hour from 10 am to 4 pm). Ferries depart from Sliema on the hour and half-hour, and leave from Valletta at quarter past and quarter to. The fare is 35c one-way.

Ċirkewwa & Mġarr-Comino

The Comino Hotel's ferry makes eight crossings a day from Ċirkewwa in Malta (between 7.30 am and 6.30 pm) and Mġarr in Gozo (between 6.30 am and 11 pm). The ferry is free to hotel guests, but costs Lm2 return for non-residents. The ferry does not run from November to March when the hotel is closed.

ORGANISED TOURS

A number of companies operate bus tours and they are highly competitive, so shop around the travel agencies. The tours will restrict you to the well-trampled tourist traps, but they can give you a good introduction to the islands nonetheless.

There are dozens of tours on offer, from half-day tours to the Blue Grotto or Valletta's Sunday market, to full-day trips to the Three Cities, Mosta and Mdina, and Gozo. In December there are tours of Christmas lights and village nativity scenes (cribs). Tours cost from Lm1.50 to Lm3.95, and can be arranged through most hotels and travel agents. Your tour guide will expect a tip.

Captain Morgan Cruises (☎ 343373) Dolphin Court, Triq ix-Xatt, Sliema (near The Ferries) is the biggest tour operator on the islands. It offers a wide range of boat trips including day trips to Comino and Gozo, harbour cruises, wine-tasting trips and jazz party cruises. Captain Morgan can also arrange jeep safaris around the more remote parts of Malta (Lm19.95) and Gozo (Lm21.95). These are full-day trips where you drive your own jeep and follow the tour leader, who is in radio contact.

Malta Aircharter (☎ 22999138 in Malta, ☎ 557905 in Gozo), in conjunction with Captain Morgan, operates helicopter sightseeing tours of the islands. There are about five flights a week. The 20-minute tour (Lm28.95) follows the north-east coast of Malta from Valletta up to Comino and takes a quick look at southern Gozo before returning via Mdina. The 40-minute tour (Lm36.95) takes in the full coastlines of Malta and Gozo, with a longer look at Valletta, St Paul's Bay and Mdina. For full details of Captain Morgan tours, times and prices, check out the Web site at www.captainmorgan.com.mt.

Excursions to Sicily

Virtù Ferries' high-speed passenger catamaran service to Pozzallo (see Ferry in the Getting There & Away chapter) makes it possible to make a day trip to Sicily. The ferry leaves Valletta at 7 am, arriving in Pozzallo at 8.30 pm, where you join a coach which takes you on a guided tour to see the active volcano Mt Etna and the ancient Greco-Roman city of Taormina. The return ferry leaves Pozzallo at 9.30 pm and arrives back in Valletta at 11 pm. The cost, excluding lunch, is around Lm33. You can book a trip through most hotels and travel agents in Malta.

Valletta & Floriana

Malta's capital, Valletta, was built by the Knights of the Order of St John in the 16th and 17th centuries. Its founder, Grand Master Jean Parisot de la Valette (see boxed text 'The Founder of Valletta'), decreed that it should be 'a city built by gentlemen for gentlemen', and it retains much of its aristocratic elegance to this day. The city is the seat of Malta's government, and is home to many of its most important museums. Floriana, most of which dates from the 18th century, is a landward suburb of Valletta with many interesting 17th- and 18th-century buildings.

On the south-eastern side of the Grand Harbour lie the fortified peninsulas of Vittoriosa and Senglea, and the town of Cospicua (known collectively as the Three Cities, or the Cotonera). They are older and in some ways more interesting than Valletta itself, as this area was where the Knights of St John first settled when they arrived in Malta in 1530.

HISTORY

Before the Great Siege of 1565, the Sceberras peninsula was uninhabited and unfortified except for Fort St Elmo at its farthest point. Fearing a further attempt on Malta by the Turks, Grand Master La Valette set about the task of financing and building new fortifications and a new city on what was then just a barren limestone ridge.

The foundation stone of Valletta was laid on 28 March 1566. Around 8000 slaves and artisans toiled on the slopes of Sceberras, levelling the summit, cutting a drainage system into the bedrock, and laying out a regular grid of streets – Valletta was to be the first planned city in Europe. A great ditch – 18m deep, 20m wide and nearly 1km long – was cut across the peninsula to protect the landward approach, and massive curtain walls and bastions were raised around the perimeter of the city.

Spurred on by the fear of a Turkish assault, the Knights completed the fortifica-

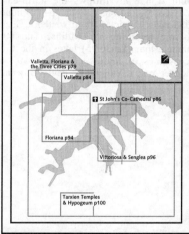

Valletta, Floriana & the Three Cities p79

Valletta p84

St John's Co-Cathedral p86

Floriana p94

Vittoriosa & Senglea p96

Tarxien Temples & Hypogeum p100

tions in a mere five years. With the defences in place, the new city was bestowed with churches, palaces, residential streets and, of course, a hospital. Valletta was considered a masterpiece of architecture and town planning, and today it remains one of Europe's finest and most distinctive cityscapes.

The threat of a Turkish attack in 1634 prompted Grand Master Antoine de Paule to begin the construction of a second line of landward defences, the Notre Dame Ditch, about 1km south-west of Valletta's Great Ditch. These were designed by the Italian engineer Pietro Paolo Floriani, who gave his name to the town which grew up within these walls in the 18th century.

ORIENTATION

Valletta and Floriana occupy the long finger of the Sceberras peninsula that divides Grand Harbour to the south from Marsamxett Harbour to the north. City Gate Terminus (Malta's main bus station) lies between the two towns.

Valletta is a compact town barely a kilometre long and 600m wide, with a regular grid of narrow streets confined within the massive medieval fortifications at the tip of the peninsula. The main street, Triq ir-Repubblika (Republic St), runs in a straight line north-east from the City Gate (adjacent to City Gate Bus Terminus) to Fort St Elmo, passing through Misraħ l-Assedju l-Kbir (Great Siege Square), Misraħ ir-Repubblika (Republic Square) and Pjazza San Ġorġ (St George's Square).

Two other major streets run parallel to Repubblika – Triq il-Merkanti (Merchants' St) two blocks to the south-east, and Triq l-Ifran (Old Bakery St) two blocks to the north-west. Triq ir-Repubblika and Triq il-Merkanti roughly follow the spine of the peninsula, and the side streets fall steeply downhill on either side. The main sights, St John's Co-Cathedral and the Grand Master's

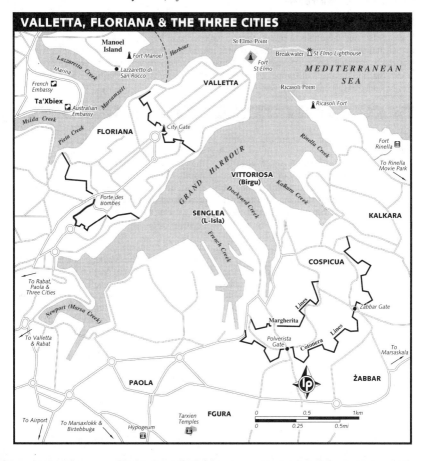

VALLETTA, FLORIANA & THE THREE CITIES

The Founder of Valletta

Jean Parisot de la Valette (1494-1568) was a French nobleman from Provence. He joined the Order of St John at the age of 20, and served it faithfully for the rest of his life, holding the title of Grand Master from 1557 until his death. He was a hardened fighter who had been captured by Barbary pirates in 1541 and spent a year as a galley slave, and a natural leader whose greatest achievement was the defence of Malta against the Turks in the Great Siege of 1565.

In the aftermath of the Great Siege, La Valette immediately set about the fortification of the Sceberras peninsula and the construction of a new

MARTIN HARRIS

city. Three years later, with the streets of Valletta already laid out, he suffered a stroke after a day's hawking at Buskett Gardens, and died in August 1568 at the age of 73. His tomb in the crypt of St John's Co-Cathedral bears a Latin inscription which translates as: 'Here lies Valette, worthy of eternal honour. He who was once the scourge of Africa and Asia, and the shield of Europe, whence he expelled the barbarians by his holy arms, is the first to be buried in this beloved city, whose founder he was.'

Palace, are to the south of Repubblika within 500m of City Gate.

Floriana lies immediately south-west of Valletta, and consists mostly of government buildings and offices. The broad avenue of Vjal ir-Re Edwardu VII (King Edward VII Avenue) and Triq Sarria runs south-west from City Gate Terminus for 500m, dividing the government buildings of Beltissebħ to the north from the long, open rectangle of Pjazza San Publiju (St Publius Square) to the south. The main street of Floriana, the imposing Triq Sant'Anna, lies two blocks south of the square. The main traffic route from Valletta to the rest of Malta exits from the south-west end of Triq Sant'Anna.

The terminal for passenger ferries from Sicily is on Pinto Wharf on the south-east side of Floriana, beneath the fortifications. There is no public transport from here into town, unless you call a taxi. The shortest walking route heads north-east along the quay, then doubles back up it-Telgħa Tal-Kurċifiss (Crucifix Hill) into Floriana. It's a stiff climb carrying a backpack – allow at least 15 minutes.

All street signs in Valletta are bilingual, with both Malti and English; in Floriana they are in Malti only. Note that houses are numbered in sequence along one side of the street, and then back in the opposite direction along the other side, which means that No 20 can sometimes be across the street from No 200!

Maps

Most maps of the Maltese islands include an inset street plan of Valletta. Half a dozen different tourist maps of Valletta can be bought cheaply from the souvenir shops and bookshops on Triq ir-Repubblika. The most useful is the *Handy Leisure Map of Malta & Gozo* with the red cover (75c). You can pick up free street maps of Valletta and Floriana at the Tourist Information Office.

INFORMATION
Tourist Offices

The Tourist Information Office (☎ 237747) is in the City Arcade in Misraħ il-Ħelsien (Freedom Square), immediately on the right as you enter the town through City Gate. It's open 8.30 am to 6 pm Monday to Saturday, and 8.30 am to 1 pm on Sunday. There is also an office at Malta International Airport (☎ 249600) that's open 24 hours.

Money
There are plenty of places to change money and cash travellers cheques on and near Triq ir-Repubblika in Valletta. The Thomas Cook office (☎ 235948) at 20 Triq ir-Repubblika is open 9 am to 6 pm Monday to Friday, and 9 am to 12.30 pm on Saturday. There are foreign exchange desks and ATMs at the HSBC bank branches at 15 Triq ir-Repubblika and 32 Triq il-Merkanti; the latter also has a 24 hour machine that will exchange foreign banknotes automatically.

The American Express representative in Valletta is the travel agency A&V von Brockdorff (☎ 232141) at 14 Triq San Zakkarija, open 9 am to 5 pm Monday to Friday. Staff will change cash and provide travel services, but won't cash travellers cheques, not even AmEx ones.

Post & Communications
At the time of writing, the main post office in Valletta (☎ 224422) had moved from its normal home in the Auberge d'Italie in Triq il-Merkanti to a building under the St James' Cavalier in Pjazza Kastilja, opposite the Auberge de Castile. It's open 8 am to 6 pm Monday to Saturday.

There are also several international courier companies in Malta, including DHL (☎ 800148), FedEx (☎ 661226), TNT (☎ 666999) and UPS (☎ 803670). Most have their offices at Luqa, near the airport, but can arrange pick-ups throughout the island. Packages for DHL can be dropped off at the Thomas Cook office at 20 Triq ir-Repubblika.

There are public telephones, both coin- and card-operated, scattered throughout Valletta – about a dozen public phones are conveniently located at City Gate and neighbouring City Arcade. All have international direct dialling. The Maltacom office in Valletta, where you can buy phonecards and make international calls, is in Triq Nofs in-Nhar; it's open 7 am to 6 pm Monday to Friday.

There is a cybercafe at the YMCA (☎ 240680), 178 Triq il-Merkanti, Valletta, where Internet access costs 75c per half-hour. The YMCA is open 10 am to 10 pm Monday to Saturday.

Travel Agencies
There are dozens of travel agents in Valletta. NSTS Travel (☎ 244983), 220 Triq San Pawl, specialises in student and youth travel, and can arrange budget holiday packages, water-sports facilities and English-language courses. The office is open 9 am to 5 pm Monday to Friday, with a 12.30 to 2.30 pm break in winter. SMS Travel & Tourism (☎ 232211), 311 Triq ir-Repubblika, is a good general agency, offering excursions, guided tours, and plane and ferry tickets.

Bookshops
There are several good bookshops in Valletta. Sapienzas (☎ 233621) and Aquilina

Medieval Town Planning
The Knights who oversaw the construction of Valletta grabbed the opportunity to try out their ideas for urban improvement. In league with Francisco Laparelli, who designed the city, and Gerolamo Cassar, who designed many of its buildings, they laid out certain rules governing the construction of their city.

The buildings were made tall enough to shade the streets from the hot sun, and the regular grid of straight streets allowed cooling sea breezes to circulate. Drainage ditches were cut beneath street level to carry away household waste, and were flushed with seawater twice a day. Every house had to have a well to catch rainwater, and waste had to be disposed of in the underground ditches; facades had to be built to certain specifications to maintain uniformity of appearance; any porches or projections that narrowed the street were prohibited; and every building had to have a sculpture on each corner. Most of these features remain to this day.

(☎ 233774) at 26 and 58 Triq ir-Repubblika respectively have a good selection of history books, travel guides, reference and fiction. The most comprehensive range of titles on Maltese history, art and architecture will be found in the Manoel Theatre booking office (☎ 222618) at the corner of Triq it-Teatru l-Antik and Triq l-Ifran.

A wide range of British, German and Italian newspapers and magazines is available from a hole-in-the-wall news-stand in Triq il-Merkanti near the Auberge d'Italie.

Libraries

The Bibliotheca (National Library of Malta; ☎ 236585) overlooks Misraħ ir-Repubblika at 36 Triq it-Tezorerija, Valletta. The Central Public Library (☎ 2240440) is at Triq Hannibal Scicluna in Floriana.

Universities

The University of Malta (☎ 333903) was founded as a Jesuit college in 1592, and became a state institution in the 18th century. It now has around 7500 students, and boasts a prestigious medical school. The modern campus is at Tal-Qroqq near Msida, about 3km west of Valletta.

Cultural Centres

Valletta and Floriana have a number of cultural centres, which offer a variety of exhibitions, lectures, language courses and cultural events.

Alliance Francaise de Malte (☎ 220701 or 238456) 108 Triq San Tumas, Floriana
The British Council (☎ 226227) c/o British High Commission, 7 Triq Sant'Anna, Floriana
German-Maltese Circle (☎ 246967) 141 Triq San Kristofru, Valletta
Italian Cultural Institute (☎ 221462) Pjazza San Ġorġ, Valletta
Russian Cultural Centre (☎ 222030) 33 Triq il-Merkanti, Valletta

Laundry

There are no coin-operated laundrettes in Valletta and Floriana. However, the Square Deal Launderette (see the Sliema & St Julian's chapter) is a five-minute boat trip away from Valletta on the Marsamxetto

Ferry (see Getting There & Away later in this chapter).

Toilets

There are clean public toilets at the entrances to Upper Barrakka Gardens and Hastings Gardens in Valletta, and at Argotti Gardens in Floriana.

Emergency

Valletta's police station (☎ 225495) is on Triq Nofs in-Nhar opposite the site of the old Opera House. The headquarters of the Malta Police (☎ 224001/2/3) are on Pjazza Vincenzo Buġeja in Floriana.

Dangers & Annoyances

Although Valletta is far safer than most European capitals, there have been reports of the occasional mugging in the quieter side streets late at night.

VALLETTA

Exploring Valletta's narrow streets and steep stairs is a good way of working up a thirst before retiring to the cool shade of a cafe for a well-earned drink. The first of the two routes described here can be completed in about 20 minutes (plus time spent visiting the various sights), but you should allow at least an hour plus sightseeing time for the second.

Walking Tour 1

Begin at the City Gate bus station and walk through the City Gate into Misraħ Ħelsien (Freedom Square). To the right rise the cracked steps and shattered column stumps of the ruined **Royal Opera House**. This once imperious building (you can check out an old photograph on the wall of the Cafe Royale across the street) was built in the 1860s, but was destroyed during a German air raid in 1942. Its gutted shell has been left as a reminder of the war, while controversy rages as to what should be done with the site.

Bear right between the Opera House and the high walls of the **St James' Cavalier**, which now houses the Malta Arts Centre. Pause to admire the facade of the **Auberge**

de Castile et Leon, designed by the architect Andrea Belli in 1741. It adorns a 16th-century building that was once the home of the Spanish and Portuguese langue of the Knights of St John, but now houses the offices of the Maltese prime minister (not open to the public).

Go left along Triq il-Merkanti (Merchants' St), passing on the left the **Auberge d'Italie** – the ornate arms above the entrance are those of Grand Master Gregorio Carafa. Take the next street on the left (Triq Melita) and then turn right along the narrow Triq San Zakkarija (St Zachary's St). At the far end you emerge into Misraħ San Ġwann (St John's Square) beneath the imposing facade of St John's Co-Cathedral (see separate entry later in this section). There is a pleasant outdoor cafe on the right here.

After visiting the cathedral, head south on Triq San Ġwann (St John's St) and turn left along Triq il-Merkanti. This section of the street has a busy weekday **market**. A short detour down the steep steps of Triq Santa Luċija (St Lucia's St) leads to the side entrance of the **Church of St Paul's Shipwreck** (the main door on Triq San Pawl is often closed), which dates from the 16th century. It has many treasures, including a dazzling gilded statue of St Paul, a golden reliquary containing some bones from the saint's forearm, and part of the column on which he is said to have been beheaded in Rome. Continue along Triq il-Merkanti past the fresh produce market and turn left on Triq l-Arċisqof (Archbishop St), which leads to Pjazza San Ġorġ (St George's Square).

The Wartime Experience audiovisual show is housed in the ornate but dilapidated Hostel de Verdelin (built in 1662) on Triq L-Arċisqof on the north-east side of the square. The 45-minute show is made up of archive film from WWII, which movingly records the ordeal suffered by the Maltese people during the siege of 1940-43. The show begins at 11 am, 1 pm and 3 pm Monday to Friday, and 11 am on Saturday and public holidays. It alternates with the Valletta Experience, which screens at 10 am, noon, 2 pm and 4 pm (10 am and noon only

on Saturday and public holidays). Admission is Lm2, and 75c for children.

Downhill and to the right at 74 Triq ir-Repubblika is the the family home of the Marquis de Piro, the **Casa Rocca Piccola** (☎ 231796). The marquis has opened part of his 16th-century palazzo to the public, and guided tours give an insight into the privileged lifestyle of the aristocracy. Tours are hourly from 10 am to 1 pm Monday to Saturday, and cost Lm2/1 for adults/students.

Head south-west on Triq ir-Repubblika, past the long facade of the Grand Master's Palace (see separate entry later in this section), which dominates the south-east side of Pjazza San Ġorġ. Misraħ ir-Repubblika (Republic Square) is crammed with cafe tables, and overlooked by the grand **Biblioteca**, Malta's national library, and a pigeon-spotted statue of Queen Victoria. Grab a coffee at the bar of Caffe Cordina on the right, before heading back along Triq ir-Repubblika towards City Gate. This leads past the imposing colonnade of the **Law Courts** and the 16th-century Auberge de Provence, which houses the interesting National Museum of Archaeology (see separate entry later in this section).

Walking Tour 2

This walk follows the outer fortifications of Valletta, and offers some great views of Grand Harbour, the Three Cities, Marsamxett Harbour and Sliema. Allow at least an hour plus time for sightseeing.

Begin at City Gate and go up the stairs on the left immediately inside the gate. This leads up to the bridge above the gate, with a good view along Triq ir-Repubblika in one direction, and across the bus station to Floriana in the other. Head north-west along Triq il-Papa Piju V (Pope Pius V St), past **St John's Cavalier**, which houses the Embassy of the Order of St John. Continue along Triq il-Mithna (Windmill St) to St Michael's Bastion. Nip into **Hastings Gardens** here for a superb view over Marsamxett Harbour to Sliema and Manoel Island.

Descend steeply via Triq San Andrija (St Andrew's St) and a flight of steps to Triq San Marku (St Mark's St) and bear left onto

VALLETTA

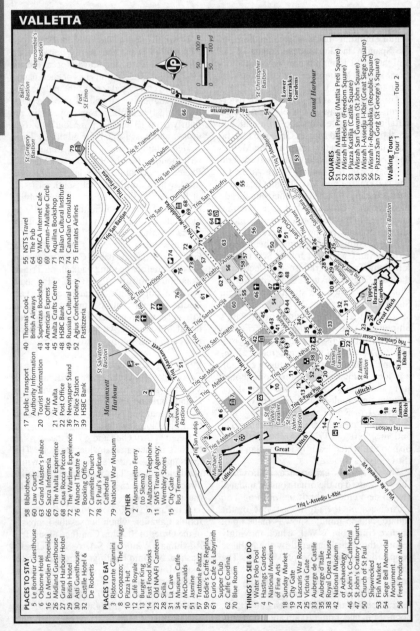

SQUARES
S1 Misraħ Mattia Preti (Mattia Preti Square)
S2 Misraħ il-Ħelsien (Freedom Square)
S3 Piazza Kastilja (Castile Square)
S4 Misraħ San Ġwann (St John Square)
S5 Misraħ l-Assedju l-Kbir (Great Siege Square)
S6 Misraħ ir-Repubblika (Republic Square)
S7 Pjazza San Ġorġ (St George's Square)

Walking Tours
.... Tour 1 ------- Tour 2

PLACES TO STAY
5 Le Bonheur Guesthouse
6 Osborne Hotel
16 Le Meridien Phoenicia
26 Midland Guesthouse
27 Grand Harbour Hotel
29 British Hotel
30 Asti Guesthouse
32 Castille Hotel &
De Roberts

58 Bibliotheca
60 Law Courts
63 Grand Master's Palace
66 Sacra Infermeria
67 The Malta Experience
68 Casa Rocca Piccola
72 The Wartime Experience
76 Manoel Theatre &
Booking Office
77 Carmelite Church
St Paul's Anglican
Cathedral
79 National War Museum

PLACES TO EAT
3 Ristorante Giannini
8 Cocopazzo; The Carriage
10 Pizza Hut
12 Café Royale
13 Burger King
14 Fast Food Kiosks
23 Old NAAFI Canteen
28 Sicilia
31 La Cave
34 Museum Caffe
41 Jasmine
51 Jasmine
57 Trattoria Palazz
59 Eddie's Caffe Regina
61 Curio Cafe & Labyrinth
Supper Club
62 Caffe Cordina
70 Blue Room

OTHER
2 Marsamxetto Ferry
(to Sliema)
9 Maltacom Telephone
Office
11 SMS Travel Agency;
Wembley Stores
15 City Gate
Bus Terminus

17 Public Transport
Authority Information
Office
20 Tourist Information
Office
21 Air Malta
22 Post Office
36 Newspaper Stand
37 Police Station
39 HSBC Bank
40 Thomas Cook;
British Airways
43 Sapienzas Bookshop
44 American Express
45 Malta Crafts Centre
48 HSBC Bank
49 Russian Cultural Centre
52 Aġius Confectionery
Pastizzeria

55 NSTS Travel
64 The Pub
69 YMCA Internet Cafe
71 German-Maltese Circle
73 Aquilina Bookshop
73 Italian Cultural Institute
74 Canadian Consulate
75 Emirates Airlines

THINGS TO SEE & DO
1 Water Polo Pool
4 Hastings Gardens
7 National Museum
of Fine Arts
18 Sunday Market
19 City Gate
24 Lascaris War Rooms
25 Victoria Gate
33 Auberge de Castille
35 Auberge d'Italie
38 Royal Opera House
42 National Museum
of Archaeology
46 St John's Co-Cathedral
47 St John's Oratory Church
50 Church of St Paul
Shipwrecked
53 Fish Market
54 Siege Bell Memorial
Monument
56 Fresh Produce Market

Triq Marsamxett (Marsamxett St), the main road that runs along the top of the city walls. Head past the water polo pool on the shore below, and look out for the steep staircase of Triq it-Teatru l-Antik (Old Theatre St) on the right, beneath the prominent spire of St Paul's Anglican Cathedral. A stiff climb leads up to **Manoel Theatre** (☎ 246389), which was built in 1731 and is one of the oldest theatres in Europe. Take a guided tour to see the restored auditorium with its gilt boxes and huge chandelier. Tours begin at 10.30 and 11.30 am Monday to Friday, and 10.30 am only on Saturday. They cost Lm1.65 including entry to the theatre's museum.

Continue along Triq Marsamxett and around the walls of the Poste D'Angleterre and Poste de France, past the entrance to the interesting National War Museum (see separate entry later in this section) to **Fort St Elmo**, named for the patron saint of mariners. Although now much altered and extended, this was the fort that bore the brunt of Turkish arms during the Great Siege of 1565. It was built by the Knights in 1552 to guard the entrances to the harbours on either side of the Sceberras peninsula. The basement and casemates were used as a location for the Turkish prison scenes in the 1978 film *Midnight Express*. The courtyard outside the entrance to the fort is studded with the lids of underground granaries. Fort St Elmo is open on weekends only, from 1 to 5 pm on Saturday and 9 am to 5 pm on Sunday. Admission is 50c, which also includes entry to Fort St Angelo in Vittoriosa.

In Guardia, a colourful and photogenic military pageant in 16th-century costume, includes a cannon-firing demonstration that will clear the wax from your ears. Parades begin at 11 am on the first and third Sunday of each month. A ticket costs Lm1.50 including a guided tour of the fort, and can be bought in advance from any tourist information office.

A little farther along Triq il-Mediterran (Mediterranean St) lies the entrance to **The Malta Experience** (☎ 243776 or 251284), a 45-minute audiovisual presentation that provides a potted history of Malta. The shows begin hourly from 11 am to 4 pm Monday to Friday, and 11 am to 1 pm on weekends and public holidays, with an extra 2 pm show from October till June. Admission is a steep Lm2.50/1.50/1.25 for adults/students/children.

The show is screened in the basement of the Mediterranean Conference Centre, which is housed in the **Sacra Infermeria**, the 16th-century hospital of the Order of St John. Here surgeons performed such advanced operations as cataract removal, trepanation and bladder stone removal, as well as the more routine amputations and treatment of war wounds. A somewhat lacklustre exhibition called **The Knights Hospitallers** (☎ 224135), with an entrance across the street from the Malta Experience, records the achievements of these medieval medics. It's open 9.30 am to 4.30 pm Monday to Friday, and 9.30 am to 1.30 pm weekends and public holidays. Admission costs Lm1.40/1.00/0.75.

About 200m past the Sacra Infermeria the road forks, and on the left is a small park and a tall pillared cupola. This is the **Siege Bell Memorial**, which commemorates those who lost their lives in the convoys of 1940-43. The 12-ton bell is rung each Sunday at noon. Take the right hand fork in the road (still Triq il-Mediterran) past the entrance to **Lower Barrakka Gardens**, which contains a little Doric temple commemorating Sir Alexander Ball, the naval captain who took Malta from the French in 1800.

Continue along Triq Santa Barbara, a charming tree-lined street with good views over the harbour to the Three Cities. The long, low building on the waterfront down below is the **fish market**, but it's usually finished trading by the time most people wake up. It's for commercial traders only, and is generally open between 4 and 7 am.

Cross the bridge above the Victoria Gate, and head through a sun-trap of a square, usually packed with cafe tables, beside the Grand Harbour Hotel. Turn left and climb up steep Triq Sant'Orsla (St Ursula St) to reach the **Upper Barrakka Gardens**. The balcony here provides a magnificent panorama of Grand Harbour and the creeks and dock-yards of Vittoriosa and Senglea.

From the gardens you can head straight across Pjazza Castile towards City Gate, or turn left out of the square along Triq Giro-lamo Cassar and look for the path on the right (signposted) that leads down into the Great Ditch beneath St James' Bastion and doubles back under the road to the **Lascaris War Rooms** (☎ 234936). These chambers, hewn out of the solid rock far beneath Las-caris Bastion, housed the headquarters of the Allied air and naval forces during WWII, and were used as the control centre for Operation Husky – the Allied invasion of Sicily in 1943. You will need to use your imagination to fill these deserted control rooms and corridors with the clatter of type-writers, the crackle of radio transmissions, and the hushed urgency that must have per-meated the air during major operations. The War Rooms are open 9.30 am to 4 pm Mon-day to Friday, and 9.30 am to 12.30 pm on

weekends and public holidays. Last admis-sion is 30 minutes before closing time; entry costs Lm1.50/0.75 for adults/children.

St John's Co-Cathedral

Malta's most impressive church was de-signed by the architect Gerolamo Cassar and built in 1573-78 as the conventual church of the Knights of St John. It took over from the church of St Lawrence in Vit-toriosa as the place where the knights would gather for communal worship. It was raised to a status equal to that of St Paul's Cathe-dral in Mdina – the official seat of the Arch-bishop of Malta – by a papal decree of 1816, hence the term 'co-cathedral'.

The facade is rather plain, and framed by twin bell-towers – a feature that has been copied by almost every church in Malta – but the interior is a colourful treasure house of Maltese baroque. The nave is long and low and every wall, pillar and rib is en-crusted with rich ornamentation, giving the

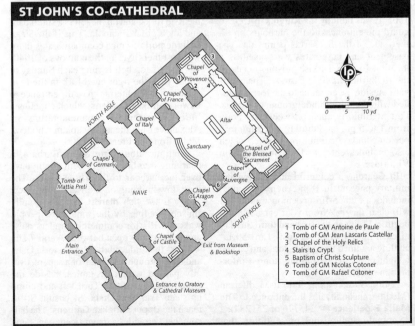

ST JOHN'S CO-CATHEDRAL

Chapel of Provence
Chapel of France
NORTH AISLE
Chapel of Italy
Altar
Chapel of Germany
Sanctuary
Chapel of the Blessed Sacrament
Tomb of Mattia Preti
NAVE
Chapel of Auvergne
Chapel of Aragon
SOUTH AISLE
Chapel of Castile
Main Entrance
Exit from Museum & Bookshop
Entrance to Oratory & Cathedral Museum

0   5   10 m
0   5   10 yd

1 Tomb of GM Antoine de Paule
2 Tomb of GM Jean Lascaris Castellar
3 Chapel of the Holy Relics
4 Stairs to Crypt
5 Baptism of Christ Sculpture
6 Tomb of GM Nicolas Cotoner
7 Tomb of GM Rafael Cotoner

effect of a dusty gold brocade – the Maltese Cross and the arms of the Order (a white cross on a scarlet background) can be seen everywhere. The floor is a vast patchwork quilt of colourful marble tomb slabs in black, white, blue, red, pink and yellow, and the vault is covered in paintings by Mattia Preti (see boxed text 'Il Cavalier Calabrese' in the Facts about Malta chapter) illustrating events from the life of St John the Baptist. The altar, at the far end, is dominated by a huge marble sculpture of the *Baptism of Christ,* with a painting of *St John in Heaven* by Preti above it.

There are six bays on either side of the nave, eight of which contain chapels dedicated to the various langues of the Order of St John. The first bay in the north aisle contains the plain marble tomb slab of Mattia Preti, whose painting *The Mystic Marriage of St Catherine* hangs in the **Chapel of Italy**, looking down on a bust of Grand Master Gregorio Carafa. The austere **Chapel of France**, with a Preti altarpiece of St Paul, was stripped of its baroque decoration in the 1840s.

The **Chapel of Provence** is dark and moody, and contains the tombs of Grand Masters Antoine de Paule and Jean Lascaris Castellar. The steps at the back lead down to the cathedral **crypt** (usually closed to the public), where the first 12 Grand Masters of Malta – from 1523 to 1623 – are interred. The reclining effigies include Jean Parisot de la Valette, hero of the Great Siege and the founder of Valletta, and his English secretary Sir Oliver Starkey, the only man below the rank of Grand Master to be honoured with a tomb in the crypt. Darker still is the **Chapel of the Holy Relics**, which contains a wooden figure of St John that is said to have come from the galley in which the Knights departed from Rhodes in 1523.

On the far side of the sanctuary, the last bay in the north aisle contains the **Chapel of the Blessed Sacrament**, closed off by a pair of solid silver gates. It contains a 15th-century crucifix from Rhodes and the keys of captured Turkish fortresses. The **Chapel of Aragon** is the most splendid in the cathedral. The tombs of the brothers – and consecutive Grand Masters – Rafael and Nicolas Cotoner compete for the title of most extravagant sculpture.

The first bay in the south aisle gives access to the **Cathedral Museum**. The first room is the Oratory, built in 1603 as a place of worship and for the instruction of novices. It is dominated by the altarpiece *The Beheading of St John the Baptist* by Caravaggio, one of the artist's most famous and accomplished paintings. The executioner – reaching for a knife to finish off the job that his sword has not quite finished – and the horrified Salome with her platter are depicted with chilling realism. On the east wall hangs *St Jerome,* another of Caravaggio's masterpieces.

The rest of the museum houses collections of church silver, vestments, illuminated choral books, and a collection of Flemish tapestries depicting Bible scenes and religious allegories. They were based on drawings by Rubens, and were commissioned by Grand Master Ramon de Perellos, whose escutcheon appears on each panel.

The cathedral is open to the public from 9.30 am to 12.45 pm and 1.30 to 5.15 pm Monday to Friday, and 9.30 am to 12.40 pm and 4 to 5 pm Saturday, except when services are being held. The museum is open 9.30 am to 12.30 pm and 1.30 to 4.30 pm Monday to Friday and 9.30 am to 12.30 pm Saturday (closed Sunday and public holidays). Entrance to the museum costs Lm1.

Grand Master's Palace

The Grand Master's Palace (☎ 221221), once the residence of the Grand Masters of the Knights of St John, is today the seat of Malta's parliament and the official residence of the Maltese president.

There are two entrances on Pjazza San Ġorġ. The right-hand arch leads to **Prince Alfred's Courtyard**, where two stone lions guard a doorway leading to the Great Hall (now occupied by Malta's parliamentary House of Representatives), and a clocktower built in 1745 marks the hours with bronze figures of Moorish slaves striking gongs. The left-hand arch leads into **Neptune's Courtyard**, named for the 17th-century bronze statue of the sea-god that stands there.

At the far right corner of Neptune's Courtyard is the ticket office and entrance to the **Armoury**, now housed in what was once the Grand Master's stables. The armour and weapons belonging to the knights were once stored at the Palace Armoury (now the Great Hall used by the parliament), and when a knight died his arms became the property of the Order. The current collection of over 5000 suits of 16th- to 18th-century armour is all that remains of an original 25,000 suits – Napoleon's light-fingered activities, over-enthusiastic housekeeping by the British and general neglect put paid to the rest.

Some of the most interesting pieces are the breastplate worn by La Valette, the beautifully damascened (steel inlaid with gold) suit made for Alof de Wignacourt, and the captured Turkish spahi armour. A second room contains displays of weapons, including crossbows, muskets, swords and pistols, but the labelling of the exhibits is disappointingly sparse.

A staircase outside the Armoury entrance provides access to the **State Apartments**. Only a few rooms are open to the public, depending on what is currently being used. The long **Armoury Corridor**, decorated with trompe l'oeil painting, scenes of naval battles, and the escutcheons of various Grand Masters, leads to the **Council Chamber** on the left. It is hung with 17th-century Gobelins tapestries gifted to the Order in 1710 by Grand Master Ramon Perellos. They feature exotic scenes of Africa, India, the Caribbean and Brazil, including an elephant beneath a cashew-nut tree; an ostrich, cassowary and flamingo; a rhino and a zebra being attacked by a leopard; and a tableau with palm trees, a tapir, a jaguar, and an iguana.

Beyond lie the **State Dining Room** and the **Supreme Council Hall**, where the Supreme Council of Order met. It is decorated with a frieze depicting events from the Great Siege of 1565, and the minstrels' gallery bears paintings showing scenes from the Book of Genesis. At the far end of the hall a door gives access to the **Hall of the Ambassadors**, or Red State Room, where the Grand Master would receive important visitors, and where the Maltese president still receives foreign envoys. It contains portraits of the French kings Louis XIV, Louis XV and Louis XVI, the Russian Empress Catherine the Great, and several Grand Masters. The neighbouring **Pages' Room**, or Yellow State Room, was used by the Grand Master's 16 attendants, and now serves as a conference room.

The Armoury and State Apartments are open 8 am to 12.45 pm weekdays in summer, and 8.30 am to 3.45 pm weekdays in winter (closed weekends and public holidays). The palace is closed to the public when parliament is in session. Admission costs Lm1.

National Museum of Archaeology

Housed in the 16th-century Auberge de Provence, the National Museum of Archaeology (☎ 239545) is undergoing renovation and expansion. In December 1999 only the Neolithic and Bronze Age galleries on the ground floor were open, but labelling was still not complete. Here you can see the beautiful and often mysterious objects that have been found at Malta's prehistoric sites, along with displays showing the technology used to build Malta's prehistoric temples, and the evolution of temple design from simple stone huts to the elaborate layout of Ġgantija.

The exhibits include female figurines found at Ħaġar Qim – perhaps representing a fertility goddess – with massive rounded thighs and arms, but tiny, doll-like hands and feet, wearing a pleated skirt and sitting with legs tucked neatly to one side. The so-called *Venus de Malta*, also from Ħaġar Qim, is about 10cm tall and displays more realistic modelling. Best of all is the *Sleeping Lady*, found at the Hypogeum and dating from around 3000 BC – here the well-endowed Venus is seen lying on her side with her head propped on one arm, apparently in the depths of blissful sleep.

The first floor, which is scheduled to open by summer 2000, will explore the Bronze Age, Phoenician, Roman and Medieval periods, while the basement will

Many figurines found at Malta's prehistoric sites are now housed in museums.

contain a shop, cafe and temporary exhibitions. Audio tours, disabled access and improved labelling are also promised.

The museum is open 7.45 am to 2 pm daily from 16 June to 30 September, and 8.15 am to 5 pm Monday to Saturday and 8.15 am to 4 pm on Sunday from 1 October to 15 June (closed on public holidays). Admission costs Lm1, but under-19s and over-65s get in free. Photography is prohibited.

National Museum of Fine Arts

Malta's Museum of Fine Arts (☎ 233034) occupies Admiralty House – a baroque *palazzo* that was used as the official residence of the Admiral Commander-in-Chief of the British Mediterranean Fleet from the 1820s until 1961. Lord Louis Mountbatten also had his headquarters here in the early 1950s.

The museum's collection of paintings – mostly Italian and Maltese – ranges from the 15th to the 20th century. Highlights include Rooms 12 and 13, which display works by **Mattia Preti** (see boxed text 'Il Cavalier Calabrese' in the Facts about Malta chapter). Look out for the dramatic *Martyrdom of St Catherine,* an incredulous *Doubting Thomas* poking a finger into

Christ's wound, and *St John the Baptist* dressed in the habit of the Knights of St John. Room 14 contains portraits of several Grand Masters by the 18th-century French artist Antoine de Favray, including the imperious *Manoel Pinto de Fonseca.* Room 19 has many 19th-century scenes of Valletta.

Opening hours and admission fees are the same as for the National Museum of Archaeology, which is described earlier in this section.

National War Museum

Malta's National War Museum (☎ 222430), housed in the north-west corner of Fort St Elmo (entrance on Triq il-Fontana) was opened in 1975 to commemorate the island's ordeal during WWII. The collection of relics, photographs and equipment include the Gloster Gladiator biplane called *Faith* (minus wings), the Jeep *Husky* used by General Eisenhower, and the wreckage of a Spitfire and a Messerschmitt Me-109 fighter aircraft recovered from the sea bed. The pictures of bomb damage in Valletta give some idea of the amount of rebuilding that was needed after the war. Pride of place goes to the George Cross medal that was awarded to the entire population of Malta in 1942.

Opening hours and admission fees are the same as for the National Museum of Archaeology, described earlier in this section.

Places to Stay

Although there are no more than a dozen hotels in Valletta, it's a good place to base yourself if you are more interested in history and culture than a beach holiday. The main museums and other attractions are within easy walking distance, and buses depart from the City Gate Terminus to all parts of the island. Most of the accommodation is within 10 minutes' walk of the City Gate.

Guesthouses Housed in a former convent, the *Asti Guesthouse (☎ 239506, 18 Triq Sant'Orsla)* has basic rooms and shared bathrooms, but prices are good at Lm5.50 per person for B&B.

The *Midland Guesthouse* (☎ 236024, 255 Triq Sant'Orsla), down the hill from the Asti Guesthouse, offers similar accommodation at Lm6 per person in summer and Lm5.50 in winter.

At the top of the town, *Le Bonheur Guesthouse* (☎ 238433, 18 Triq l-Inġinieri) is a friendly, family-run place in a quiet street. Rooms with en suite shower cost Lm5.50 per person for B&B. There's a bar and restaurant on the ground floor.

Hotels The *British Hotel* (☎ 224730, fax 239711) gives its official address as 267 Triq Sant'Orsla, but the main entrance faces Grand Harbour on Triq il-Batterija. Rooms are clean, but basic and rather lacking in charm. However, the breakfast tables enjoy a wonderful view of the harbour, and there's a small rooftop terrace. Doubles with private bath cost Lm8 per person and singles Lm10 including breakfast. A discount of 10% is offered on stays of at least seven days.

Grand Harbour Hotel (☎ 246003, fax 242219, 47 Triq il-Batterija) is just downhill from the British. Its high/low season rates are Lm9.90/8.80 B&B for a double with private bath and WC, Lm8.80/7.70 with private shower and shared WC. Single supplement is Lm2, and there's a 10% discount for stays of at least seven days.

The three-star *Castille Hotel* (☎ 243677, fax 243679, 348 Triq San Pawl) enjoys a grand position in an atmospheric old *palazzo* next door to the Auberge de Castile. Rooms with bath and TV cost Lm25 per person for B&B in high season, Lm16 in low.

The *Osborne Hotel* (☎ 243656/7, fax 247293, 50 Triq Nofs in-Nhar) is also housed in a knight's palace. Cosy and comfortable rooms are Lm11 per person low season, rising to Lm14 in high season based on sharing a twin room.

Places to Eat

Valletta is essentially a business district, and there are many restaurants and cafes that are open at lunchtime that close in the evenings. However, there are still a few good places to have dinner.

Restaurants *De Robertis* (☎ 243677) on the top floor of the Castille Hotel (see Places to Stay) commands a magnificent view over Grand Harbour and the Three Cities. It doesn't quite deliver the goods on a la carte dishes like Oysters Kilpatrick (Lm2.75) and Tournedos Rossini (Lm5.30), but the three-course set menu for Lm4.50 is good value. Full meals are served from noon to 2.30 pm and 7 to 10 pm daily; afternoon tea is also available.

Better to head downstairs to *La Cave* (☎ 243677), an atmospheric wine cellar beneath the Castille Hotel. It offers large, crunchy pizzas big enough for two for Lm2.35 – the *pizza Maltija* is topped with goat's cheese, olives and Maltese sausage. Wash it down with local wine at Lm2.80 a bottle. La Cave is open from noon to 2.45 pm and 6.30 to 10.45 pm daily, and there's the added attraction of live Latin American music on Thursday night.

Curio Cafe (☎ 248002, 44 Triq id-Dejqa) is tucked away in an alley a block north of Triq ir-Repubblika but is worth seeking out. Set in the Labyrinth antique shop and art gallery, the ground floor bistro offers generous salads (Lm1.60 to Lm2.50), delicious home-made pies (60c to 70c) and great coffee (35c). There's a more extensive menu in the basement supper club. The cafe's open 10 am until midnight, Monday to Saturday.

Restaurant de Vilhena (☎ 246389) in the basement of the Manoel Theatre foyer on Triq l-Ifran is a great place for lunch or a pre-theatre dinner. Starters like leek and artichoke soup with mushroom and cheese croute cost Lm1.50, while mains like pan-fried chicken with roast vegetables and chive-flavoured mashed potato, or pancetta and asparagus risotto are Lm2.75.

Cocopazzo (☎ 235706, Valletta Bldgs, Triq Nofs in-Nhar) is a friendly little place where the morning's seafood catch is displayed on ice in a large wooden bowl. *Lampuki* (dolphin fish or mahi-mahi) fillet in tomato sauce with olives and capers costs Lm4, a Caesar salad is Lm2.50, pasta dishes are Lm2.75, and fillet steak in a red wine sauce is Lm5. It's open for breakfast and lunch 9 am to 3 pm weekdays, 11 am to 3 pm Saturday, 12.30 to 3 pm Sunday, and for dinner 6.30 to 10 pm every day.

The entrance to **The Carriage** (☎ 247828) is right next door to Cocopazzo, but the restaurant is on the top floor of the building. It's mainly a business lunch spot, with crisp decor and efficient service and a set weekday lunch menu for Lm6.50. The food is an imaginative blend of French and Italian with oriental influences, and there are good vegetarian options. The Carriage opens for dinner from Thursday to Saturday, but you shouldn't expect much change out of Lm25 for two.

Ristorante Giannini (☎ 237121, 23 Triq il-Mithna) is another upmarket choice, set in an elegant townhouse with a great view over Marsamxett Harbour. One of Malta's top restaurants, it's a good place for a business lunch or a romantic dinner. The menu is a mix of Italian and Maltese. Expect to pay around Lm13 a head including wine.

Trattoria Palazz (☎ 226611, 43 Triq it-Teatru l-Antik) is in an attractive cellar beneath the Bibliotheca just off Republic Square. Main course pastas start at Lm2.95, steaks are Lm5.50, and lobster is Lm9.50. Traditional Maltese dishes like rabbit stew and bragioli are Lm3.85. It's open for lunch and dinner, but closed Sunday.

The **Blue Room** (☎ 238014, 59 Triq ir-Repubblika) is a Chinese restaurant, but the decor of cheerful blue-checked tablecloths and bright polished pine makes a refreshing change from red and gold flock wallpaper and paper lanterns. Starters are around Lm1.20, mains Lm2.60 to Lm2.80, and rice 60c. Specialities of the house include sizzling earthenware pots of pork and tofu for Lm4.50. It's a popular place, and worth booking at weekends. It's open noon to 3 pm and 7 to 11 pm, but closed lunchtime on Monday and Saturday.

Jasmine (☎ 226078, 279 Triq San Pawl) is another good choice, serving Cantonese specialities. The dining room is tiny – there are only four small tables downstairs and another six upstairs – but it offers takeaway too. Main courses cost around Lm2.30, and it's open daily for lunch and dinner.

Sicilia (☎ 240659) is a tiny bar and restaurant that spills out onto a little suntrap of a square at the foot of Triq San Ġwann (St John's St). Check the blackboard for the dish of the day – calamari with salad and chips and a glass of wine costs Lm2.50. It's open 8 am to 5 pm Monday to Friday only.

Cafes & Fast Food The prime people-watching spot in Valletta is Misraħ ir-Repubblika, where several cafes command the ranks of tables around the statue of Queen Victoria. The oldest and best is **Caffe Cordina**, established in 1837 and now a local institution. You have the choice of waiter service at the tables in the square, or joining the locals at the zinc counter inside – pay first at the till, and give the receipt to the guy behind the bar. A cappuccino is 40c.

Eddie's Caffe Regina is also on Misraħ ir-Repubblika, and offers fresh lampuki for lunch in season. Coffee is 50c and a pint of local beer is 90c.

Café Royale, on Triq ir-Repubblika across from the ruins of the Royal Opera House, has tasty pastries filled with ham, cheese and tomato, or spinach and ricotta, for just 60c, and excellent Sicilian coffee for 35c to 40c. Sicilian ice cream is also on offer for 40c a scoop.

Museum Caffe (24 Triq Melita) is a convivial little nook with a wooden beamed ceiling and narrow side benches that's been in business since 1921. Here you can get a pie or pasta and a coffee or soft drink for less than Lm1. It's open for breakfast and lunch only Monday to Friday.

Café Diva is set in the foyer of the Manoel Theatre on Triq l-Ifran, in the elegant covered courtyard of the old Bonici Palace. Coffees are 50c, and a decadent banana and honey milk shake is 75c.

For a touch of WWII nostalgia, head for the **Old NAAFI Canteen** in the Great Ditch beneath Triq Girolamo Cassar (opposite the entrance to the Lascaris War Rooms), and order a mug of strong, sweet, milky tea and a bacon roll for under Lm1. It's open 9.30 am to 5 pm daily.

The major fast food outlets are near the top of the town – **Burger King** is right on Freedom Square just inside the City Gate, **McDonalds** is at 24 Triq ir-Repubblika, and **Pizza Hut** is at 19-20 Triq Nofs in-Nhar. But cheaper and tastier fast food can be found at the **kiosks** beside City Gate Bus Terminus, where you can buy hot pastizzi for a mere 8c each, and passable pizza for 25c a slice.

Self-Catering *Wembley Stores* at 305 Triq ir-Repubblika has a wide selection of tinned and dried food, and there is a *fresh produce market* on Triq il-Merkanti behind the Grand Master's Palace, where you can buy fruit and vegetables, fish, meat, sausages and cheese. It's open 5 am to 7 pm Monday to Saturday, but closes at 2 pm on Wednesday. The *Agius Confectionery Pastizzeria (273 Triq San Pawl)* is good for cakes and pastries.

Entertainment

Valletta is not famous for its nightlife. On most evenings, the town appears to close down after 8 pm, as local people head home or retire to a neighbourhood bar, and tourists sit down to dinner in their hotels. However, there are still some venues in town that are worth a visit.

The *Labyrinth Supper Club (☎ 248002, 44 Triq id-Dejqa)* often has live entertainment in its basement club. Acts can range from jazz quartets to poetry recitals. It's open from 7.30 pm till midnight or later, Monday to Saturday. *La Cave* (see Restaurants) in the basement of the Castille Hotel has live Latin American music on Thursday evening.

Fans of the late British actor Oliver Reed might want to raise a glass to their hero in the succinctly named *The Pub*, in Triq l-Arċisqof opposite the Grand Master's Palace. This is the homely little hostelry where the wild man of British film enjoyed his final drinking session before last orders were called forever in May 1999.

Manoel Theatre (☎ 237396 or 246389, 115 Triq it-Teatru l-Antik) is Malta's national theatre, and the islands' principal venue for drama, concerts, opera, ballet, and the hugely popular Christmas pantomime. The booking office on the corner of Triq l-Ifran and Triq it-Teatru l-Antik is open 10 am to noon and 5 to 7 pm Monday to Friday and 10 am to noon on Saturday. The season runs from October to May.

Shopping

There are small shopping centres all along Triq ir-Repubblika, but little of interest to visitors. The Malta Crafts Centre in Misraħ San Ġwann (St John's Square) has a range of locally produced crafts, including glassware and lace.

A **street market** is held in Triq il-Merkanti (between Triq San Ġwann and Triq it-Teatru l-Antik) from around 7 am until 1 pm Monday to Saturday. The merchandise is mainly clothes, shoes, watches and jewellery, along with pirated CDs and computer games. A much bigger market takes place in St James' Ditch, just south of the City Gate bus station, every Sunday.

Getting There & Away

Air The Air Malta office (☎ 240686) in Valletta is in Misraħ il-Ħelsien, near the Tourist Office. It's open 8 am to 5.30 pm Monday to Friday and 8 am to 1 pm on Saturday. Other airlines with offices in the capital include British Airways (☎ 242233) at 20/2 Triq ir-Repubblika (next to the Thomas Cook office) and Emirates (☎ 251384) at 144 Triq l-Ifran.

Bus All bus routes lead to Valletta. The City Gate bus station has services to all parts of the island. For information on routes, fares and timetables, ask at the Public Transport Authority kiosk on the south side of the terminus.

Boat The Marsamxetto ferry (☎ 338981) provides a quick and easy way to travel between Valletta and Sliema. The crossing only takes about five minutes, and there are departures every hour (every half-hour from 10 am to 4 pm). Ferries depart from Sliema on the hour and half-hour, and from Valletta at quarter past and quarter to.

Getting Around

To/From the Airport Bus No 8 runs between the airport and the City Gate terminus in Valletta, passing through Floriana on the way – the fare is 15c, and the journey takes about 40 minutes. The airport bus stop is immediately outside the entrance to the Departures Hall.

Ignore any taxi drivers who tell you that the bus stop is a 20-minute walk away, or that the bus won't be along for another hour – they're just touting for business. You'll find a taxi information desk in the airport arrivals hall. The set fare for a taxi from the airport to Valletta or Floriana is around Lm6.

Public Transport Bus No 99 makes a circuit of Valletta from City Gate to Fort St Elmo along the outer road that follows the top of the city walls, but walking is generally the fastest and easiest way to get about.

Car & Motorcycle A car is more of a hindrance than a help in Valletta and Floriana. The streets around City Gate are clogged with cars, buses and taxis most of the day, and cars without a resident's permit are not allowed to park in Valletta – instead, you must use the big underground car park in Floriana, which is just south-west of the bus station.

FLORIANA

The suburb of Floriana grew up in the 18th century within the landward defences of Valletta. The northern part is taken up with government offices, while the south side is mostly residential.

Walking Tour

Begin at the City Gate Bus Terminus and walk south-west along the central garden strip of Vjal ir-Re Edwardu VII (King Edward VII Avenue) and Triq Sarria. The **monument to Christ the King**, opposite the Meridien Phoenicia Hotel, commemorates the International Eucharistic Congress held in Malta in 1913.

Cross Triq L-Assedju L-Kbir and continue along **Il-Mall**. Now occupied by tree-lined gardens, the 400m-long Mall was laid out in the 17th century on the orders of Grand Master Lascaris, so that the younger knights might play at pall-mall (an ancestor of croquet), in the forlorn hope that this might keep them from the temptations of wine, women and gambling.

The long open space on the south side of the Mall is Pjazza San Publiju (St Publius Square). The circular slabs that stud its paved surface are the lids of underground **granaries**. The square is dominated by the **Church of St Publius** dedicated to the patron saint of Floriana. Publius was the

Karrozzin

The karrozzin – a traditional horse-drawn carriage with seats for four passengers – has been in use in Malta since 1856. Many of the carriages are treasured family possessions passed down from father to son, and are cared for with obsessive pride. If you can manage to get up early enough, you can see the owners turn up for a day's work with the karrozzin on the back of a pick-up truck and the horse towed behind in a horse-box. With a quick buff of the leather and brass, they back the horse into the harness, and they're all set.

JULIET COOMBE

You can pick up a karrozzin in Valletta at City Gate, Pjazza San Ġorġ and Fort St Elmo; at The Ferries in Sliema; outside the Hilton Hotel in St Julian's; and Mdina's main gate. Haggle with the driver and agree on a fare before getting in. About Lm5 is average for a tour of the local sights.

Roman governor of Malta in AD 60 when St Paul was shipwrecked on the island. He was converted to Christianity and became Malta's first bishop. Built in the 18th century, the church was badly damaged by WWII bombs.

Continue along Triq Sarria to the circular **Sarria Chapel**, built in 1678 and designed and decorated by Mattia Preti. Across the street is the **Wignacourt Water Tower**, part of an aqueduct system that brought water to Valletta from the central hills. Beside the tower is the entrance to the **Argotti Botanical Gardens**.

Follow the street round to the left past the Sarria Chapel and downhill to the **Lion Fountain**, and turn right on the main road out of town. A five-minute walk leads to the **Porte des Bombes**, an ornamental gateway dating from 1697-1720 that once formed part of the Floriana Lines fortifications. It's decorated with reliefs of cannons and the arms of Grand Master Perellos under whose reign it was built.

Return to the Lion Fountain and then continue straight on along the grand, arcaded Triq Sant'Anna (St Anne's Street) to return to Valletta.

FLORIANA

OTHER
1 Gozo Ferry
2 Gozo Channel Co. Office
4 Police Headquarters
5 Department of Works
   (for large scale maps)
9 City Gate Bus Terminus
15 Boffa Hospital
16 Bank of Valletta & ATM
17 British High Commission
18 US Embassy
28 Bus Stop
30 Italian Embassy
32 Alliance Francaise de Malte
33 Japanese Consulate
34 Passenger Ferry Terminal
   (Ferries to Sicily)

········ Walking Tour

Marsamxett Harbour

Hannibal Scicluna

Beltissebh (Government Buildings)

Pieta Creek

To Ta'Xbiex & Sliema

Jubilee Gardens

Piazza L Preziosi

To Hamrun

Grand Harbour

Pinto Wharf

To Fort St Elmo

PLACES TO STAY & EAT
7 Le Meridien Phoenicia Hotel
29 Bon Appetit Cafe

THINGS TO SEE & DO
3 Sa Maison Garden
6 Central Public Library
8 Christ the King Monument
10 Triton Fountain
11 Commonwealth Air Forces Memorial
12 Sunday Market
13 War Memorial
14 Herbert Ganado Gardens
19 Bust of GM Manoel de Vilhena
20 Church of St Publius
21 Sarria Chapel
22 Wignacourt Water Tower
23 Methodist Church
24 Argotti Botanical Gardens
25 St Philip Gardens
26 Portes des Bombes
27 Lion Fountain
31 George V Gardens

0   50   100 m
0   50   100 yd

Places to Stay & Eat

Le Meridien Phoenicia (☎ *225241, fax 235254,* ✉ *info@phoenicia.com.mt*) is technically in Floriana, but it is only a minute's walk from Valletta's City Gate. Built in the late 1940s, it is one of Malta's grandest and most comfortable hotels. The five-star facilities include 24-hour room service, free car parking, a business centre, and a private seven-acre garden terrace with heated outdoor pool. A standard single/double room costs Lm65/75, while a suite with a harbour view will set you back a whopping Lm150.

There aren't too many places to grab something to eat in Floriana. The *Bon Appetit Cafe* on Triq Sant'Anna will provide coffee and a pastry at the end of your walk.

Getting There & Away

Floriana is just a five-minute walk from Valletta. All buses to and from Valletta also pass through Floriana. The main bus stop on Triq Sant'Anna has an information board displaying the various route numbers and destinations.

There are two ferry terminals in Floriana. The daily car ferry to Gozo departs from Pieta Creek in Marsamxett Harbour (see the Getting Around chapter), while passenger ferries from Sicily dock at the Passenger Ferry Terminal on Pinto Wharf (see the Getting There & Away chapter).

Around Valletta & Floriana

THE THREE CITIES

When the Knights of St John first arrived in Malta in 1530, they made their home in the fishing village of Birgu, on a finger of land on the south side of the Great Harbour, overlooking the inlet (now known as Dockyard Creek) that was called the Port of the Arab Galleys. Here they built their auberges and repaired and extended the ancient defences. By the 1550s, Birgu (Fort St Angelo) and the neighbouring point of L-Isla (Fort St Michael) had been fortified, and

Fort St Elmo had been built on the tip of the Sceberras peninsula. Bormla, at the head of Dockyard Creek, was not fortified until the 17th century.

From this base, the Knights withstood the Turkish onslaught during the Great Siege of 1565, but in the years that followed they moved to their new city of Valletta across the harbour. During WWII, the Three Cities and their surrounding docks were bombed almost daily throughout 1941 and 1942, and suffered terrible damage and bloodshed. Today, the towns of Vittoriosa, Senglea and Cospicua, as they are now known, are close-knit working communities largely dependent on their dockyards for employment. They are refreshingly un-touristy, and offer a welcome escape from the commercial hustle of Valletta and Sliema.

The Three Cities were originally named Birgu, L-Isla and Bormla but their names were changed after the Great Siege of 1565. Birgu became Vittoriosa (Victorious), L-Isla became Senglea (after Grand Master Claude de la Sengle), and Bormla became Cospicua (as in conspicuous courage). Local people and some road signs still use the old names, and all three together are sometimes referred to as 'The Cotonera', a reference to the Cotonera Lines – the landward fortifications surrounding the Three Cities that were built in the 1670s at the instigation of Grand Master Nicolas Cotoner.

There are no tourist information offices or currency exchanges in the Three Cities.

Vittoriosa

Vittoriosa is only 800m long and 400m at its widest, so it's hard to get lost. However, street signs are in Malti, while most tourist maps are in English only, which can be confusing. From the Poste de France, Triq il-Mina l-Kbira (Main Gate St) leads to the town's main square Misraħ ir-Rebħa (Victory Square). From the square, Vittoriosa Wharf and the Maritime Museum are downhill to the left, while Triq San Filippu (St Philip's St) leads straight on towards Fort St Angelo at the tip of the peninsula.

VITTORIOSA & SENGLEA

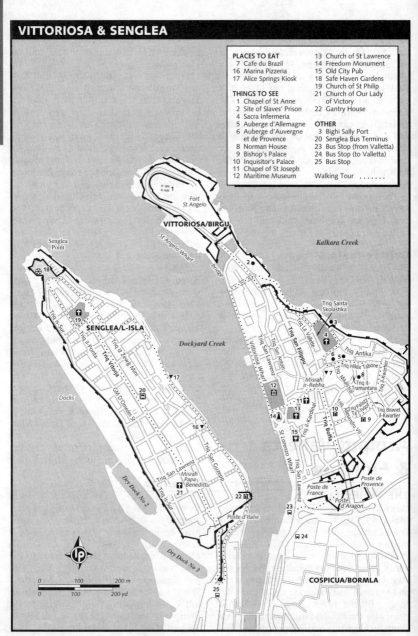

PLACES TO EAT
7 Cafe du Brazil
16 Marina Pizzeria
17 Alice Springs Kiosk

THINGS TO SEE
1 Chapel of St Anne
2 Site of Slaves' Prison
4 Sacra Infermeria
5 Auberge d'Allemagne
6 Auberge d'Auvergne et de Provence
8 Norman House
9 Bishop's Palace
10 Inquisitor's Palace
11 Chapel of St Joseph
12 Maritime Museum

13 Church of St Lawrence
14 Freedom Monument
15 Old City Pub
18 Safe Haven Gardens
19 Church of St Philip
21 Church of Our Lady of Victory
22 Gantry House

OTHER
3 Bighi Sally Port
20 Senglea Bus Terminus
23 Bus Stop (from Valletta)
24 Bus Stop (to Valletta)
25 Bus Stop

Walking Tour . . . .

Fort St Angelo

VITTORIOSA/BIRGU

Kalkara Creek

Senglea Point

St Angelo Wharf

bridge

Triq Santa Skolastika

Triq is-Sur
Triq il-Ponta
Triq iz-Zewg Mini
Triq Vittorja

SENGLEA/L-ISLA

Dockyard Creek

Triq il-Vitlorja

Triq San Anton

Vittoriosa Wharf

Triq San Lawrenz

Triq San Filippu

Il-La Valette

Triq Antika

Triq Hilda Tabone

Triq il-Tramuntana

Triq Mdina Vil.

Triq it-Tramuntana

Triq il-Kwartier

Triq Biswiet il-Kwartier

Docks

GM D'Omedes St

Misrah ir-Rebha

Triq Palazz Ta' Lippu

Triq Boffa

Triq il-Kardinal

Triq San Guzepp

Misrah Papa Benedittu

Triq San Lawrenz

Triq is-Sur

Poste de France

Poste d'Aragon

Poste de Provence

St Lorenzo Wharf

St Lawrenz

Poste d'Italie

Dry Dock No 2

Dry Dock No 3

COSPICUA/BORMLA

0 100 200 m
0 100 200 yd

Steep side street, Valletta

A place to reflect: Upper Barrakka Gardens

The imposing dome of the Carmelite Church dominates the Valletta skyline.

Valletta's Auberge de Castile, once home to a medieval Knight, is now the office of the Prime Minister.

English-style letterbox, Valletta

Guarding the fort, Valletta

Senglea lights up

Door knocker with Maltese Cross, Valletta

Keeping an eye on the vedette, Senglea

Walking Tour Begin at the bus stop at the corner of Triq San Lawrenz (St Lawrence St) and Triq 79. Cross the road towards the Poste d'Aragon and enter the bastion through the **Advanced Gate**, inscribed with the date 'MDCCXXII' (1722) and a relief of crossed cannons. Cross the bridge over the moat, which has been planted with orange trees and is now the Coronation Gardens, and pass through the Couvre Port into the Poste de France (there's a good view of Senglea from the battlement up the ramp to the left).

Go through Porte de Provence and head left along Triq Boffa (Boffa St), past the **Inquisitor's Palace** to Misrah ir Rebha (**Victory Square**) with its two monuments: the Victory Monument, erected in 1705 in memory of the Great Siege; and a statue of St Lawrence, patron saint of Vittoriosa, dating from 1880.

Go left into the nearby chapel where the little **Oratory of St Joseph** – now a fascinating museum – contains relics of Grand Master La Valette, and continue down past the **Church of St Lawrence**. Built on the site of an 11th-century Norman church, St Lawrence's served as the conventual church of the Knights of St John from 1530 until the move to St John's Co-Cathedral in Valletta.

At the foot of the hill, pass to the left of the large building across the street. The palm and cactus garden on the left contains the **Freedom Monument**, which commemorates the departure of the last British forces in Malta in 1979. Bronze figures show a bugler playing the Last Post as his comrade lowers the flag, and a British sailor saying goodbye to a Maltese girl while, rather unromantically, shaking her hand.

Turn right along the waterfront, past the interesting **Maritime Museum** (see description later in this section), which is housed in the old naval bakery. Continue along Vittoriosa Wharf, which is currently the subject of a planning proposal to develop the 'Cotonera Waterfront' as a marina for so-called 'super-yachts'. The largely derelict 17th-century buildings on your right include the Knights' Treasury, the Captain-General's Palace, and a hostel for galley captains. At

the far end of the quay you can cross the bridge over the moat and follow a path beyond St Angelo Wharf to the rocky point beneath the walls of **Fort St Angelo**, where old cannons serve as bollards and the remains of WWII gun installations can be seen. The bridge was the original approach to the fort's **main gate**, which can be seen above the wharf.

Go through a tunnel at the far end of the final building on Vittoriosa Wharf (originally the powder magazines for the Order's galley fleet). You emerge into an open space on the site of the former **Slave Prisons**, where Turkish and Arab galley slaves were incarcerated. Turn right below the walls and look out for a narrow staircase on the right. Climb the stairs and turn right along the top of the wall to the main street, and follow it across the ditch into Fort St Angelo (see description later in this section).

Retrace your route back towards the stairs, but keep straight on along Triq Santa Skolastika (St Scholastica St) towards the massive blank walls of the **Sacra Infermeria**, the first hospital to be built by the Knights on their arrival in Malta. It now serves as a convent. Go left down a stepped alley (signposted Triq il-Miratur) and turn right along the walls. The ramp descending into a trench in front of the Infermeria leads to the **Bighi Sally Port**, where the wounded were brought by boat to the infirmary under the cover of darkness during the Great Siege.

Turn right (also Triq il-Miratur), then go left and left again along Triq Hilda Tabone (Britannic St). To your right lies a small maze of charming alleys with some of the oldest surviving buildings in the city. Wander up Triq it-Tramuntana (North St) to the so-called **Norman House** at No 11 (on the left) and look up at the 1st floor. The twin-arched window, with its slender central pillar and zigzag decoration, dates from the 11th century, and is in a style described as Siculo-Norman (similar windows survive in Il-Kastell on Gozo).

At the far end of Triq Hilda Tabone turn right along Triq il-Kwartier (Barrack St), and bear right at the corner of the imposing **Armoury**. Turn left and then right along

Triq Palazz Ta'l-Isqof (Bishop's Palace St) past the **Bishop's Palace**. Return to Triq Boffa (Boffa St).

Maritime Museum The old naval bakery, built in 1578, now houses Malta's Maritime Museum (☎ 660052 or 805287). The exhibits include Roman anchors, traditional Maltese fishing boats, models of the Knights' galleys and British naval vessels. There are also displays of old navigational instruments, log books and signal books.

The museum is open 7.45 am to 2 pm daily from 16 June to 30 September, and 8.15 am to 5 pm Monday to Saturday and 8.15 am to 4 pm on Sunday from 1 October to 15 June (closed on public holidays). Admission costs Lm1, but under-19s and over-65s get in free.

Fort St Angelo The tip of the Vittoriosa peninsula has been fortified since at least the 9th century, and before that it was the site of Roman and Phoenician temples. The Knights took over the medieval fort in 1530 and rebuilt it and strengthened it – Fort St Angelo served as the residence of the Grand Master of the Order until 1571, and was the headquarters of La Valette during the Great Siege. Further defences were added in the late 17th century by the engineer Don Carlos Grunenberg, whose florid coat-of-arms still sits above the gate overlooking St Angelo Wharf.

The British took over the fort in the 19th century, and from 1912 until 1979 it served as the headquarters of the Mediterranean Fleet, first as *HMS Egmont* and from 1933 as *HMS St Angelo*. The upper part of the fort, including the Grand Master's Palace and the 15th-century Chapel of St Anne, is now occupied by the modern Order of St John. You can wander around the rest of the fort, which is an unusual mixture of medieval fortress and abandoned 20th-century officers' mess, complete with sad-looking swimming pool and tennis court.

Fort St Angelo is open from 10 am to 2 pm on Saturday only. Admission is 50c, and the ticket includes entry to Fort St Elmo in Valletta.

Places to Eat Remember to bring a packed lunch. The only place where you can get a beer or a coffee is the *Cafe du Brazil* on Victory Square.

Getting There & Away Bus Nos 1, 4 and 6 from Valletta will take you to the bus stop on Triq 79 beneath the Poste d'Aragon; No 2 goes all the way to Victory Square. There's a bus every 15 or 20 minutes.

Senglea

Senglea is even more difficult to get lost in than Vittoriosa, as the streets form a grid pattern. The town was pretty much razed to the ground during WWII, and little of historic interest remains, but there are great views of Valletta and Vittoriosa, and the little *vedette* (watchtower) at the tip of the peninsula is one of the classic sights of Malta.

Senglea's vedette enjoys commanding views.

Walking Tour From the bus stop in the square outside the fortifications, walk up the ramp and pass through the gate at the Poste d'Italie, and continue along Triq Vitorija (Victory St). At the first square is the **Church of Our Lady of Victory**, which was completely rebuilt after WWII. Follow Triq Vitorija all the way to the **Church of St Philip**, and follow the narrow alleys around to the left to reach Safe Haven Gardens at the tip of the peninsula.

The vedette here is decorated with carvings of eyes and ears symbolising watchfulness, and commands a view over the whole length of Grand Harbour and the southern flank of Valletta.

Bear left when you leave the Safe Haven Gardens, and follow Triq iż-Żewġ Mini (Two Gates St) past St Philip's Church. Turn left down Triq Sant'Anġlu and then right and descend to the quayside. Follow the waterfront, with its moored *dgħajsas* (traditional rowing boats or water taxis) and views of Vittoriosa Wharf, back to the starting point.

Towards the end of the quay the road passes under the bastion, and a walkway goes around the outside beneath the so-called **Gantry House**. This was where the galleys of the Knights of St John were moored while their masts were removed using machinery mounted on the wall above the walkway.

Places to Eat You can grab an inexpensive burger, hot dog or ice-cream at the *Alice Springs Kiosk* or its neighbour on the quayside. If you're in the mood for something a little more substantial, try the *Marina Pizzeria* (☎ 664398) a little farther along the waterfront.

Getting There & Away Bus No 3 runs between Valletta and the central square in Senglea every half hour or so. Alternatively, catch bus No 1 or 4 to Vittoriosa and get off at Dry Dock No 1 (at the head of Dockyard Creek) and walk back up the hill and turn right. It's only a 15-minute walk from the main gate at Vittoriosa around to the main gate at Senglea.

Cospicua

Cospicua was comprehensively flattened during WWII, and there is nothing to see in the town itself. However, if you're interested in medieval fortifications, you can spend half a day exploring the two concentric rings of 17th-century defences known as the Margherita Lines and the Cotonera Lines. A good map (*The Maze Street Atlas* by Frans Attard) and a specialist book (*The Knights' Fortifications* by Stephen Spiteri) are recommended.

THE HYPOGEUM & THE TARXIEN TEMPLES

The suburb of Paola, about 2km south-west of Cospicua, conceals two of Malta's most important prehistoric sites. The **Hypogeum** is an incredible underground necropolis, discovered during building work in 1902. It is thought to date from around 3600 to 3000 BC, and an estimated 7000 bodies may have been interred here. Unfortunately, carbon dioxide exhaled by visiting tourists began to damage the delicate limestone walls of the burial chambers, and the Hypogeum was until recently closed to the public for several years (you can see a model of it in the National Museum of Archaeology in Valletta). It has now been reopened and 50-minute tours of the complex are available. There is also an exhibition and audiovisual display. It is open daily.

The **Tarxien Temples** (pronounced tar-sheen) are hidden up a back street several blocks east of the Hypogeum – keep your eyes peeled, as the entrance is inconspicuous. These megalithic structures were excavated in 1914, and are thought to date from between 3600 and 2500 BC. There are four linked temples, built with massive stone blocks up to 3m by 1m by 1m in size,

The decorated stone blocks of Tarxien

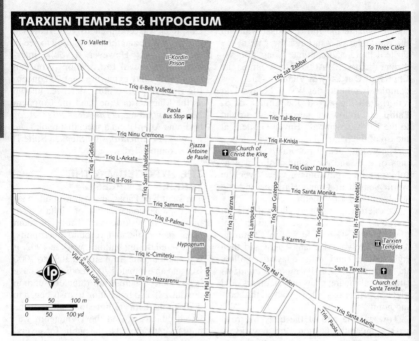

TARXIEN TEMPLES & HYPOGEUM

decorated with spiral patterns and pitting, and reliefs of animals including bulls, goats and pigs. The large statue of a broad-hipped female figure was found in the right-hand niche of the first temple.

The Tarxien Temples are open daily from 7.45 am to 2 pm in summer, and from 8.15 am to 5 pm (4 pm on Sunday) in winter. Admission is Lm1. More than a dozen buses pass through Paola, including Nos 1, 2, 3, 4 and 6. Get off at the main square, Pjazza Paola – the Hypogeum is a five-minute walk away, Tarxien is 10 minutes.

FORT RINELLA
Fort Rinella (☎ 640131), 1.5km north-east of Vittoriosa, was built by the British in the late 19th century as one of two coastal batteries designed to counter the threat of Italy's new ironclad battleships. The batteries (the second one was on Tigne Point in Sliema) were equipped with the latest Armstrong 100-ton guns – the biggest

muzzle-loading guns ever made. Their 100-ton shells had a range of 6.4km and could penetrate 38cm of armour plating. The guns were never fired in anger, and were retired in 1906. Fort Rinella has been restored by a group of amateur enthusiasts from the Malta Heritage Foundation, and is now one of Malta's most interesting military museums.

Admission costs Lm1 for adults, 75c for pensioners, 50c for students and 25c for children. A family ticket (two parents plus children) costs Lm2. To get there, take bus No 4 from Valletta or the Three Cities, or bus No 627 from Buġibba.

RINELLA MOVIE PARK
The Rinella Movie Park (☎ 667755) at Fort St Rocco, 500m east of Fort Rinella, is a poor attempt at creating the equivalent of Los Angeles' Universal Studios in the middle of the Med. Unless you have a gang of unruly kids to entertain, give it a wide berth.

However, entrance to the car park is free, where you have a grandstand view of the huge Mediterranean Film Studios water tanks below – the biggest film production water facilities in Europe – where water scenes from such films as *The Spy Who Loved Me, Never Say Never Again* and *Raise the Titanic* were shot.

The park is open from 10 am to 6 pm Wednesday to Sunday and on public holidays. Admission costs a hefty Lm4 for adults, and Lm2 for students and children aged 2 to 12. A family ticket for two adults and two children is Lm10. To get there by public transport, take Bus No 4 from Valletta, which passes the entrance to the park.

Sliema & St Julian's

The seaside suburb of Sliema was once the preserve of the Maltese upper classes, a cool retreat from the heat and bustle of Valletta. Although the waterfront streets have now been taken over by concrete hotels, restaurants, shops and bars, the back streets remain largely residential, and a Sliema address is still something of a status symbol in Maltese society.

St Julian's to the north is the focus of recent tourist development, with new four- and five-star hotels and apartment complexes rising along the rocky shoreline, notably at Portomaso and St George's Bay. Paċeville is in the heart of St Julian's, and is recognised as the nightlife capital of Malta. If you want to explore Valletta and the Three Cities, but are planning on taking a package holiday to save some money, then Sliema is the most convenient place to stay as there is a fast and regular ferry service to the capital.

ORIENTATION
Sliema occupies the peninsula to the north of Valletta, from which it is separated by Marsamxett Harbour. The main thoroughfare on the south side of the peninsula is Triq ix-Xatt (The Strand), which continues south along the Gżira waterfront and around the Ta'Xbiex peninsula to the marina at Msida. The focal point of Sliema, known as The Ferries, is at the north-eastern end of The Strand, where you will find the bus terminus and the ferry to Valletta. From here, Triq it-Torri (Tower Rd) strikes north across the neck of the peninsula and then follows the coastline north and west to Balluta Bay and St Julian's.

St Julian's (San Ġiljan) lies between Balluta Bay and St George's Bay. The compact grid of streets packed with pubs and clubs to the north of Spinola Bay between Triq San Ġorġ and Triq id-Dragunara is known as Paċeville (pronounced patchy-ville). North of St Julian's lies the rapidly developing district of St George's Bay.

HIGHLIGHTS

- Dining on Spinola Bay
- Winning at the casino
- Losing it in Paċeville
- Escaping on a boat trip

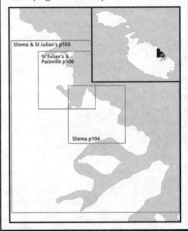

Sliema & St Julian's p103

St Julian's & Paċeville p106

Sliema p104

INFORMATION
Money
Thomas Cook (☎ 322747) offices can be found at il-Piazzetta, Triq it-Torri, Sliema, and in Triq Elija Zammit in Paċeville. American Express (☎ 334051) has its main Malta office at Airways House, Triq il-Kbira, Sliema. There are plenty of banks and ATMs throughout both Sliema and St Julian's. For currency exchange outside office hours you could try Eurochange at the corner of Triq id-Dragunara and Triq Ball in Paċeville; it's open from 8.15 am to 10 pm daily.

Post & Communications
The main post office is on Triq Manwel Dimech in Sliema. There are Maltacom offices at the south end of Triq it-Torri in

Sliema (open 8 am to 11 pm) and on Triq San Ġorġ in Paċeville (open 24 hours).

Waves Internet Café and Cocktail Bar (☎ 342242, @ waves@waldonet.net.mt), 139 Triq it-Torri, Sliema, has four terminals, a pool table and pinball machines. It charges Lm1 per half hour minimum and 10c a page for printing, and is open daily from noon till late. Jokers (☎ 333653, @ camilmac@waldonet.net.mt), 71 Triq ix-Xatt, Sliema, offers the latest in video games as well as Internet access.

Għall Kafe (☎ 319686, @ info@melita .net) at 118 Triq San Ġorġ in Paċeville, is Malta's biggest Internet cafe, with over 20 terminals. It charges Lm1 for 40 minutes, or Lm2 for 100 minutes, and printing is free.

Laundry

You can do your own washing at the Square Deal Launderette (40 Triq ix-Xatt, Sliema) for Lm2.50 a load, plus 40c per 10 minutes of tumble-drier time. Add Lm1 for a service wash. It's open 8 am to 5 pm Monday to Friday, and 8 am to 2 pm Saturday.

Swan Laundry and Dry Cleaning is on Triq it-Torri in Sliema and Triq Ġorġ Borg Olivier in St Julian's (service washes only).

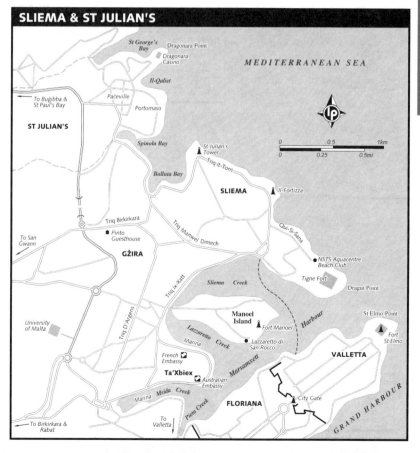

SLIEMA & ST JULIAN'S

Dangers & Annoyances

The tidal wave of alcohol and testosterone that swills through the streets of Paċeville at weekends occasionally overflows into outbreaks of violence. Some people also find that the noise levels in and around Paċeville at night are high enough to be a nuisance. Unless you plan to party the night away, you will probably prefer to seek accommodation in a quieter part of town. If you decide to rent a car, bear in mind that finding a place to park, especially in the streets of Paċeville, is a bit of a nightmare.

THINGS TO SEE & DO
Sliema

There's not a lot to see in Sliema itself, but there are good views of Valletta from Triq ix-Xatt (The Strand) and Tigne Point, especially at dusk as the floodlights are switched on. Triq ix-Xatt and Triq it-Torri (Tower Rd) make for a pleasant waterfront stroll, with plenty of bars and cafes to quench a thirst in. In the evenings these streets fill up with promenading families out for their daily *passeggiata* (evening stroll).

Tigne Point, east of Sliema, was one of the sites where the Turkish commander

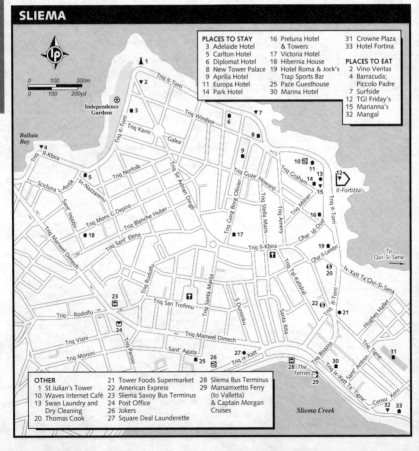

SLIEMA

PLACES TO STAY
3 Adelaide Hotel
5 Carlton Hotel
6 Diplomat Hotel
8 New Tower Palace
9 Aprilia Hotel
11 Europa Hotel
14 Park Hotel
16 Preluna Hotel & Towers
17 Victoria Hotel
18 Hibernia House
19 Hotel Roma & Jock's Trap Sports Bar
25 Paċe Guesthouse
30 Marina Hotel
31 Crowne Plaza
33 Hotel Fortina

PLACES TO EAT
2 Vino Veritas
4 Barracuda; Piccolo Padre
7 Surfside
12 TGI Friday's
15 Marianna's
32 Mangal

Independence Gardens

Balluta Bay

Il-Fortizza

To Qui-Si-Sana

Sliema Creek

OTHER
1 St Julian's Tower
10 Waves Internet Café
13 Swan Laundry and Dry Cleaning
20 Thomas Cook
21 Tower Foods Supermarket
22 American Express
23 Sliema Savoy Bus Terminus
24 Post Office
26 Jokers
27 Square Deal Launderette
28 Sliema Bus Terminus
29 Marsamxetto Ferry (to Valletta) & Captain Morgan Cruises

Dragut Reis ranged his cannon to pound Fort St Elmo into submission during the Great Siege. The tip of the peninsula is still known as Dragut Point. There is little to see today except the classic view of the Valletta fortifications. The overgrown remains of Tigne Fort are scheduled for redevelopment.

There are two towers on Triq it-Torri. **St Julian's Tower** is one of the network of coastal watchtowers built by Grand Master de Redin in the 17th century. **Il Fortiżża** was built by the British in the 19th century, and has now been taken over by a couple of restaurants.

Sliema's **beaches** are mostly shelves of bare rock, and clambering in and out of the sea can be a bit awkward. In places along Triq it-Torri and at Qui-Si-Sana, square pools have been cut into the soft limestone – these were made for the convenience of upper class Maltese ladies, but have since fallen into disuse. There are better facilities at the many private **lidos** along the coast, including swimming pools, sun-lounges, bars and water sports – admission costs around Lm2 to Lm3 per day.

In summer, you can watch the local **water polo** teams in action at the Balluta Bay and Il-Fortiżża pools.

Around Sliema

Sliema merges southward into the suburb of Gżira. A short bridge gives access to **Manoel Island**, most of which is taken up by boatbuilding yards and the dilapidated ruins of Fort Manoel. The island was used as a quarantine zone by the Knights of St John, and their 17th-century plague hospital, the **Lazzaretto di San Rocco**, can still be seen on the south side – it served as an isolation hospital during WWI and was last used during an epidemic in 1936. **Fort Manoel** was built in the early 18th century under Grand Master Manoel de Vilhena. It suffered extensive bomb damage during WWII, when nearby Lazzaretto Creek was used as a submarine base.

Ta'Xbiex (pronounced tashb-yesh), to the south of Manoel Island, is an upmarket suburb of gracious villas, mansions and embassies, with yacht marinas on either side.

St Julian's

Amid the heaving bars and packed restaurants of central St Julian's lies the elegant **Palazzo Spinola**, built for the Italian knight Rafael Spinola in the late 17th century. Surrounded by a walled garden (the entrance is on Triq il-Knisja), it now houses an elegant (and expensive) restaurant. Another aristocratic residence that has found a new lease of life is the **Villa Dragonara**, set on the southern headland of St George's Bay. Built in the late 19th century for the Marquis Scicluna, a wealthy banker, it is now occupied by the Dragonara Casino.

Paċeville is the in-your-face (and off-your-head) cluster of pubs, clubs and restaurants that forms the focal point for the wilder side of Malta's nightlife. This is party-all-night and sleep-all-day territory, and anyone over the age of 25 will feel old beyond their years. There is new development all around – notably the ultra-posh Portomaso complex on the site of the old Fort Spinola – as the tourist authorities try to push Malta's image upmarket, but Paċeville is likely to retain its raucous, rough-and-ready atmosphere for some time to come.

Most of the **beaches** around St Julian's are of the bare rock or private lido variety, but there is a genuine, if crowded, sandy beach at the head of St George's Bay.

ACTIVITIES
Water Sports

Traditional touristy stuff like banana-rides, paragliding and paddle-boat hire are available at most of the private lidos along the shore. The NSTS Aquacentre Beach Club (☎ 338568) on the Qui-Si-Sana waterfront offers a wide range of waterborne activities, including windsurfing (Lm14 for six hours, including instruction), water-skiing (Lm5 for 10 minutes), dinghy sailing (Lm20 for four hours in a three-person boat), motor-boating (Lm24 for four hours), snorkelling (Lm1.50 an hour) and scuba-diving (Lm15 per dive).

Oki-Ko-Ki Banis (☎ 339831 or 375874), right beside the Hotel Cavalieri on Triq Spinola in St Julian's, offers water-skiing lessons and speedboat hire, as well as boat trips to Comino.

ST JULIAN'S & PACEVILLE

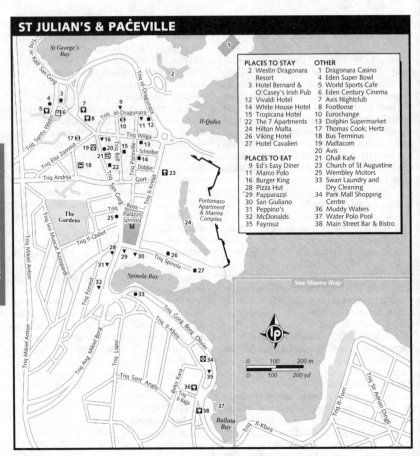

PLACES TO STAY
2 Westin Dragonara Resort
3 Hotel Bernard & O'Casey's Irish Pub
12 Vivaldi Hotel
14 White House Hotel
15 Tropicana Hotel
22 The 7 Apartments
24 Hilton Malta
26 Viking Hotel
27 Hotel Cavalieri

PLACES TO EAT
9 Ed's Easy Diner
11 Marco Polo
16 Burger King
28 Pizza Hut
29 Papparazzi
30 San Giuliano
31 Peppino's
32 McDonalds
35 Fayrouz

OTHER
1 Dragonara Casino
4 Eden Super Bowl
5 World Sports Cafe
6 Eden Century Cinema
7 Axis Nightclub
8 Footloose
10 Eurochange
13 Dolphin Supermarket
17 Thomas Cook; Hertz
18 Bus Terminus
19 Maltacom
20 Avis
21 Ghall Kafe
23 Church of St Augustine
25 Wembley Motors
33 Swan Laundry and Dry Cleaning
34 Park Mall Shopping Centre
36 Muddy Waters
37 Water Polo Pool
38 Main Street Bar & Bistro

Boat Trips

Captain Morgan Cruises (☎ 343373), at The Ferries in Sliema, has a boat trip for every traveller's taste and pocket. There's a tour of the Grand Harbour, which costs Lm6.25 for adults and Lm4.95 for children under 12. There's also an all-day cruise right around Malta available, which will set you back around Lm13.95 for adults and Lm8.75 for children under 12. Other options include day trips to the Blue Lagoon on Comino, 'underwater safaris' on a glass-bottomed boat, wine-tasting cruises and jazz party cruises.

Yachting

Experienced sailors can join the throng of white sails on the harbour by chartering a yacht from Captain Morgan (☎ 343373). Prices begin at Lm795 to Lm980 a week for a six- to eight-berth yacht, depending on the season.

PLACES TO STAY

Most of the accommodation in Sliema and St Julian's is aimed squarely at the package holiday and luxury hotel market, but you'll find that there are some bargains to be had during the low season.

PLACES TO STAY – BUDGET

Cheap hostel accommodation can be found at *Hibernia House* (☎ *333859, fax 230330, Triq Mons G Depiro, Sliema)*, which charges Lm2.85 for a bed in a shared dorm. To get there from Valletta, take bus 62 or 67 to Balluta Bay and walk up Triq Manwel Dimech for 300m – Triq Mons G Depiro is on the left.

The *Paċe Guesthouse* (☎ *343357, fax 347325, 10 Triq Sant'Agata, Sliema)* is set back from the waterfront above The Strand. A double room with shower costs Lm5.50 per person.

Pinto Guesthouse (☎ *313897, Triq il-Qalb Imqaddsa, St Julian's)* is a steep walk up from Balluta Bay, but worth the hike for the clean, spacious rooms and excellent view. The price is Lm6 per person including breakfast in high season, and Lm3.85 in low.

The *Adelaide Hotel* (☎/*fax 330361,* @ *adelaide@cheerful.com, 230 Triq it-Torri, Sliema)* is a small, family hotel overlooking Balluta Bay, with a quiet garden at the back. Rates are Lm7 per person (Lm7.70 in July and August) based on sharing a double or twin; the single supplement is Lm2.50. Some rooms have an en suite bath or shower, but most have shared WC. Prices include a continental breakfast; a cooked British breakfast is Lm2.50 extra. The hotel is closed from November to March.

The *Tropicana Hotel* (☎ *337557, fax 342890)* is on Triq Ball in the heart of Paċeville. All rooms have air-con and private shower and WC. High/low season rates are Lm10/8 per person including breakfast.

For self-catering, try *The 7 Apartments* (☎ *377543, fax 374663)* on Triq San Ġorġ in Paċeville. Prices for a fully furnished self-catering apartment with satellite TV and swimming pool begin at Lm75 a week.

PLACES TO STAY – MID-RANGE

Marina Hotel (☎ *336461)*, on the Tigne waterfront in Sliema, has good views across the harbour to Valletta. All rooms have private bath, and summer rates begin at Lm20 per person.

Hotel Roma (☎ *317633, fax 319112)*, on Triq Għar il-Lembri in Sliema, has double

rooms with shower for Lm35 in high season, and Lm24 in low.

Europa Hotel (☎ *330080, fax 311288, 138 Triq it-Torri, Sliema)* charges Lm17 per person in high season, and Lm13 in low.

All rooms at the friendly and efficient *Aprilia Hotel* (☎ *315131, fax 344307,* @ *aprilia@digigate.net, 36 Triq Ġorġ Borg Olivier, Sliema)* have en suite bathrooms, balconies, TV, air-con and heating. Rates are Lm19/12 per person B&B in high/low season, sharing a double or twin; there's a 50% surcharge for single occupancy. If you book a minimum stay of seven nights, at least three months in advance, you can get a 30% discount on these rates.

The *Carlton Hotel* (☎ *315764/5, fax 316736)*, at the northern end of Triq it-Torri in Sliema, charges Lm11.25/7 per person for a double room with breakfast. It has a roof terrace with bar and pool.

New Tower Palace (☎ *337271, fax 311235)*, also on Triq it-Torri, was renovated in 1999. All rooms have en suite bathrooms and balconies, and there's a sun terrace on the 7th floor. High/low season rates are Lm22/18 for a double.

Hotel Bernard (☎ *373900, fax 314726,* @ *hotelbernard@hotelbernard.com.mt)* is a stylish new hotel on Triq ix-Xatt San Ġorġ close to St George's Bay and Paċeville. All rooms have private bath, TV and air-con, and the hotel has a business centre. It's excellent value at Lm19/10 per person high/low season, including breakfast.

The *Viking Hotel* (☎ *316702 or 340930, fax 345757)* on Triq Spinola, St Julian's, charges Lm10/7 per person for doubles and Lm12/9 for singles with shower and fan. There's a 24-hour bar.

Right in the centre of Paċeville is the *White House Hotel* (☎ *378016, fax 378032,* @ *info@whitehousehotel.com)*, which is on Triq Paċeville. Comfortable and clean rooms with bath or shower, TV and air-con cost Lm10/7 per person for a double and Lm12/7.50 for a single.

PLACES TO STAY – TOP END

Park Hotel (☎ *343780, fax 343770)* on Triq Graham in Sliema has comfortable rooms with bath, TV and air-con. There is also a 24-hour cafe, indoor pool, outdoor rooftop pool, sauna and massage centre. High/low season rates for B&B are Lm29.25/18 for a single, and Lm39/24 for a double.

Preluna Hotel & Towers (☎ 334001, fax 342292, ✉ preluna@waldonet.net.mt, 124 Triq it-Torri, Sliema) is Malta's tallest building, and commands spectacular views along the coast. High/low season B&B rates for standard rooms begin at Lm38/32 for a double or twin, and Lm26/24 for a single. Add Lm14 to Lm18 to these prices if you want a room with a sea view.

Vivaldi Hotel (☎ 378100, fax 378101, ✉ ndbrg@gtvivaldi.goldentulip.nl) is an attractive new place aimed at the business and luxury tourism market. High season rates are Lm50/60 a single/double.

The *Diplomat Hotel* (☎ 345361, fax 345351, ✉ diplomat@vol.net.mt, 173 Triq it-Torri, Sliema) has small but attractive rooms, a rooftop swimming pool, and a 24-hour cafeteria. High/low season prices for a twin room are Lm45/34, and for a single Lm30/23, including breakfast. A sea view costs Lm5 extra, and there's a 10% discount for bookings made by email.

The excellent *Hotel Fortina* (☎ 343380, fax 339388, ✉ info@hotelfortina.com) is on Triq ix-Xatt ta'Tigne, overlooking Sliema Creek. It has two swimming pools, a fitness centre and a beach-front lido, Room rates begin at Lm41/31 per person in high/low season, based on sharing a double room. A supplement of Lm10 is charged for single occupancy.

The *Victoria Hotel* (☎ 334711, fax 334771, ✉ victoria@waldonet.net.mt), at the top of Triq Ġorġ Borg Olivier in Sliema, has a quiet location away from the seafront, and luxurious four-star facilities that include a swimming pool, sun terrace and free parking. Rack rates are Lm45/55 for a single/double room in summer, and Lm33/44 in winter.

The family-oriented *Hotel Cavalieri* (☎ 336255/8, fax 330542) is in a quiet location at the end of Triq Spinola in St Julian's. It has a pool, gym, sauna and a private lido with water-sports facilities, as well as diving

and sailing schools. It charges Lm55/45 for a double/single.

The *Crowne Plaza* (☎ 343400, fax 311292, ✉ hotel@crowneplazamalta.com) on Triq Tigne in Sliema has views of the Med on one side and Valletta on the other, although the brochures don't show the ugly wasteland awaiting development farther out on the point. Still, it's an excellent place to stay, occupying the site of an 18th-century fortress and partly housed in the century-old Officers' Mess of the Royal Malta Artillery. There's a fresh-water outdoor pool, heated indoor pool and beach club.

Westin Dragonara Resort (☎ 381000, fax 381348, ✉ westindrag@kemmunet.net.mt) is a vast, 300-room complex on Dragonara Point, St Julian's. The extensive amenities include two outdoor and one indoor pool, a gym, two jacuzzis, two tennis courts and a diving school. There are also 14 rooms designed for wheelchair users. All this does not come cheap. High/low season rack rates are Lm102/92 for a double room, but for a minimum stay of three nights the prices drop to Lm70/50 for a double and Lm45/35 for a single. You can also add on Lm10 for a sea view, and Lm6.50 for a buffet breakfast. Deals can be done for longer stays and low season holidays.

Hilton Malta (☎ 336201, fax 341539), in the middle of the new Portomaso marina and apartment complex, opened in 1999. It has, well, everything you would expect from a Hilton, though the views will be spoiled a little until all the construction work is finished. Rates for a standard double room begin at Lm80.

PLACES TO EAT
Restaurants

There's no shortage of restaurants in Sliema and St Julian's. *Mangal* (☎ 341046) is a good Turkish place on the Tigne waterfront with a view across the harbour to Valletta. *Meze* (starters) like stewed aubergine, stuffed pepper and cheese pastries go for Lm1 to Lm2, and main courses of lamb kebabs or grilled fish run to Lm3 to Lm5.

Surfside (☎ 345384) is on the Triq it-Torri seafront near the New Tower Palace Hotel.

The menu is mainly seafood, served in a dining room overlooking the sea. There's also a bar and cafe with Internet access.

Vino Veritas at 59 Triq Sir Adrian Dingli (on the corner with Triq it-Torri) is popular with both locals and tourists. It has good vegetarian options, like vegie lasagne and risotto, for around Lm1.75, and a lively wine bar.

TGI Friday's (☎ 346897/8) is housed in Il-Fortiżża on Triq it-Torri in Sliema. The standard menu of pizzas, steaks and burgers is made up for by the atmospheric vaults of the old watchtower.

Marianna's (☎ 318943), across the road from TGIF, is a loud and lively Tex-Mex restaurant. A piled plateful of nachos is Lm2.50, and a chilli-choked enchilada is Lm3.50. Diners are often tempted in with a free margarita.

The *Barracuda (☎ 331817, 195 Triq il-Kbira)*, on the western fringes of Sliema, is a smart seafood and pasta place with good views across Balluta Bay. Try the pasta with parma ham, apple and calvados sauce. Beneath the Barracuda is *Piccolo Padre (☎ 344875)*, a lively pizzeria-cum-art gallery that is almost always crowded. The traditional crunchy pizzas (Lm1.50) are worth queuing for.

Fayrouz (☎ 320837) is a Lebanese place on Triq Ġorġ Borg Olivier near the Park Mall Shopping Centre. The shish kebabs, falafel, tabbouleh and baba ganoush are delicious, but the decor is a little uninspiring. Fill up at lunch for about Lm2 to Lm3.

Peppino's (☎ 373200, 31 Triq San Ġorġ, St Julian's) first floor dining room is a good spot for a romantic dinner. The food is Italian with an emphasis on seafood and pasta, and the service is attentive but unobtrusive. There's also a good wine bar on the ground floor. The restaurant is open noon till 3 pm and 7 to 11 pm, Monday to Saturday.

The terrace at *Papparazzi (☎ 374966)* is a prime people-watching spot, with a fine view of Spinola Bay. The bistro serves good pastas, pizzas, steaks and burgers at prices around the Lm2 to Lm5 mark, and has excellent coffee.

There are more than half a dozen restaurants in the block next to Papparazzi. One of

the best is *San Giuliano (☎ 332000)*, an up-market Italian place with a superb view over the bay. The menu is mainly seafood, pasta, steak and veal; main courses cost around Lm4 to Lm8.

The *Marco Polo (☎ 331995)* on Triq id-Dragunara in Paċeville is an excellent, if expensive, Asian restaurant, offering a range of Chinese and Singaporean dishes. Main courses cost around Lm4 to Lm8.

Fast Food

The ubiquitous *McDonalds* is on the square at the head of Spinola Bay, and *Pizza Hut* is just up the hill on Triq San Ġorġ. There's a *Burger King* on the corner of Triq San Ġorġ and Triq Wilga in Paċeville, but a much better option for late-night munchies is *Ed's Easy Diner* on Triq id-Dragunara, where you can get good burgers and hot dogs for around the Lm1 mark.

Self-Catering

The *Tower Foods Supermarket* at 46 Triq it-Torri, Sliema, sells a wide range of groceries, frozen foods and fresh fruit and veg. In Paċeville, head for the *Dolphin Supermarket* on Triq Wilga.

ENTERTAINMENT
Bars

Sliema and St Julian's have a bar for everyone, from the teenage clubber to the old-age pensioner. Paċeville is the place for full-on partying, while the St Julian's and Sliema waterfronts have everything from posh wine bars to traditional British pubs.

Vino Veritas (see Places to Eat earlier in this section) is a laid-back wine bar and restaurant that has weekly live jazz sessions, while *Muddy Waters* opposite the water polo pool in Balluta Bay has a great juke box and regular live bands in summer.

Main Street Bar & Bistro (☎ 373377/88) on the Balluta Bay waterfront is a fashionable new bar where you can graze on snacks with Indian, Chinese, Thai, Mexican and Caribbean flavours. The bar is famous for its computerised till and drinks-pricing system, which reflects the stock market. Prices vary through the night, depending on how

SLIEMA & ST JULIAN'S

Beautiful Buses & Classic Cars

Malta's buses are a tourist attraction in themselves. Many of them are classic Bedfords, Thames, Leylands and AECs dating from the 1950s, '60s and '70s, brightly painted in a livery of yellow, white and orange; the Gozo buses have a more restrained colour scheme of grey, white and red. Although the old buses are undeniably picturesque, the downside is that they can also be noisy and uncomfortable, with clattering diesel engines and creaky-squeaky suspension that can rattle the fillings out of your teeth.

There are also hundreds of classic British cars still on the road, not because of any great enthusiasm for vintage vehicles, but because they are cheap and just seem to keep on going. Keen-eyed car enthusiasts can spot Ford Anglias, Ford Consuls, Cortina Mk1s, Triumph Heralds, Morris Minors, Hillman Minxes, Austin 1100s, old Bedford and Commer vans, and any number of Austin Minis, all in varying states of repair.

There are vintage trucks too. Many truck drivers decorate their vehicles with brightly coloured paint jobs, and adorn them with names like The Only One, Roy Rodgers, Buffalo Chief and Eskimo Prince.

---

popular a drink is – as more people buy a particular type of drink, its price increases, while the cost of unpopular drinks plummets. Current prices are displayed on TV screens. Unfortunately, the only return on your investment is likely to be a hangover. It's open daily 10 am to 1 am.

O'Casey's Irish Pub (☎ 373900), beneath the Hotel Bernard in St George's Bay, is much as you'd expect of an Irish theme bar anywhere in the world – it's crowded, lively, friendly, and well-stocked with cold Guinness.

Footloose, just up the hill in Paċeville, is a loud and cavernous sticky-carpet bar where the party crowd fill up on Bacardi Breezers before diving into one of the neighbouring clubs.

Jock's Trap Sports Bar (☎ 317633) on Triq Għar il-Lembi, Sliema (beneath the Hotel Roma) is a lively drinking den where sports fans can catch the big match on large-screen TVs. It's open 8 pm to 1 am daily (or whenever a major sports event is being screened).

The **World Sports Cafe** (☎ 382382), opposite the Eden Century cinema in St

George's Bay, offers similar sporting attractions in more stylish surroundings. It also has an extensive menu of snacks, burgers, nachos etc.

Casino

The **Dragonara Casino** (☎ 382362/3/4), out on the point beyond the Dragonara resort, is housed in a 19th-century mansion that, appropriately enough, once belonged to wealthy banker. The tables offer roulette, blackjack, chemin de fer, stud poker and punto banco, and there's a slot-machine gallery at the back. But give up any dreams of breaking the bank – there's a Lm5000 maximum jackpot. The minimum age for tourists is 18 (it's 25 for Maltese citizens), and you'll need your passport or ID card to get in. The dress code is 'smart casual', admission is free, and the casino is open daily from 10 am until 2 am or later.

Nightclubs

There are several clubs concentrated at the north end of Triq San Ġorġ in Paċeville, and farther down the hill on Triq ix-Xatt Ta' San Ġorġ, but their names come and go with the seasons. The only one that has managed to stand the test of time is *Axis (☎ 318078)*, Malta's biggest and best venue, with three separate clubs and seven bars providing space for 2500 people. It's open Friday and Saturday from 10.30 pm, with laser shows at 11.30 pm and 1.30 am.

Cinema
The *Eden Century (☎ 376401)* on Triq ix-Xatt Ta'San Ġorġ in St George's Bay has 16 screens showing first-run films.

Ten-Pin Bowling
The *Eden Super Bowl (☎ 319888)*, across the road from the Eden Century cinema, offers a 20-lane, ten-pin bowling alley.

GETTING THERE & AWAY
Bus Nos 62, 64 and 67 run regularly between Valletta and Sliema, St Julian's and Paċeville. Nos 60 and 63 go to the Savoy terminus in Sliema (near the Post Office on Triq Manwel Dimech). Bus No 645 goes from The Ferries in Sliema through St Julian's and on to St Paul's Bay, Mellieħa and the Gozo Ferry at Ċirkewwa. Bus No 70 runs from The Ferries through Paċeville and along the coast to the Buġibba terminus.

The Marsamxetto Ferry shuttles regularly between Sliema and Valletta (see Getting There & Away in the Valletta chapter).

GETTING AROUND
Wembley Motors (☎ 374141 or 374242) at 50 Triq San Ġorġ, St Julian's, provides a reliable 24-hour radio taxi service, and can also arrange car hire.

Ada Car Rental (☎ 691007 or 310004) is at 171 Triq it-Torri, Sliema, beneath the Diplomat Hotel. Hertz (☎ 314636) has an office beside Thomas Cook in Triq Elija Zammit in Paċeville, and Avis (☎ 246640) is just around the corner in Triq San Ġorġ.

North-West Malta

The Victoria Lines escarpment – a steep slope that follows the line of a geological rift known as the Great Fault – cuts across the island from the bay of Fomm ir-Riħ in the west to Baħar iċ Ċagħaq in the east, dividing north-west Malta from the more densely populated central region.

The north-west is more rugged than the rest of the island, with extensive outcrops of the hard Upper Coralline Limestone. Geological faulting has produced a series of barren rocky ridges and fertile, flat-floored valleys. Most of Malta's beach resorts – Buġibba, Qawra, St Paul's Bay, Mellieħa Bay and Golden Bay – are in the north-west, and some more remote corners offer good coastal walking. The rocky shores of the north-west boast some of the country's best diving outside of Gozo.

BAĦAR IĊ-ĊAGĦAQ

Baħar iċ-Ċagħaq (**ba**-har eetch **cha**-ag) – also known, less tongue-twistingly, as White Rocks – lies halfway between Sliema and Buġibba. It has a rather scruffy rock beach and a couple of water-based attractions. The **Splash & Fun Park** (☎ 375021) has a large seawater swimming pool and a selection of ugly (and somewhat dilapidated-looking) fibreglass water-slides and flumes. There's also a children's playground inhabited by bizarre-looking plastic dinosaurs in bright primary colours. The park is open 9.30 am to 6 pm in summer only (Lm3.25/2.25 for adults/children).

Mediterraneo Marine Park (☎ 372218) is home to a group of performing Black Sea dolphins, rescued from an old Soviet marine park that went bust. The dolphins go through their routine at 11.30 am Monday to Friday, with an afternoon show at 2.30 pm on Sunday and public holidays. Doors open one hour before showtime (Lm3.50/2 for adults/children).

On Qrejten Point, west of the bay, is **Qalet Marku Tower**, one of several 17th-century watchtowers along this coastline.

HIGHLIGHTS

- Hiking along the coast between Mistra Bay and Għajn Ħadid
- Exploring Malta's marine life on an Underwater Safari cruise
- Enjoying the views from the wild headland of Ras il-Qammieħ
- Sunbathing on Għajn Tuffieħa beach on a quiet spring day

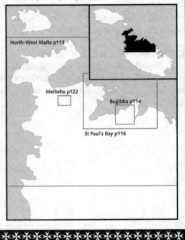

North-West Malta p113

Mellieħa p122

Buġibba p114

St Paul's Bay p116

To get to Baħar iċ-Ċagħaq, take bus No 68 from Valletta, or No 70, 645 or 652 from Sliema or Buġibba.

ST PAUL'S BAY & BUĠIBBA

St Paul's Bay is named for the saint who was shipwrecked here in AD 60 (see boxed text 'St Paul in Malta'). The unsightly sprawl of Buġibba and Qawra, on the eastern side of the bay, is the biggest tourist development on Malta. Buġibba is the heartland of the island's 'cheap-n-cheerful' package holiday trade, and is absolutely mobbed in summer. It is not the prettiest of places, and there are no sandy beaches, but

NEIL WILSON

St Paul's Islands were named after the shipwrecked saint who brought Christianity to Malta.

NEIL WILSON

Film set turned tourist attraction, Popeye Village in Anchor Bay is popular with the kiddies.

The watchful Eye of Osiris, St Paul's Bay

St Paul's Bay is a fisherman's paradise.

Mosta Dome, miraculously still standing after three bombs struck the roof during WWII

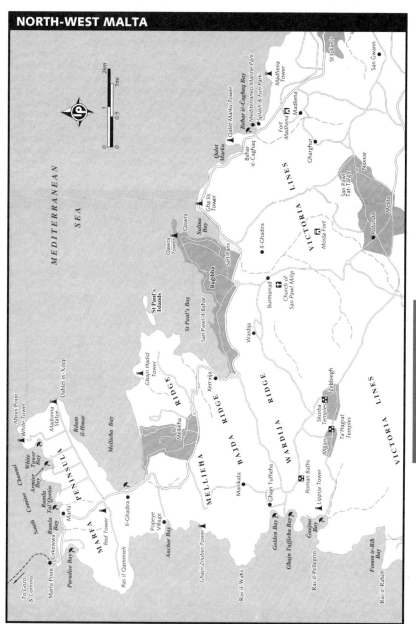

at least it's cheap, especially in winter when there are some real accommodation bargains to be found.

Orientation & Information

The tourist towns of Buġibba and Qawra (**aow**-ra) occupy the peninsula on the southeastern side of St Paul's Bay. Buġibba merges westward into the fishing village of St Pawl il-Baħar in Maltese). The smaller resort of Xemxija lies at the head of the bay on the north-west shore, about 3.5km from Buġibba. St Paul's Islands guard the north-western point of the

bay. The main coast road from Valletta and Sliema to Mellieħa and the Gozo ferry bypasses Buġibba and St Paul's Bay village.

You can change money in Buġibba at Thomas Cook on Triq Bajja and beside the New Dolmen Hotel. There's an HSBC bank with ATM and 24-hour currency exchange machine on Misraħ il-Bajja (Bay Square).

The post office is on the corner of Triq il-Ħalel and the waterfront, and you can check your email at the cybercafe in the Mirabelle Restaurant on Triq Bajja. It's open 8 am to 11 pm and charges Lm1 for 40 minutes. For laundry, try the RCE Launderette

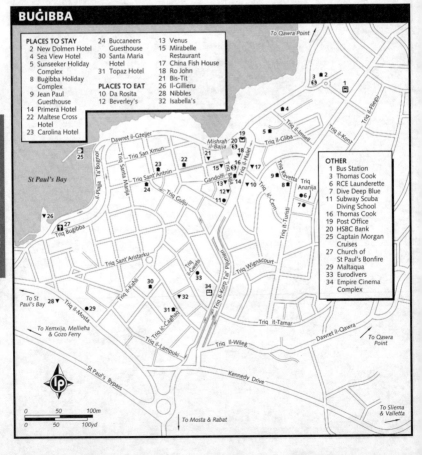

The Victoria Lines

The Victoria Lines are fortifications built by the British in the late 19th century. They were supposedly built to protect the main part of the island from potential invaders landing on the northern beaches, but they didn't see any military action and some historians think they were commissioned simply to give the British garrisons something to do. The lines were named for Queen Victoria's Diamond Jubilee in 1897.

The Victoria Lines run along a limestone escarpment that stretches from Fomm ir-Riħ in the west to Baħar iċ-Ċagħaq in the east. Three forts – Madliena Fort, Mosta Fort and Binġemma Fort – are linked by a series of walls, entrenchments and gun batteries. The best-preserved section, known as the Dwejra Lines, is north of Mdina. Using the Maltese government 1:25,000 maps (see Maps in the Facts for the Visitor chapter), it is possible to walk the length of the Victoria Lines between Madliena Fort in the east and Binġemma Fort in the west, a distance of around 12km. The views, especially northwards towards Gozo and Comino, are excellent.

(☎ 580599) on Triq Ananija. It's open 8.30 am to 5.30 pm daily from June to September, and 10 am to 2 pm in winter.

Things to See & Do

There's not much to see in Buġibba except acres of painted concrete and sunburnt flesh, and not much to do other than lie around in the sun, go swimming or get towed around the bay on a variety of inflatable objects. Perhaps the best option is to head for the harbour at the exotically named Plajja Tal'Bognor (Bognor Beach) and get away from it all on a **boat trip**.

Salina Bay, to the east of Qawra Point, is a popular venue for local anglers. The narrow head of the bay is filled with **salt pans**, which have been in use since at least the 16th century. On the eastern edge of the bay, beside the steps leading from the main coast road up to the Coastline Hotel, are the remains of a 16th-century redoubt and **fougasse** (see boxed text 'The Fougasse').

Buġibba merges westwards into the old fishing village of St Paul's Bay, which has retained something of its traditional Maltese character, and has a few historical sights to boot. The 17th-century **Church of St Paul's Bonfire** stands on the waterfront to the south of Plajja Tal'Bognor, supposedly on the spot where the saint first scrambled ashore. During the festa of St Paul's Shipwreck (10 February), a bonfire is lit outside the church.

The **Wignacourt Tower**, built in 1610, guards the point to the west of the church, and houses a tiny museum with exhibits on local history, including a small selection of guns and armour. It's open 10 am to 2 pm on Sunday only (admission free). West again, near the fishing-boat harbour at the head of the bay, is **Għajn Rasul** (Apostle's Fountain), where St Paul is said to have baptised the first Maltese convert to Christianity. On the festa of Sts Peter and Paul (29 June), people gather at the fountain before taking fishing boats out to **St Paul's Islands**, where they hear mass beneath a large white statue of St Paul that was erected in 1845.

Activities

Boat Trips Captain Morgan (☎ 343373) offers an hour-long 'underwater safari' in a glass-bottomed boat exploring the marine life around St Paul's Islands, and the wrecks of HMS *Kingston* (sunk during WWII) and the MV *Hanini* (once a private yacht). There's also a full-day cruise to Comino and Gozo on the graceful gaff-rigged schooner *Charlotte Louise*, with stops for swimming and snorkelling.

Underwater safaris set off at 10 am, 11.30 am, 1 pm and 2.30 pm Monday to Saturday from May to October, daily from July to September, with an extra cruise at 3.45 pm in August only. In March, April and November there are departures at 10 am, noon and 2 pm Monday to Friday

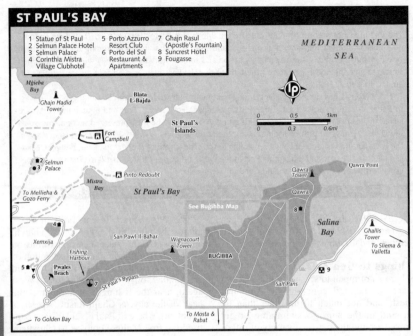

ST PAUL'S BAY

1 Statue of St Paul
2 Selmun Palace Hotel
3 Selmun Palace
4 Corinthia Mistra Village Clubhotel
5 Porto Azzurro Resort Club
6 Porto del Sol Restaurant & Apartments
7 Ghajn Rasul (Apostle's Fountain)
8 Suncrest Hotel
9 Fougasse

only. Tickets cost Lm4.95 for adults, and lm3.95 for kids under 12.

The *Charlotte Louise* cruises depart at 10 am and return at 6 pm daily from June to September, and Monday to Saturday in May and October. The price (Lm23.95 for adults, Lm19.75 for children) includes a buffet lunch, free bar and use of snorkelling equipment.

Scuba-Diving There are several diving schools in St Paul's Bay and Buġibba, including Maltaqua (☎ 571873) on Triq il-Mosta, Subway Scuba Diving School (☎ 572997) on Triq il-Korp Tal'Pijunieri, Dive Deep Blue (☎ 583946) at 100 Triq Ananija, Octopus Garden (☎ 582586) at the New Dolmen Hotel, Eurodivers (☎ 483926) on Triq Ġwiebi, and Strand Diving Services (☎ 574502) on Triq Ramon Perellos. For more information on diving, see the boxed text 'Diving in Malta' in the Facts for the Visitor chapter.

Places to Stay – Budget

Most of the accommodation around St Paul's Bay is taken up by package holiday companies from April to October, so book in advance if you want to stay in summer. In the low season you can get some good deals, especially for stays of a week or more.

The *Jean Paul Guesthouse* (☎ 572452, ☎/fax 576142, @ lilianam@orbit.net.mt) in Triq Kavetta is a friendly place just a few minutes' walk from the seafront. There are single, double and family rooms available, all with en suite bathroom, for Lm6.75 per person B&B.

Buccaneers Guest House (☎ 571671) is another friendly place, at the corner of Triq Sant'Antnin and Triq Ġulju. The rooms are plain but comfy, and there's a lively bar and restaurant.

Maltese Cross Hotel (☎ 573517, fax 372437, 70 Triq Sant'Antnin) is in a central location just off Misraħ il-Bajja. It has good-value rooms with private shower for

Lm8 per person B&B. There's a rooftop sun terrace with a view of the bay.

Sea View Hotel (☎ 573105, fax 581788), on Dawret il-Gżejjer (Islet Promenade) north of Misraħ il-Bajja, has rather small and basic rooms, but all have balconies and en suite shower, and there's a small pool out the back. It charges a reasonable Lm7 per person B&B in high season, and Lm4.50 in low; a sea view costs an extra Lm1 in summer only, and the single room supplement is Lm2. There's a further charge of Lm2 per person if you stay only one night.

Places to Stay – Mid-Range

The three-star *Primera Hotel (☎ 573880 or 571757, fax 5812290)* is bang in the centre of Buġibba at the corner of Triq Pijunieri and Triq il-Ħalel. The comfortably appointed rooms have en suite bath, satellite TV and air-con, and there's also a heated indoor pool and another tiny one on the rooftop. Room rates range from Lm10 per person B&B in winter to Lm12 in summer, with a single-room supplement of Lm3 a night.

Carolina Hotel (☎ 571534/6 or 583808/9, fax 573602, ✆ carolina@mail.mol.net.mt) in Triq Sant'Antnin has an outdoor rooftop pool and a heated indoor pool with jacuzzi. All rooms have private bathrooms, and cost Lm15 per person per night in July and August, dropping to Lm6 in November and December, based on sharing a twin or double room. A balcony with a sea view will add an extra Lm5 a night to the bill.

Sunseeker Holiday Complex (☎ 575619, fax 581573) in Terjqet il-Kulpara offers self-catering apartments for weekly lets. High season prices range from Lm88 a week for a two-person flat, to Lm155 a week for a six-person flat. From November to April these prices drop to Lm60 and Lm88 respectively. The complex has indoor and outdoor pools, sauna, jacuzzi and mini-market.

Buġibba Holiday Complex (☎ 580861, fax 580867, ✆ info@bhc.com.mt) in Triq it-Turisti is one of the veterans of the Buġibba tourist trade, having been around for more than a decade. It has hotel rooms and self-catering apartments, three swimming pools, cocktail bar, restaurant and pizzeria. Twin

St Paul in Malta

The Bible (Acts 27-28) tells how St Paul was shipwrecked on Malta (most likely around AD 60) on his voyage from Caesarea to stand trial in Rome. The ship full of prisoners was caught in a storm and drifted for 14 days before breaking up on the shore of an unknown island. All aboard swam safely to shore, '… and when they were escaped, then they knew that the island was called Melita'.

The local people received the shipwrecked strangers with kindness, and built a bonfire to warm them. Paul, while adding a bundle of sticks to the fire, was bitten by a venomous snake – a scene portrayed in several religious paintings on the island – but suffered no ill effects. The Melitans took this as a sign that he was no ordinary man.

Acts 28 goes on to say that Paul and his companions met with 'the chief man of the island, whose name was Publius; who received them, and lodged them three days courteously', during which time Paul healed Publius' sick father. The castaways remained on Melita for three months before continuing their journey to Rome, where Paul was imprisoned and sentenced to death.

According to Maltese tradition, Paul laid the foundations of a Christian community during his brief stay on the island. Publius, later canonised, was converted to Christianity and became the bishop of Malta and later of Athens. The site of the shipwreck is traditionally taken to be St Paul's Island (known in Maltese as Selmunett). The house where Publius received the shipwrecked party may have occupied the site of the 17th-century church of San Pawl Milqi (St Paul Welcomed) on the hillside above Burmarrad, 2km south of Buġibba, where excavations have revealed the remains of a large Roman villa and farm.

The Fougasse

A *fougasse* was a cheap and primitive mortar-like weapon – a deep, circular pit hewn from the solid rock, and angled at around 45 degrees to the vertical, pointing towards the sea. An explosive charge with a long fuse was placed at the bottom of the pit, and assorted large stones and other shrapnel piled on top. When enemy ships came within range, the fuse was lit and the resulting explosion would send a shower of heavy rocks raining down on the invading fleet. Several dozen fougasses were dug along the northern coast of Malta during the early days of the Knights' occupation, and a few can still be seen – notably the one preserved on the shore of Salina Bay near the Coastline Hotel.

hotel rooms cost Lm17/11 per person B&B in high/low season; the single room supplement is Lm8/5 per night. A one-bedroom apartment (sleeping up to four people) costs Lm35/18.90 a night self-catering.

Topaz Hotel (☎ 572416/9, fax 571123, 🖂 topazmalta@vol.net.mt) on Triq iċ-Ċagħaq is a large complex of air-conditioned hotel rooms and self-catering apartments set around a courtyard with two swimming pools about 1km from the sea. Hotel room B&B rates range from Lm5.50 per person in November to February, to Lm14 in August, with an Lm4 or Lm5 supplement for single occupancy. A self-catering studio apartment that sleeps two costs from Lm6 (per apartment per night) in January to Lm18 from July to September.

The hotel rooms at *Santa Maria Hotel* (☎ 576576, fax 576793) in Triq ir-Ramel are block-booked by Airtours, but it also has self-catering apartments from Lm6.30 a night for a two-person studio in November to April, rising to Lm14.70 in July to September.

Places to Stay – Top End

The *New Dolmen Hotel* (☎ 581510, fax 581532, 🖂 ndhmalta@vol.net.mt) on the waterfront about 500m north-east of Misraħ il-Bajja takes its name from the remains of a prehistoric temple which has been incorporated – none too sympathetically – into the hotel garden. It has all the comforts you would expect of a four-star hotel, and charges high/low season rates of Lm21.75/11 per person B&B, based on sharing a twin room and staying at least six nights. The single occupancy supplement is Lm6/4.50.

The vast, 434-room, four-star *Suncrest Hotel* (☎ 577101, fax 575478, 🖂 joseph _tonna@suncresthotel.com) on the Qawra waterfront facing Salina Bay is the biggest and flashiest hotel in Buġibba. The staff are friendly and helpful, there's 24-hour room service, and guests have free use of a wide range of leisure facilities, including no fewer than four swimming pools (three outdoor, one indoor), a gymnasium, a jacuzzi, a sauna, a massage parlour, a squash court and a floodlit tennis court. High/low season rates (per room, not per person) are Lm50/ 35 for a twin and Lm35/25 for a single.

Places to Eat

Buġibba is awash with cheap eating places, many offering 'full English breakfast' and 'typical English fish and chips', as well as pizzas, burgers and kebabs. But there's a reasonable selection of other cuisines, and a few good Maltese places too.

Da Rosita (☎ 571158) in Triq il-Ħalel, is a bright and breezy, family-run Italian-Maltese restaurant. The varied menu includes pasta, fish, shellfish, steaks and vegetarian dishes. A starter of giant mussels costs Lm2.40, and a main course of traditional *bragioli* is Lm3.75.

China Fish House (☎ 574303) on Triq il-Ħalel is run by a young lady from Chongqing, and the cuisine is authentically Chinese. Butterfly prawns, a house speciality, are Lm4.75, and aromatic crispy duck with pancakes is Lm4.50. A set dinner for two is Lm9.50.

Ro John (☎ 574454), the Indian restaurant across the street from the China Fish House on Triq il Ħalel, has wisecracking waiters and classic curries like lamb tikka massala (Lm2) and king prawn chilli (Lm3.50). *Octopus balti* (Lm3) adds a bit of Maltese colour to the menu.

Venus (☎ 571604), on the corner of Triq Bajja and Gandolfi, is a good place for a romantic dinner. The menu adds an imaginative twist to traditional ingredients – try the baked goat's cheese with smoked apples, pecans and rosemary bread (Lm2.25) followed by roast rabbit with garlic and star anise (Lm4.25).

Beverley's (☎ 575037) on Triq Pijunieri specialises in fresh fish and Maltese dishes. Every Wednesday is Maltese night, with a set dinner menu at Lm4.50 a head. Typical courses might include octopus in garlic, grilled fish, Maltese chicken pie or *pudina* (Maltese bread pudding).

Isabella's (☎ 572834) is a Mexican-American eatery on Triq L-Ibħra. Burgers start at Lm3.25, a rack of ribs is Lm4.25, and for Lm4.25 you can get a tongue-tingling *mole poblano* (chicken cooked in a sauce with tomatoes, lots of chillis and some bitter chocolate – yes, chocolate!).

Bis-Tit (☎ 585820) on Triq Sant'Antnin is a bit out of the ordinary. Run by a Nigerian couple, it offers an exotic menu of African dishes such as *efo riro,* a spicy confection of shredded prawns and vegetables, in the Lm3.75 to Lm4.75 price range.

Il-Gillieru (☎ 573480 or 573269) enjoys a five-star location on a terrace overlooking the harbour. It's been around for decades and is a local institution famed for its fresh seafood – the *aljotta* (fish soup) is excellent. It's not cheap – expect to pay Lm25 for dinner for two – so save it for a special occasion.

If you want a change from hotel breakfasts and fancy a Maltese-style start to the day, you can grab a coffee (55c) and a couple of *pastizzi* (10c each) at ***Nibbles*** cafeteria on Triq Mosta. Staff also sell pastries and confectionery.

Entertainment
There are basically two species of *bars* in Buġibba. There's the 'typical British pub' with a name like The Victoria, The Red Lion or The Crown and Thistle, where you can down pints of bitter, play darts and sing along with the karaoke machine. And there are bars with names like Bonkers, Staggers, Scandals and (this is true) Big Bum, where your mission for the evening is to get sloshed and go berserk. Take your pick from the dozens of bars along Triq il-Turisti and the streets around Misraħ il-Bajja.

The ***Oracle Casino*** (☎ 570057), at the New Dolmen Hotel on the Qawra seafront, is smaller and less formal in atmosphere than the Dragonara in St Julian's. It's open from noon until the small hours every day. The minimum age is 18 for visitors (25 for Maltese citizens), and admission is free. The dress code is 'smart casual' and you'll need your passport or ID card.

The four-screen ***Empire Cinema Complex*** (☎ 581909 or 581787) on Triq il-Korp Tal'Pijunieri in Buġibba shows first-run movies, and has a video games arcade in the basement. Tickets cost Lm2.40 for adults, and Lm1.40 for children

Getting There & Away
Bus Nos 49 and 58 run frequently between Valletta and Buġibba. Nos 43, 44 and 48 call at Buġibba and St Paul's Bay before terminating at Mellieħa, Mellieħa Bay and Ċirkewwa respectively.

Direct bus services from Buġibba (avoiding Valletta) include Nos 48 (to Ċirkewwa), 51 (to Golden Bay), 70 (to Sliema), 86 (to Mosta and Rabat), 427 (to Mosta, Attard and Marsaxlokk) and 627 (to Sliema, Paola and Marsaxlokk).

The Buġibba bus station is on Triq it-Turisti near the New Dolmen Hotel.

XEMXIJA
The small, south-facing resort of Xemxija (shem-**shee**-ya), on the north side of St Paul's Bay, takes its name from *xemx,* the Maltese word for sun. There are a couple of private lidos along the waterfront, but Pwales Beach at the head of St Paul's Bay is just a narrow strip of gravelly sand.

About 300m west of the roundabout at the top of the hill in Xemxija a minor road leads to **Mistra Bay**, which has a tiny, gravelly beach and a tourist restaurant. It's not very pretty, and the bay itself is filled with fish-farm pens, but there's good swimming and snorkelling off the rocks and good hiking along the coast beyond the **Pinto Redoubt**, a 17th-century gun battery at the far end of the bay.

Places to Stay & Eat

Porto del Sol (☎ 573970) at the foot of the hill on the main road is an attractive family-run restaurant with views of the bay. It's popular with locals, and well-known for its excellent seafood – expect to pay around Lm20 to Lm25 for dinner for two including wine. Upstairs, there are 10 *self-catering apartments*, all with balconies overlooking the bay. A two-person studio apartment costs Lm5.50 per night from November to March, Lm6 April to June and in October, and Lm11 July to September. A two-bedroom apartment (sleeps up to five) costs Lm8/9/14.

Porto Azzurro Resort Club (☎ 585171, fax 585170) on Triq Ridott, the street that cuts back left above the Porto del Sol, has indoor and outdoor pools, a fitness centre, sauna and jacuzzi, and a mini-market. Self-catering studio apartments with a double bed cost from Lm11 a night in low season. There's a restaurant too, but it's best avoided – the food is miserable.

The *Corinthia Mistra Village Clubhotel (☎ 580481, fax 582941)* has a great location on top of the ridge above Xemxija. It has over 200 one- and two-bedroom apartments set in landscaped gardens, swimming pools, sun terraces, a gym, sauna and massage parlour, tennis and squash courts, mini-market, launderette and children's club.

GĦAJN TUFFIEĦA

The fertile Pwales Valley stretches 4km from the head of St Paul's Bay to Għajn Tuffieħa (ayn too-fee-ha, meaning 'Spring of the Apples') on Malta's west coast. Here, two of Malta's best sandy beaches draw crowds of sun-worshippers. The misleadingly named **Golden Bay** – the sand is more grey-brown than golden – is overlooked by the white battlements of the Golden Sands Hotel, and is the busier and more developed of the two beaches.

Around the headland and to the south, guarded by a 17th-century watchtower, is **Għajn Tuffieħa Bay**. It is reached via a long, long flight of steps from a car park beside the derelict Old Riviera Hotel, which is slowly sliding downhill towards the sea. The 250m strip of red-brown sand, backed by slopes covered in acacia and tamarisk trees, is more attractive than its neighbour, and is now protected by law – camping and sleeping on the beach are prohibited.

There are good coastal walks south to Ġnejna Bay (see Mġarr later in this chapter), and north to Anchor Bay.

Places to Stay & Eat

The **Golden Sands Hotel** *(☎ 573961/2 or 580848, fax 580875)* has a great location overlooking the beach, but the atmosphere is a little antiseptic. A twin room costs Lm16/9.50 per person for half-board in high/low season. The single room supplement is Lm2.50, and a sea-view balcony costs an extra Lm2 a night.

Tucked away behind Golden Bay is the **Hal Ferh Holiday Village** *(☎ 573882/3, fax 573888)*. The walled-in compound was originally a British military barracks, but the rooms and self-catering apartments are bright and comfortable. Rates for hotel rooms range from Lm9.75 per person in April and October to Lm16.75 in July and August. A one-bedroom apartment costs Lm14 to Lm20.25 per night, and a two-bedroom apartment is Lm18.75 to Lm25.75. Prices include free use of water sports facilities, minigolf and the tennis court. The complex is closed from November to March.

The **Apple's Eye Restaurant**, on a terrace overlooking Golden Bay, peddles standard tourist fare such as burgers and pizzas for Lm1.80 to Lm2.25.

Getting There & Away

By car, turn south at the roundabout at the west end of the St Paul's-Buġibba Bypass, or catch bus No 51 from Buġibba, No 652 from Sliema, or No 47 from Valletta.

MĠARR & ŻEBBIEGĦ

The village of Mġarr (mm-**jarr**), 2km south-east of Għajn Tuffieħa, would be unremarkable were it not for the conspicuous dome of the famous **Egg Church**. The Church of the Assumption was built in the 1930s with money raised by local parishioners, largely from the sale of locally produced eggs.

A minor road leads west from Mġarr past the ornate early 19th-century **Zammitello Palace** – originally a manor house, and now a wedding hall – to **Ġnejna Bay**. The red sand beach is backed by terraced hillsides and enjoys a distant view of the Ta'Ċenċ cliffs on Gozo. There is good swimming off the rocks on either side of the bay. The **Lippija Tower** on the northern skyline makes a good target for a short walk.

On the road between Għajn Tuffieħa and Mġarr you will find the remains of the **Roman Baths**. There are only scant remnants of floor mosaics, the fire-bricks beneath the caldarium (hot room), and the stone toilet seats from the latrine, but it's worth a look if you're in the area. There's usually an attendant on hand to give a guided tour – leave a tip of around 50c.

Back in Mġarr, the site of the **Ta'Ħaġrat Temples** is concealed down a side street near the police station (on the road towards Żebbiegħ), but it's hardly worth seeking out. The site is fenced off and there's nothing to see except a few tumbled stones. The **Skorba Temples** in the neighbouring village of Żebbiegħ are slightly more interesting, but probably only to archaeology enthusiasts. The excavation of the site was important in providing evidence of village habitation on Malta in the period 4500-4100 BC, now known as the Skorba Phase. Fragments of pottery and figurines found on the site are displayed in the National Museum of Archaeology in Valletta.

Malta's Top 10 Swimming Spots

Għajn Tuffieħa Bay, North-West Malta (p120)
Ġnejna Bay, North-West Malta (p121)
Rdum il-Ħmar, North-West Malta (p125)
Fomm ir-Riħ, Central Malta (p133)
Għar Lapsi, Central Malta (p137)
Peter's Pool, South-East Malta (p143)
Dwejra Bay, Gozo (p158)
Wied il-Għasri, Gozo (p159)
Ir-Ramla, Gozo (p163)
Blue Lagoon, Comino (p164)

❋❋❋❋❋❋❋❋❋❋❋❋❋❋❋❋❋❋❋❋

Il-Barri (☎ 5733235), also known as Charlie's, and the *Sunny Bar* (☎ 573705), both on the village square in Mġarr, are favourite local venues for a *fenkata* (see boxed text in the Facts for the Visitor chapter).

MELLIEĦA

The town of Mellieħa (mell-**ee**-ha) perches picturesquely atop the ridge between St Paul's Bay and Mellieħa Bay. Although it was founded in the 15th century, the site was abandoned for several hundred years because of its vulnerability to attacks by corsairs landing in the bay below. The town was re-occupied in the 19th century.

Because of its distance from the beach, Mellieħa escaped the tidal wave of development that blighted Sliema and Buġibba in the early days of Malta's package holiday boom. Although there are now several large hotels in town, Mellieħa today exudes a certain atmosphere of exclusivity, enhanced by the rash of expensive new villas spreading along the slopes overlooking Mellieħa Bay.

Orientation & Information

Triq Ġorġ Borg Olivier – Mellieħa's main drag – runs north-south along a narrow gorge in the limestone plateau of the Mellieħa ridge, and descends via a series of hair-pin bends towards Mellieħa Bay. The older part of the town lies to the west of this street, with the Church of Our Lady of Victory at the northern end. Newer houses, luxury villas and apartments spread along the ridge to the east. The bus terminus is in Misraħ iż-Żjara Tal'Papa, beneath the church. The main road to Ċirkewwa and the Gozo Ferry bypasses Mellieħa to the south and west.

There are branches of the Bank of Valletta and HSBC on the main street, each with an ATM.

Things to See

The Church of Our Lady of Victory sits prominently on a rocky spur overlooking Mellieħa Bay. Stairs lead down on the eastern side of the church to a little pedestrian plaza beside the **Shrine of the Nativity of Our Lady of Mellieħa**. It has been a place

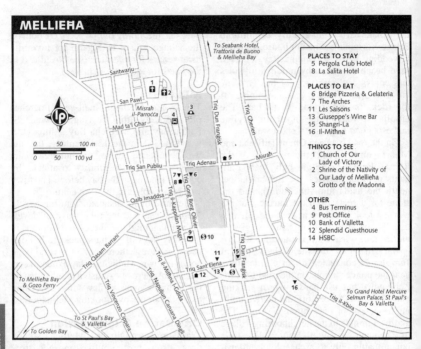

MELLIEĦA

To Seabank Hotel,
Trattoria de Buono
& Mellieħa Bay

Santwarju

San Pawl
Misraħ
il-Parroċċa

Mad ta' l Għar

0   50   100 m
0   50   100 yd

Triq Dun Franġisk

Triq Għerien

Triq San Publiu

Triq Adenau

Misraħ

Triq Ġorġ Borg Olivier

Qalb Imaddsa

Triq il-Kappillan Magri

Triq Qasam Barrani

Triq il-Mithna l-Qdida

Triq Napuljun Casana Dingli

Triq Vincenzo Cipara

Triq Sant'Elena

Triq Dun Franġisk

To Mellieħa Bay
& Gozo Ferry

To St Paul's Bay
& Valletta

To Golden Bay

To Grand Hotel Mercure
Selmun Palace, St Paul's
Bay & Valletta

Triq il-Kbira

PLACES TO STAY
5 Pergola Club Hotel
8 La Salita Hotel

PLACES TO EAT
6 Bridge Pizzeria & Gelateria
7 The Arches
11 Les Saisons
13 Giuseppe's Wine Bar
15 Shangri-La
16 Il-Mithna

THINGS TO SEE
1 Church of Our
   Lady of Victory
2 Shrine of the Nativity of
   Our Lady of Mellieħa
3 Grotto of the Madonna

OTHER
4 Bus Terminus
9 Post Office
10 Bank of Valletta
12 Splendid Guesthouse
14 HSBC

of pilgrimage since medieval times, and its walls are covered with votive offerings. The fresco of the Madonna above the altar is said to have been painted by St Luke.

Across the main street from the shrine, a gate in the wall and a flight of steps lead down to the **Grotto of the Madonna**, another shrine dedicated to the Virgin. It is set deep in a cave lit by flickering candles, beside a spring with waters that are said to heal sick children. Baby clothes hung on the walls are votive offerings given in thanks for successful cures.

A 15-minute walk leads down the steep hill to **Mellieħa Bay**, the biggest and best sand beach in the Maltese islands. It's also, predictably, one of the most popular. The warm, shallow waters of the bay are great for swimming and safe for kids, so the sea gets almost as crowded as the sand. Add the water-skiers, rental canoes, banana-rides, parascending boats and the fact that the reliable north-easterly breeze blowing into the

bay in summer makes it ideal for windsurfing, and you begin to realise that Mellieħa Bay is not the place to get away from it all.

Ironically, on the other side of the road from Malta's busiest beach is **Il-Għadira** (il-aa-**dee**-ra, meaning 'the marsh'), Malta's first national nature reserve. This area of shallow, reedy ponds surrounded by scrub is an important resting area for migrating birds.

Places to Stay

Splendid Guesthouse (☎ 523602, fax 521273, ✉ splendid@waldonet.net.mt) is at the southern end of Triq il-Kappillan Magri. All 14 rooms have private showers, fan and heater, and there's a sun-bathing terrace on the rooftop. Rates for B&B are Lm6.50 per person for a single room, Lm5.50 per person for a double. There's an extra Lm2 per person per night for stays of less than three nights. The Splendid is closed in winter.

Then there's the three-star *La Salita Hotel* (☎ 520923, fax 520930), which dominates the main street in the middle of Mellieħa. All 75 rooms have en suite bath and satellite TV – those on the northern side have sea views and cost Lm1 to Lm2 extra – and there's a tennis court and rooftop pool. B&B in a twin room costs Lm16.50/10.50 per person in high/low season; single occupancy incurs a Lm5/4 supplement.

The **Pergola Club Hotel** (☎ 522582, fax 521436/7, ✆ pergola@maltanet.net) is across the bridge opposite La Salita. It has very comfortable hotel rooms and self-catering apartments, all with en suite bath, satellite TV and a balcony overlooking the swimming pool. Twin/single hotel rooms cost Lm12/15 per person in high season, dropping to Lm7.50/10 in low season. Apartments for two-four people cost Lm18/25 per apartment per day, dropping to Lm12/18.

Seabank Hotel (☎ 522233, fax 521635, ✆ seabank@digigate.net) is situated on Mellieħa Bay, right next to Malta's biggest sandy beach. It has four-star facilities, including sauna, jacuzzi, fitness room and diving school. Summer rates are Lm22 per person in a twin room including a buffet breakfast, plus Lm6 per room for a sea view.

Grand Hotel Mercure Selmun Palace (☎ 521040, fax 521159) lies 2km east of Mellieħa town centre, next to the grand, fort-like 18th-century Selmun Palace. There are 150 rooms in a modern block behind the palace, overlooking a garden courtyard, and six luxury suites in the palace itself. The hotel has outdoor and indoor pools, two tennis courts and a luxury restaurant in the palace. High/low season hotel room rates are Lm32/20 per person for half-board, sharing a twin room; the single supplement is Lm10. Living it up in the palace suites will cost Lm44/32 per person for half-board.

Places to Eat

The atmospheric **Il-Mitħna** (☎ 520404) is housed in an early 17th-century windmill, the only survivor of three that used to sit atop Mellieħa Ridge. The menu has straightforward dishes like linguini with mushrooms and cream (Lm2.60), grilled swordfish (Lm4.50) and chicken breast with green peppercorns (Lm4.80).

The **Shangri-La** (☎ 523342) on Triq Franġisk Zahra is a good Chinese restaurant that offers takeaway as well as sit-down meals. Steamed fish with black bean sauce is Lm5, mushrooms with oyster sauce are Lm1.50 and aromatic crispy duck (half) with pancakes is Lm4.60.

Giuseppe's Wine Bar (☎ 574882) on Triq Sant'Elena is run by Malta's favourite TV chef Michael Diacono. The menu varies according to what Mr Diacono picks up at market that morning, but is always imaginative and tasty. It opens for dinner only, and is closed on Sunday; booking is recommended.

Les Saisons (☎ 521641), across the street from Giuseppe's, specialises in fresh fish, rabbit and meat dishes – pan-fried fillet of pork in wine with green pepper, bacon and coriander is Lm4.95. The lunch menu includes dishes like fresh tomato soup (Lm1.50), and pasta with green pesto and olive oil (Lm1.90).

The Arches (☎ 523460 or 520533) in the main street is large and rather formal, with outdoor dining in summer. The food is both expensive and delicious – try pumpkin and walnut soup with a cappuccino of mushrooms (Lm3.20) followed by rack of lamb with a mustard, hazelnut and herb crust and potato salad with bourbon and raspberry vinaigrette (Lm6.50).

For a snack or light lunch, try the **Bridge Pizzeria & Gelateria** across the street from La Salita Hotel. It serves pizzas (around Lm2) and ice cream at outdoor tables.

Downhill from Mellieħa, at the roundabout where the bypass re-joins the coast, is **Trattoria de Buono** (☎ 521332), which is part of the Tunny Net Complex. It has excellent fresh lunches at reasonable prices, like a spread of *bresaola* (Italian sausage), salami and parma ham with olives, salad and bread (Lm1.65), or pasta with olive oil, garlic, artichokes, mixed peppers and black kidney beans (Lm1.80). Dinner dishes range from conchiglie with four cheeses (Lm2.25) to pan-fried king prawns with garlic and cognac (Lm7).

NORTH-WEST MALTA

Getting There & Away
Bus Nos 43, 44 and 45 from Valletta pass through Mellieħa. No 43 terminates here, No 44 continues to Mellieħa Bay, and No 45 goes on to Ċirkewwa. From Buġibba, catch bus No 48 or 645.

Around Mellieħa
The crest of Mellieħa Ridge offers some good walking to the east and west of the town. To the east, the fortress-like **Selmun Palace** dominates the skyline above St Paul's Bay. It was built in the 18th century for a charitable order called the Monte di Redenzione degli Schiavi (Mountain of the Redemption of the Slaves), whose business was to ransom Christians who had been taken into slavery on the Barbary Coast. The palace, which now houses a hotel and restaurant, mimics the style of the Verdala Palace (see Around Mdina & Rabat in the Central Malta chapter).

The rough road that winds around to the right of Selmun Palace leads in just over 1km to derelict **Fort Campbell**, an abandoned coastal defence built by the British between WWI and WWII. The headland commands a fine view over St Paul's Islands, and you can hike down to the coastal salt pans of Blata il-Bajda (White Rocks) and around to Mistra Bay, or westwards along the clifftop to the ruined tower of Għajn Ħadid above the little beach at Mġieba Bay.

A left turn at the foot of the hill leading down to Mellieħa Bay puts you on the road to **Anchor Bay**, about 1.5km away on the west coast. This steep-sided, pretty little bay was named after the many Roman anchors that were found on the sea-bed by divers, some of which can be seen in the National Maritime Museum (see Vittoriosa in the Valletta & Floriana chapter).

However, in 1979 it was transformed – less than convincingly, it must be said – into the fishing village of Sweethaven and was used as the set for the Hollywood musical *Popeye*, starring Robin Williams. The film was a turkey – as was the idea of retaining the set as a tourist attraction. The place is about as interesting as, well, an

abandoned film set, and the marketing is aimed squarely at kids.

Popeye Village, as it is also called, is open 9 am to 5 pm daily (7 pm from April to September), and the cost of admission is Lm2.75/2.25/1.75 for adults/students/children. You can get a good view of the village from the southern side of the bay without paying a penny.

Bus No 441 runs hourly from Mellieħa Bay to Anchor Bay between 10 am and 4 pm.

MARFA PENINSULA
The Marfa peninsula is Malta's final flourish before dipping beneath the waters of the Comino Channel. It's a barren ridge of limestone, steep on the south side and dipping more gently north and east from the high point of Ras il-Qammieħ (129m). A minor road leads west from the top of the hill up from Mellieħa Bay, passing the **Red Tower**, built in 1649 for Grand Master Lascaris as part of the chain of signal towers that linked Valletta and Gozo. It now houses a coastguard station and sports a rather incongruous radar scanner. The road continues to the wild headland of **Ras il-Qammieħ**, which commands great views north to Gozo and south along the western sea-cliffs of Malta.

Opposite the Red Tower road, another potholed track leads east along the spine of the peninsula, with side roads giving access to various little coves and beaches. These places are very popular with local people, and are best avoided at weekends when the crowds can be enormous.

First up is **Ramla Bay**, with its small, sandy beach monopolised by the hotel of the same name. Immediately to its east is **Ramla Tal'Qortin**, which has no sand and is surrounded by an unsightly sprawl of Maltese holiday huts amid a forest of TV aerials and telephone cables.

The next two roads lead down to **Armier Bay** and **Little Armier Bay** and meet in the middle. The scrap of sand at Little Armier is probably the most pleasant beach around here, but it's still a bit scruffy looking. The last road goes to **White Tower Bay**, which has another seaweed-stained patch of sand

and a rash of peppermint-green holiday huts. A track continues past the tower to the low cliffs of Aħrax Point, from which a pleasant coastal walk leads 1km south to a statue of the Madonna on Daħlet ix-Xilep.

To the east of the road, near the turn-off to White Tower Bay, is a picnic area among the trees where it is possible to scramble down to the shore of **Rdum il-Ħmar** on the north shore of Mellieħa Bay. There is a tiny scrap of beach here, and good rocks to swim and snorkel around.

The main road from Valletta ends at Ċirkewwa, which consists of little more than a desalination plant, a hotel and the Gozo ferry terminal. A left turn just before the Paradise Bay Hotel leads to **Paradise Bay**, a narrow patch of sand below cliffs with a private lido and a grand view of the ferry slip.

Places to Stay & Eat

Squeezed onto the tip of Marfa Point is the four-star *Paradise Bay Hotel* (☎ *573981, fax 573115,* ❷ *info@paradise-bay.com).* All rooms have private bathroom, balcony, satellite TV and a trouser press – the latter is no doubt connected to the 'no shorts' dress code at dinner. There are also three outdoor pools and one indoors, as well as two tennis courts, water-sports facilities and a diving school. B&B rates for a twin room range from Lm8 per person in low season to around Lm17 in high, with a Lm3.50 single supplement and an extra Lm1 for a 'bay view' room.

Ramla Bay Resort (☎ *522181, fax 575931,* ❷ *ramlabay@digigate.net)* is also four-star, with 118 hotel rooms and 45 self-catering apartments, a private beach and floodlit tennis court. High season rates range from Lm16 to Lm22 per person.

The Marfa peninsula is a bit of a culinary wasteland, with few eating places outside the two hotels. There's *Ray's Pizzeria* at Little Armier Bay, and the *Paradise Bay Lido* at the beach opposite the Gozo ferry terminal. The *cafe* at the ferry terminal serves sandwiches, pies and soggy, microwaved pizzas for 50c. The food on the ferry is even worse.

Getting There & Away

Bus No 45 runs regularly between Valletta and Ċirkewwa, and takes about an hour. By car, you can make the trip in about 40 to 45 minutes. Bus Nos 48 and 645 run from Ċirkewwa to Buġibba and Sliema respectively. Bus No 50 runs from Valletta to Armier Bay in summer only. A taxi from Malta International Airport to Ċirkewwa should cost no more than Lm13.

For details of the ferry services to Gozo and Comino, see the Getting Around chapter earlier in this book.

NORTH-WEST MALTA

Central Malta

MDINA & RABAT

Mdina, once the ancient walled capital of Malta, perches loftily on a crag about 10km west of Valletta. Rabat, its suburban counterpart, sprawls untidily to its south.

History

The citadel of Mdina was fortified from the earliest times. As long ago as 1000 BC the Phoenicians had built a protective wall here, and called their settlement Malet, meaning 'place of shelter'. The Romans built a large town here and called it Melita. It was given its present name when the Arabs arrived in the 9th century – *madina* is Arabic for 'walled city'. They built strong walls and dug a deep moat between Mdina and its suburbs (known as *rabat* in Arabic).

In medieval times Mdina was known as Città Notabile – the Noble City. It was the favoured residence of the Maltese aristocracy, and the seat of the *università* or governing council. The Knights, who were largely a sea-based force, made Valletta and the Grand Harbour their centre of activity, and Mdina sank into the background as a retreat of the Maltese nobility. Today, with its massive walls and peaceful, shady streets, it is often called the Silent City.

Unfortunately, the Silent City appears to be succumbing to a rising tide of tawdry tourist traps, all hitching a ride on the back of the successful Mdina Experience audiovisual show. You can soak up enough history from the streets and stones without paying to see endless gory tableaux of dying knights and tortured prisoners, complete with 'authentic smells'.

Orientation & Information

Mdina is the walled city; Rabat is the name given to the town outside the walls. Mdina's main street, Triq Villegaignon, runs from the Main Gate to Pjazza tas-Sur (Bastion Square), passing St Paul's Cathedral on the right. A second gate, called the Greek's

HIGHLIGHTS

• Wandering the back streets of Mdina
• Staring in awe at Mosta Dome
• Strolling along the top of the Dingli cliffs
• Joining in with the L-Imnarja festivities at Buskett Gardens

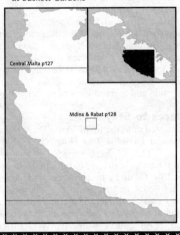

Central Malta p127

Mdina & Rabat p128

Gate, lies at the western corner of Mdina, opposite the Museum of Roman Antiquities. In Rabat, Triq San Pawl begins opposite the Greek's Gate and runs south to St Paul's Church and the town square.

The bus terminus is on Is-Saqqajja, 150m south of Mdina's Main Gate. Visitors' cars are not allowed into Mdina, but there is ample parking outside the Main Gate and on Triq il-Mużew. There are petrol pumps between the Main Gate and the Point de Vue Guesthouse and Restaurant.

You'll find an HSBC bank and ATM at the corner of Is-Saqqajja, across from the Point de Vue. You can also change money at the Maltese Falcon souvenir shop in Triq Villegaignon near the cathedral. The post office is in Rabat opposite the Main Gate,

CENTRAL MALTA

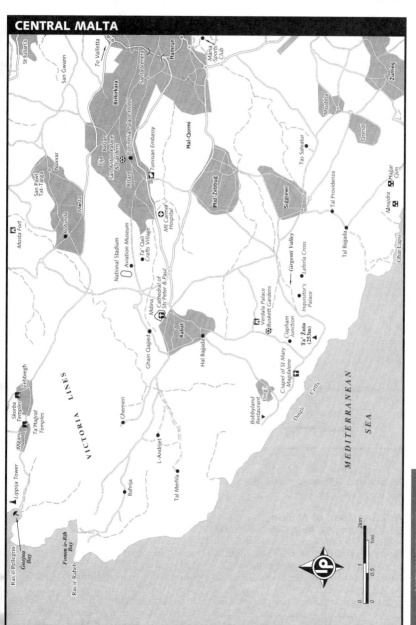

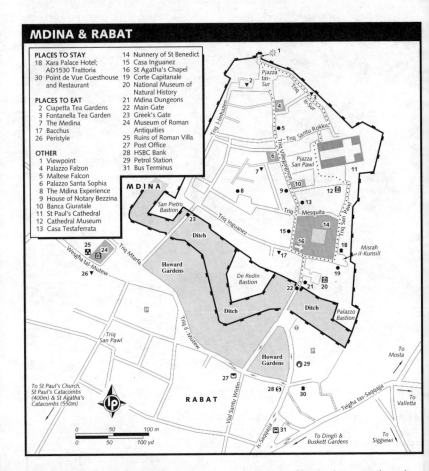

MDINA & RABAT

PLACES TO STAY
18 Xara Palace Hotel;
     AD1530 Trattoria
30 Point de Vue Guesthouse
     and Restaurant

PLACES TO EAT
2 Ciapetta Tea Gardens
3 Fontanella Tea Garden
7 The Medina
17 Bacchus
26 Peristyle

OTHER
1 Viewpoint
4 Palazzo Falzon
5 Maltese Falcon
6 Palazzo Santa Sophia
8 The Mdina Experience
9 House of Notary Bezzina
10 Banca Giuratale
11 St Paul's Cathedral
12 Cathedral Museum
13 Casa Testaferrata

14 Nunnery of St Benedict
15 Casa Inguanez
16 St Agatha's Chapel
19 Corte Capitanale
20 National Museum of
     Natural History
21 Mdina Dungeons
22 Main Gate
23 Greek's Gate
24 Museum of Roman
     Antiquities
25 Ruins of Roman Villa
27 Post Office
28 HSBC Bank
29 Petrol Station
31 Bus Terminus

on the corner of Triq il-Mużew and Vjal Santu Wistin. There are public toilets outside the Main Gate.

Walking Tour of Mdina

Enter Mdina by the **Main Gate**, which was built in 1724 and bears the arms of Grand Master Manoel de Vilhena. The outline of the original gate can be seen in the wall to the right of the bridge. Immediately inside the gate on the right are the **Mdina Dungeons**, which house a series of gruesome tableaux depicting torture and dismemberment, accompanied by a rather wearing

sound-track of screaming, groaning, chopping and choking noises. It's a last resort for a very wet day.

An imposing gateway on the right leads into the courtyard of **Palazzo de Vilhena**, built as a summer residence for the Grand Master in the early 18th century. The palace served as a hospital from 1860 until 1956, and since the 1970s has housed the National Museum of Natural History (see separate entry later in this section).

Go left and then right onto Triq Villegaignon. On the right-hand corner of the street is **St Agatha's Chapel**, which dates

A slice of fishing life, Marsaxlokk

The natural arch of the famed Blue Grotto

How the enormous megaliths of Ħaġar Qim were originally put in place remains a mystery.

Door knocker, Neptune with seahorses, Mdina

Doorway, Mdina

Modern-day Mdina, once the capital of Malta, is now known as the 'Silent City'.

The Mdina Uprising

After the French invasion of Malta in June 1798, Napoleon stayed on the island for only six days before continuing his journey to Egypt, where his fleet was defeated by the British Navy at Aboukir. He left behind a garrison of only 4000 troops under the command of General Vaubois.

With revolutionary fervour, the French tried to impose their ideas on Maltese society. They abolished the nobility, defaced their escutcheons, persecuted the clergy and looted the churches. But on 2 September 1798, when they attempted to auction off the treasures of Mdina's Carmelite Church – on a Sunday – the Maltese decided that enough was enough. In a spontaneous uprising, they massacred the French garrison at Mdina, throwing its commander, a Capitaine Masson, off a balcony to his death.

The French retreated to the safety of Valletta, where the Maltese, under the command of Canon Caruana of St Paul's Cathedral, besieged them. Having learnt of Napoleon's misfortune in Egypt, the Maltese asked for help from the British, who imposed a naval blockade on Malta under the command of Captain Alexander Ball. The Maltese forces suffered two hard years of skirmishing and stand-off until the French finally capitulated on 5 September 1800.

from the early 15th century. The entire block on the right here is occupied by the **Nunnery of St Benedict**, whose members live in strict seclusion. No man is permitted to enter the convent, and the sisters are not allowed to leave. Even after death they remain, buried in a cemetery within the walls of the nunnery.

On the left is the **Casa Inguanez**, the ancient seat of Malta's oldest aristocratic family, who have lived here since the 14th century. A detour to the left down Triq Mesquita leads to the **Mdina Experience**, a 25-minute audiovisual presentation that does for Mdina's history what the Malta Experience in Valletta does for Malta's. Farther along Triq Villegaignon on the right, the **Casa Testaferrata** is residence of the Marquis of St Vincent Ferreri, another member of the Maltese nobility. Across the street on the left is the **House of Notary Bezzina**. It was from Bezzina's balcony the French commander Masson was lobbed to his death in 1798 (see boxed text 'The Mdina Uprising').

Next up on the right is the beautiful baroque facade of the **Banca Giuratale**, built in 1730, which once housed Mdina's city council. Beyond that, Pjazza San Pawl opens out on the right, dominated by the elegant baroque facade of St Paul's Cathedral (see separate entry later in this section).

Facing it is the **Palazzo Santa Sophia**, which bears a stone tablet with the date 1233. Though probably inaccurate, the building is still the oldest in Mdina.

Keep on along Triq Villegaignon past the Carmelite Church and monastery to the **Palazzo Falzon**, also called (inaccurately) the Norman House. The building dates from 1495, and was used for a time by Grand Master De L'Isle Adam when the Knights first arrived in Malta in 1530. Look up to see the beautiful medieval windows. The ground floor houses a private museum with displays of 16th- and 17th-century weapons, furniture and cooking utensils.

Triq Villegaignon ends at Pjazza tas-Sur (Bastion Square). The **views** from the city walls take in all of northern and central Malta, including St Paul's Bay, Mosta Dome and the Valletta bastions. On an exceptionally clear day, you might even see the peak of Mt Etna in Sicily, 225km away to the north-north-east (scan the horizon just to the left of Mosta Dome).

Follow the walls to the right along Triq is-Sur, pausing for a cuppa at the Fontanella Tea Garden (see Places to Stay & Eat later in this section) if you wish, and bear right at Triq Santu Rokku into Pjazza San Pawl. The entrance to the cathedral is on the far side. The **Cathedral Museum**, housed in the former seminary, contains

A statue of madonna and child stands outside Mdina's Carmelite Church.

important collections of coins, silver plate, vestments, manuscripts and religious paintings, as well as a series of woodcuts by the German artist Albrecht Durer.

Go to the left of the Cathedral Museum along Triq San Pawl, which leads to the pretty little square of Misrah il-Kunsill. Facing the Xara Palace Hotel is the **Corte Capitanale**, the former Court of Justice – note the figures on the balcony representing Justice and Mercy. Turn right to return to the Main Gate, or continue to the end of Triq Inguanez and exit through the Greek's Gate to visit the Museum of Roman Antiquities (see separate entry later in this section).

St Paul's Cathedral

The Cathedral of St Paul is said to be built on the site of the villa belonging to Publius, the Roman governor of Malta who welcomed St Paul in AD 60. The original Norman church was destroyed by an earthquake, and the restrained baroque edifice you see today was built in 1697-1702 by Lorenzo Gafa. Note the fire and serpent motifs atop the twin belltowers, symbolising the saint's first miracle on Malta (see the boxed text 'St Paul in Malta' in the North-West Malta chapter).

Echoing St John's Co-Cathedral in Valletta, the floor of St Paul's is covered in the polychrome marble tombstones of Maltese nobles and important clergymen, while the vault is painted with scenes from the life of St Paul. The altar painting of *The Conversion of St Paul* by Mattia Preti survived the earthquake, as did the apse above it with the fresco of *St Paul's Shipwreck* and the beautifully carved oak doors to the sacristy on the north side.

The cathedral is open to the public from 9 am to 1 pm and 1.30 to 4.30 pm Monday to Saturday. Admission is free, but leave a donation. The Cathedral Museum is open 9 am to 4 pm Monday to Saturday (Lm1).

National Museum of Natural History

The National Museum of Natural History (☎ 455951), though housed in the elegant Palazzo de Vilhena, looks a little tired these days – a rather touching notice apologises for the run-down look, and hopes that renovation will not be long in coming.

The most interesting part is the geology exhibit, which explains the origins of Malta's landscape and displays the wide range of fossils that can be found in its rocks. The teeth belonging to the ancient shark *Carcherodon megalodon aggasiz* are food for thought – measuring 18cm on the edge, they belonged to a 25m monster that prowled the Miocene seas 30 million years ago. Also on display (in the Sea-Shells Room) is the pickled body of a 16kg squid found at Xemxija in St Paul's Bay. The dusty and moth-eaten collection of stuffed animals and birds can be safely ignored.

The museum is open 7.45 am to 2 pm daily from 16 June to 30 September, and 8.15 am to 5 pm Monday to Saturday and 8.15 am to 4 pm Sunday from 1 October to 15 June (closed on public holidays). Admission costs Lm1, but under-19s and over-65s get in free.

Museum of Roman Antiquities

Mdina's Museum of Roman Antiquities (☎ 454125) was built in the 1920s over the excavated remains of a large Roman townhouse dating from the 1st century BC. The centrepiece is the original peristyle court (a once-open courtyard surrounded by columns). The mosaic floor has a geometric border around the image of two birds perched on a water bowl; a cistern in one corner was used for collecting rainwater.

Mosaic fragments mounted on the walls show nymphs punishing a satyr, grinning clowns and the famous (though surprisingly small) wide-mouthed woman surrounded by fruits and vegetables. However, there is too little labelling or explanation to make much sense of the collection of sculptures, amphorae, pottery fragments and oil lamps. More remains can be seen in the excavations behind the museum.

The museum has the same opening hours and admission prices as the National Museum of Natural History.

Rabat

The town of Rabat, which sprawls to the south of Mdina, contains little of interest except for the Church of St Paul and the nearby catacombs.

From the Museum of Roman Antiquities, walk south along Triq San Pawl for 400m to **St Paul's Church**, built in 1675. Beside the church, stairs lead down into the **Grotto of St Paul**, a cave where the saint is said to

The popular wailing woman mosaic is on display in the Museum of Roman Antiquities.

MARTIN HARRIS

The Tragedy of St Agatha

St Agatha was a 3rd-century Christian martyr from Sicily – Catania and Palermo both claim to be her birthplace – who fled to Malta to escape the amorous advances of a Sicilian governor. On returning to Sicily she was imprisoned and tortured, and her breasts were cut off with shears – a horrific punishment gruesomely depicted in many paintings and statues in Malta. She was then burnt at the stake. There is a chapel dedicated to St Agatha in Mdina.

have preached during his stay in Malta. The statue of St Paul was gifted by the Knights in 1748, while the silver ship to its left was added in 1960 to commemorate the 1900th anniversary of the saint's shipwreck.

From the church, numerous signposts point the way across the parish square and along Triq Sant'Agata towards two groups of early Christian underground tombs. First, on the left, are **St Paul's Catacombs**, which date from the 3rd century AD. The labyrinth of rock-cut tombs, narrow stairs and passages is poorly lit, so a torch comes in handy. There's not a lot to see, but it's fun to explore. You can buy a map and explanatory leaflet at the ticket desk. St Paul's Catacombs are open 7.45 am to 2 pm daily in summer (closed public holidays), and 8.15 am to 5 pm (4 pm on Sunday) in winter (Lm1).

Another 150m down the street on the right are **St Agatha's Catacombs**. These are more interesting than St Paul's as they contain a series of remarkable frescoes dating from the 12th to the 15th century. Back at ground level is an unusual little museum containing everything from fossils and minerals to coins, church vestments and Etruscan, Roman and Egyptian artefacts.

St Agatha's Catacombs are open 9 am to 5 pm Monday to Friday and 9 am to 1 pm on Saturday (closed Sunday and public holidays), and 1 to 2 pm daily from October to June. Admission costs 50c.

CENTRAL MALTA

Places to Stay & Eat

There is very little accommodation in Mdina and Rabat, but there are a few good places to eat. *Point de Vue Guesthouse and Restaurant* (☎ 454117) on Is-Saqqajja combines both in a convenient central location. The rooms are basic but good value at Lm5.50 per person for B&B, and the restaurant offers Maltese specialities like fish, rabbit and lamb, and pizzas for around Lm2.

Xara Palace (☎ 450560, fax 452612, ✉ info@xarapalace.com.mt) in Mdina's Misraħ il-Kunsill is one of Malta's most elegant and expensive hotels. Housed in a 17th-century mansion, it served as an RAF officers' mess during WWII. It was renovated and re-opened as a hotel in May 1999. There are 17 luxury suites, each complete with 21-inch TV, stereo music centre and modem connection. There's also a gym and sauna. A standard suite (sleeps two) costs Lm85.50 a night year-round, and breakfast is Lm5.50 extra.

The *AD1530 Trattoria* (☎ 450560), next door to the Xara Palace, is a pleasant place with wooden tables, yellow-washed walls and a roaring log fire in winter. At Lm3.50 the set lunch menu is reasonable value, offering the likes of bruschetta, a pizza or pasta dish, and cake or coffee.

The Medina (☎ 454004) in Triq is-Salib Imqaddes occupies an attractive garden-courtyard behind a medieval townhouse. The menu offers a mix of Maltese, Italian and French dishes – expect to pay around Lm20 for dinner for two including wine.

Bacchus (☎ 454981) in Triq Inguanez is built into a vault beneath the De Redin Bastion that used to serve as a powder magazine. Blocks of original Roman masonry can be seen in one of the walls. The menu has a French influence, with main courses in the Lm4 to Lm6 range. It's open noon till 3 pm and 6 to 11 pm, and reservations are recommended.

Fontanella Tea Garden (☎ 454264) enjoys a wonderful setting on top of the city walls. It serves delicious home-baked cakes, good sandwiches and passable coffee, but you'll need a degree in mechanical engineering to operate the sliding doors in the toilets. It's open 10 am to 6 pm daily in winter, and 11 pm in summer.

The *Ciapetti Tea Gardens* (☎ 459987) in il-Wesgħa Sant'Agata has an outdoor terrace with good views to the north. It offers sandwiches, salads and cakes as well as tea and coffee.

The *Peristyle Restaurant* (☎ 4517717), opposite the Museum of Roman Antiquities, is a bit of a tour bus venue, but the pizzas and burgers are quite palatable and not too expensive.

Shopping

Within the Empire Arts & Crafts Centre (☎ 453245) in Triq Sant'Agata (near St Paul's Catacombs) there's a wide range of local arts and crafts for sale. You can watch local glass-blowers, lace-makers and jewellers at work, and sample local wines and cheeses. It's open 9 am to 5 pm daily.

Getting There & Away

From Valletta, take bus No 80 or 81; from Sliema and St Julian's No 65; and from Buġibba and St Paul's Bay No 86. By car, the road from Valletta is well signposted. From St Paul's Bay, begin by following signs to Mosta.

AROUND MDINA & RABAT
Ta'Qali Crafts Village

The arts and crafts workshops at Ta'Qali are housed in the old Nissen huts on this WWII RAF airfield, which is badly in need of a makeover – the place looks like a building site. Although it's rather scruffy, the workshops are worth a look. You can watch glass-blowers at work, and shop for gold, silver and filigree jewellery, paintings by local artists, leather goods, Maltese lace, furniture, ceramics and ornamental glass.

Ta'Qali is open 8 am to 4 pm Monday to Friday, and entry is free. Try to get there before 10 am if you want to avoid the coach-tour crowds.

Malta Aviation Museum

The Malta Aviation Museum (☎ 416095) is tucked away in an unassuming shed between Ta'Qali Crafts Village and the National

Stadium, 2km north-east of Mdina. It's a real enthusiast's museum, with bits of engines, airframes and instruments lying around, and numerous restoration projects under way – including a WWII Hawker Hurricane IIa. You can watch locals working on the aircraft and other exhibits. Star of the show is a WWII Spitfire Mk IX; other aircraft on display include a vintage Flying Flea, a De-Havilland Vampire T11, a Fiat G91R, an immaculate Sea Vixen and a battered old Douglas Dakota DC-3.

The museum is open from 10 am to 5 pm daily, except Good Friday, Easter Sunday, 24 and 25 December and 1 January. Admission costs Lm1 for adults, 75c for children.

Fomm ir-Riħ

Fomm ir-Riħ (meaning 'mouth of the wind') is the most remote and undeveloped bay on Malta. During rough weather it can be a drab and miserable place, the grey clay slopes and limestone crags merging with the grey clouds and the wave-muddied waters. But on a calm summer's day it can be a beautiful spot, with good swimming in the clear blue waters off the southern cliffs, and few other people to disturb the peace.

It's a long hike to get there. From central Rabat, follow Triq Għeriexem (passing to the left of the Museum of Roman Antiquities) to the roundabout on the edge of town (this can also be reached via the bypass from the roundabout on the Rabat-Mosta road). Follow signs for Baħrija – if you see any (they're a bit hard to spot). After the roundabout, head left at the first fork, and right at the next (Fiddien Bridge). You then pass Fiddien Reservoir on the right, and after 1km bear left at an unsignposted fork, then left towards St Martin's and Baħrija. After passing through the centre of Baħrija village, fork right, then right again. As the road drops into a valley, turn right on a rough track with low gateposts (but no gate) – this ends 600m downhill above the southern cliffs of Fomm ir-Riħ. It's easiest by car – on foot it's an 8km hike (about one hour and 45 minutes) from the bus terminus in Rabat.

But you're not there yet. To reach the head of the bay, you need to follow a pre-carious footpath across a stream-bed and along a ledge in the cliffs. Locals say that the former Maltese prime minister, Dom Mintoff, used to ride his horse along this path – today posts have been cemented in place to prevent horses and bicycles using it.

From here, you can hike north to the wild cape of Ras il-Pellegrin and down to Ġnejna Bay (see Mġarr in the North-West Malta chapter), or west to Ras ir-Raħeb and south along the top of the coastal cliffs to the tiny village of Mtaħleb and back into Rabat.

Ta'Gagin (☎ *450825*) on the village square in Baħrija is a good place to sample authentic Maltese rabbit and chips, at Lm4 for a portion, and Lm11 for a whole rabbit. It comes with something called 'rabbit sauce', a rich gravy flavoured with juniper berries. They also have delicious steaks (Lm4) and horse-meat (Lm4). The three-course set menu is Lm5.25.

The Festival of L-Imnarja

L-Imnarja (sometimes spelt Mnarja), held on 28 and 29 June (the feast day of Sts Peter and Paul), is Malta's biggest and most boisterous festival. Its origins lie in a harvest festival dedicated to St Paul – the name is a corruption of the Italian *luminaria*, meaning 'illuminations', after the traditional bonfires that once lit up Rabat during the festival.

The festivities begin on 28 June with a huge party in Buskett Gardens, complete with folk music, singing and dancing. Vast quantities of rabbit stew are consumed, washed down with plenty of local wine. The carousing continues well into the small hours, and many people end up spending the entire night at Buskett.

The following day continues with an agricultural show at Buskett, where farmers and gardeners exhibit their produce, accompanied by local band performances. In the afternoon, bareback horse and donkey races are held at Saqqajja Hill in Rabat, attended by crowds from all over the island. The winners are awarded with *palji* – colourful banners – which are taken home to adorn the victor's village.

CENTRAL MALTA

North Country (☎ 456688) next door offers similar fare, while the *New Life Bar* across the road is the place for a cold beer or a glass of local wine.

Dingli Cliffs

Named after the famous Maltese architect Tommaso Dingli (1591-1666) – or possibly his 16th-century English namesake Sir Thomas Dingley, who lived nearby – Dingli is an unremarkable little village. But only 500m to the south-west the land falls away at the spectacular 220m-high Dingli Cliffs. A potholed tarmac road runs along the top of the cliffs. There are also some great walks south past the lonely little **Chapel of St Mary Magdalene**, built in the 17th century, to Ta'Żuta (253m) the highest point in the Maltese Islands. Here, you'll enjoy excellent views along the coast to the tiny island of Filfla.

Heading north along the cliffs, you will find the *Bobbyland Restaurant* (☎ 452895), 500m from the Dingli junction. This is a hugely popular weekend venue for local people, and the indoor and outdoor tables are regularly crowded with diners munching contentedly on fried rabbit (Lm3.50).

Bus No 81 runs every half hour or so from Valletta to Dingli via Rabat.

Verdala Palace

Verdala Palace was built in 1586 as a summer residence for Grand Master Hugues Loubeux de Verdalle. It was designed by Gerolamo Cassar in the form of a square castle with projecting towers at each corner, but this was only for show – it was intended to be a hunting retreat, not a defendable, fortified position.

The British used Verdala as the Governor of Malta's summer residence, and today it

---

The Riddle of the Ruts

One of the biggest mysteries of Malta's prehistoric period is the abundance of so-called 'cart ruts' throughout the islands. In places where bare limestone is exposed, it is often scored with a series of deep parallel grooves, looking for all the world like ruts worn by cart-wheels. But the spacing of the ruts varies, and their depth – up to 60cm – means that wheeled carts would probably get jammed if they tried to use them.

A more likely explanation is that the grooves were created by a *travois* – a sort of sled formed from two parallel poles joined by a frame and dragged behind a beast of burden, similar to that used by the Plains Indians of North America. The occurrence of the ruts correlates quite closely to the distribution of Bronze Age villages in Malta.

This still leaves the question of what was being transported. Suggestions have included salt and building stone, but it has been argued that whatever the cargo was, it must have been abundant, heavy, and well worth the effort involved in moving it. The best suggestion to date is that the mystery substance was topsoil – it was carted from low-lying areas to hillside terraces to increase the area of cultivable land, and so provide food for a growing population.

In some places the ruts are seen to disappear into the sea on one side of a bay, only to re-emerge on the far side. In other spots they seem to disappear off the edge of a cliff. These instances have given rise to all sorts of weird theories, but they are most convincingly explained as the results of long-term erosion and sea-level changes due to earthquakes – the central Mediterranean is a seismically active area, and Malta is riddled with geological faults.

Good places to see the ruts include Clapham Junction near Buskett Gardens and the top of the Ta'Ċenċ cliffs in Gozo (see p155).

occasionally houses visiting dignitaries. The **Great Hall's** frescoes depict the illustrious career of Grand Master de Verdalle and scenes from Greek mythology. A sweeping oval staircase – with steps broad and shallow enough to be climbed by a knight wearing unwieldy armour – leads to the first floor apartments, where you can see chessboards carved into the floor by bored French officers kept imprisoned here during the naval blockade of 1789-1800. The panoramic **view** from the roof takes in most of Malta.

The palace is 2.5km south of Mdina. It's open 9 am till noon and 2 to 5 pm on Tuesday and Friday only, but is occasionally closed (especially in August and September) if hosting foreign dignitaries. Check with the Tourist Information Office in Valletta if in doubt. Admission costs Lm1.

Buskett Gardens

The valley to the south of Verdala Palace harbours the only extensive area of woodland in Malta. Known as Buskett Gardens (from the Italian *boschetto*, meaning 'little wood'), its groves of Aleppo pine, oak, olive and orange trees provide shady picnic sites in summer and orange-scented walks in winter. Buskett Gardens is the main venue for the L-Imnarja festival, held on 28 and 29 June (see boxed text).

The gardens are open at all times, and are free. Bus No 81 from Valletta to Dingli via Rabat stops at the entrance. Buskett is well signposted from Rabat.

Clapham Junction

Just south of Buskett Gardens is a parking area. At its far end the road forks – head left, uphill, for 300m to where a rough track on the right is signposted 'Cart Tracks'. To the right (west) of this track is a large area of sloping limestone pavement, scored with several sets of intersecting prehistoric 'cart ruts' (see the boxed text 'The Riddle of the Ruts'). The ruts are about 1.5m apart and up to 50cm deep. The name Clapham Junction – a notoriously complicated railway junction in London – was given to the site by British visitors.

MOSTA

Mosta is a busy and prosperous town of around 13,000 people, spread across a level plateau atop the Victoria Lines escarpment. Mosta is famous for its Parish Church of St Mary, generally better known as the **Mosta Dome** or Rotunda, which was designed by the Maltese architect Giorgio Grognet de Vassé and built between 1833 and 1860 using funds raised by the local people. Its circular design with a six-columned portico was closely based on the Pantheon in Rome, and the great dome – a prominent landmark visible from most parts of Malta – is said to be one of the broadest unsupported domes in Europe. Its diameter of 39.6m is exceeded only by the Pantheon (43m) and St Peter's (42.1m) in Rome. But dome comparison is a tricky business open to dispute. The parishioners of Xewkija on Gozo claim that their church has a bigger dome than Mosta's – though the Gozitan Rotunda has a smaller diameter (25m), it is higher and has a larger volumetric capacity. So there.

Apart from the church, there's not much else to see in Mosta, but it does make a good starting point for exploring the Victoria Lines (see boxed text in the North-West Malta chapter). To reach Mosta Fort from the Rotunda, head north-west on Triq il Kostituzzjoni (to the left of the church, facing the portico), cross the bridge over Wied il-Għasel, and turn right along Triq il-Forti. Go straight on at the roundabout – the distance from the church to the fort is 2.5km.

The Miracle of Mosta

On 9 June 1942, during WWII, three enemy bombs struck the Mosta Dome while around 300 parishioners waited to hear Mass. Two bounced off and landed in the square without exploding. The third pierced the dome, smashed off a wall and rolled across the floor of the church. Miraculously, no one was hurt, and the bomb failed to detonate. A replica of the bomb can be seen in the church vestry.

CENTRAL MALTA

Ta'Marija (☎ *434444*), on Triq il-Kostituzzjoni across from the Mosta Dome, is aimed squarely at the tourist market. The menu consists of Maltese specialities including rabbit, game, steak and seafood, with main courses ranging in price from Lm3 to Lm6. The decor is a bit over the top, with deer antlers all over the walls, and the wooden bar has been built to look like a ship.

Pjazza Cafe (☎ *413379*), on the main square opposite the Mosta Dome, is more down to earth. You can fill up on pizza, pasta and burgers for about Lm2, while enjoying the view of the Dome across the square. If you feel the urge to check your email, the Pjazza doubles as an Internet cafe.

To get to Mosta by public transport, take bus No 53 or 57 from Valletta, No 65 from Sliema and St Julian's, and No 86 from Buġibba and St Paul's.

THE THREE VILLAGES

The main road from Valletta to Mosta passes through the town of Birkirkara, one of the biggest population centres on the island, and part of the huge conurbation that encircles Valletta and the Three Cities. Just west of Birkirkara is an upmarket suburban area known as the Three Villages, centred on the medieval settlements of Attard, Balzan and Lija. Although modern development has fused the three into a continuous urban sprawl, the old village centres still

MARTIN HARRIS

The imposing Mosta Dome is so enormous it can be seen from almost every corner of Malta.

CENTRAL MALTA

retain their parish churches and narrow streets, and there are some interesting historical sites to visit and explore.

Triq il-Mdina, the main road which skirts the southern edge of Attard, follows the line of the **Wignacourt Aqueduct**, built in 1610-14 to improve the water supply to Valletta. Substantial lengths of the ancient structure still stand beside the road. The **Parish Church of St Mary** in Attard, designed by Tommaso Dingli and built around the same time as the aqueduct, is one of the finest Renaissance churches on the island. Lija's **Parish Church of St Saviour**, designed in 1694, is the focus of one of Malta's liveliest festas, famed for its spectacular fireworks (6 August).

The main attraction in this area is **San Anton Palace and Gardens**, which lies between Attard and Lija. The palace was built in the early 17th century as the country mansion of Grand Master Antoine de Paule. It later served as the official residence of the British Governor of Malta, and is now the official residence of the Maltese president. The walled gardens stretch between the palace and the main entrance on Triq Birkirkara, and contain groves of citrus and avocado, as well as a magnificent old fig tree. The Eagle Fountain, just inside the main gate, dates from the 1620s. The Mask Fountain is surrounded by unusual floss-silk trees with thick, thorn-studded trunks and beautiful pink flowers.

The palace is closed to the public, but the gardens are open daily from dawn till dusk. The north entrance to the gardens, through the palace courtyard, is only open at certain times: 7 to 8.45 am, 10 am to 1 pm, and 4 to 4.30 pm. Admission is free.

To get to San Anton Gardens, take bus No 40 from Valletta.

Places to Stay & Eat

The *University Residence* (☎ 436168 or 430360, fax 434963, @ peter@dream.vol.net.mt), about 200m north of San Anton Gardens in Triq R M Bonnici, Lija, is the official student residence for the University of Malta, and is a good place to meet a mixture of travellers and local and international stu-

dents. A dorm bed costs Lm2.85 a night. To get there, catch bus No 40 from Valletta, and ask the driver to tell you where to get off.

On the other side of San Anton Gardens, and at the other end of the accommodation spectrum, the five-star *Corinthia Palace Hotel* (☎ 440301, fax 465713, @ palace@corinthia.com) is sufficiently luxurious and elegant to entertain the entourages of foreign dignitaries visiting the president of Malta. Rates begin at Lm40/50 per room for a single/double, and breakfast is another Lm5.50.

At *Il-Melita* (☎ 441077), beside the main entrance to San Anton Gardens on Triq Birkirkara, you can lounge around in comfy cane chairs and enjoy a cold drink, or order a lunch of pasta or pizza.

GĦAR LAPSI

A badly cratered road leads from Saqqajja Hill in Rabat to the outskirts of Siġġiewi, where a right turn puts you on the road to Għar Lapsi. The name means 'Cave of the Ascension', and there was once a fisherman's shrine here. The road winds steeply to the coast past an ugly desalination plant, and ends at a rough car park beside a peeling, turquoise-painted, concrete restaurant.

Fortunately, the main attraction here is not the architecture but the swimming – a little cove in the low limestone cliffs has been converted into a natural lido, with stone steps and iron ladders giving access to the limpid blue water. It's a popular place with local people. For hikers, a signpost indicates a footpath along the clifftop towards Ħaġar Qim and the Blue Grotto (see South-East Malta).

Lapsi Seaview Restaurant (no phone) may look a little worse for wear, but discriminating Maltese custom means that the swordfish, octopus and (inevitably) rabbit are good and tasty.

Getting to Għar Lapsi without a car is tricky. Bus No 94 shuttles infrequently between Siġġiewi and Għar Lapsi on Thursday and Sunday from July to September only. The alternative is a 4km hike each way. To get to Siġġiewi take bus No 89 from Valletta.

South-East Malta

The south-east of Malta has less in the way of tourist development than the rest of the island. Marsaskala is the only place in the south-east that could be described as a holiday resort, and it tends to be more popular with the Maltese than with foreign visitors. But several of Malta's most interesting historical sites are to be found here, along with some good coastal scenery and the old fishing village of Marsaxlokk.

MARSASKALA
Marsaskala, gathered around the head of its long, narrow bay, was originally a Sicilian fishing community (the name means 'Sicilian Harbour'). Today it is an increasingly popular residential area and seaside resort, especially among the Maltese.

Orientation & Information
The Triq ix-Xatt promenade is the focus of the town and where most of the restaurants and cafes are to be found. The bus terminus is on Triq Sant'Antnin at the southern end of the promenade. On the north side of the bay, Triq iż-Żonqor goes past the Church of St Anne, with its distinctive Italianate campanile, to Żonqor Point, where the National Water Polo Stadium is located. Triq is-Salini, on the south side of the bay, leads to the headland of il-Gżira, where St Thomas' Tower and the Corinthia Jerma Palace Hotel are to be found. There's a sub-post office next door to the Sottovoce restaurant on Triq ix-Xatt.

Things to See & Do
Marsaskala is not big on sights or tourist attractions. The main activities are hanging out in cafes and bars along the waterfront, strolling along the promontory, and fishing in the harbour. **St Thomas' Tower**, on the southern point of the bay, is a small fort that was built by the Knights of St John after a Turkish raiding party landed in Marsaskala Bay in 1614 and plundered the

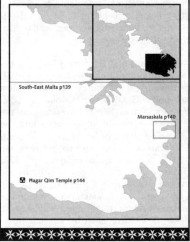

South-East Malta p139

Marsaskala p140

Ħagar Qim Temple p144

nearby village of Żejtun. At the time of writing it was being restored, and by the time you read this it may have opened as a restaurant.

St Thomas Bay is a deeply indented – and deeply unattractive – bay to the south of Marsaskala, lined with concrete and breeze-block huts and a dirty, potholed road. There's a sandy beach of sorts, and the place is popular with local people and windsurfers. It's about a 10-minute walk from Marsaskala along Triq Tal'Gardiel (past the Sun City Cinema Complex). From St Thomas Bay you can continue walking along the coast to Marsaxlokk (about 4km).

SOUTH-EAST MALTA

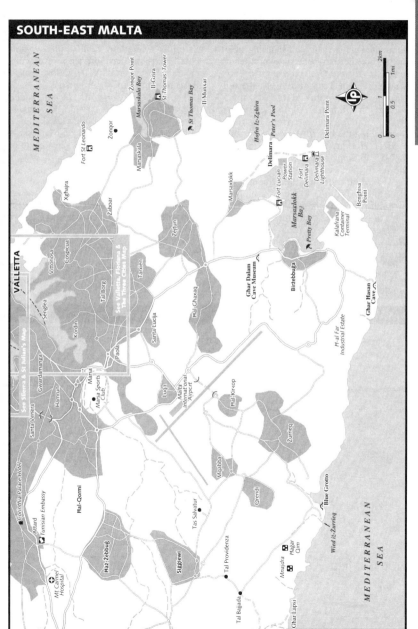

MEDITERRANEAN SEA

Zonqor Point
Marsaskala Bay
Zonqor
St Thomas' Tower
Il-Gzira
St Thomas Bay
Il-Munxar
Fort St Leonardo
Xghajra
Marsaskala
Zabbar
Zejtun
Marsaxlokk
Hofra Iz-Zghira
Peter's Pool
Delimara
Fort Lucian
Power Station
Fort Delimara
Delimara Point
Delimara Lighthouse
Marsaxlokk Bay
Pretty Bay
Kalafrana Container Terminal
Benghisa Point
VALLETTA
Cospicua
Vittoriosa
Tarxien
Tal Borg
Senglea
Kordin
Paola
Santa Lucija
Hal Chaxaq
Ghar Dalam Cave Museum
Birzebbuga
See Valletta, Floriana & The Three Cities Map
See Sliema & St Julian's Map
Marsa
Marsa Sports Club
Gwardamanga
Hamrun
Santa Venera
Luqa
Malta International Airport
Hal Far Industrial Estate
Ghar Hasan Cave
Corinthia Palace Hotel
Attard
Tunisian Embassy
Hal-Qormi
Hal Kirkop
Mqabba
Zurrieq
Mt Carmel Hospital
Haz-Zebbug
Siggiewi
Tas Salvatur
Qrendi
Blue Grotto
Wied iz-Zurrieq
Tal Providenza
Mnajdra
Hagar Qim
Tal Bajjada
Ghar Lapsi

MEDITERRANEAN SEA

2km
1mi
0.5
0

Places to Stay

The accommodation scene in Marsaskala is dominated by private self-catering apartments, but there are one or two other options. *At Alisons Guesthouse* (☎ 639814, fax 687593) in Triq Vajrita is a friendly place with 11 rooms that cost Lm5.50 per person. *Summer Nights Guesthouse* (☎ 6879560), on the waterfront, has rooms overlooking the bay for Lm6 per person.

SHIK Holiday Complex (☎ 633303, fax 637953, ✉ shik@global.net.mt) is opposite the bus terminus on the corner of Triq Sant'Anna. Self-catering apartments cost Lm9 to Lm10/Lm13 to Lm16 a night for two/four people; there's a 10% discount for stays of four weeks or more.

Etvan Hotel (☎ 633265, fax 684330, ✉ etvan@oberonlabs.com) on Triq il-Bahhara has comfortable twin rooms with en suite bathroom from Lm5 per person in low season to Lm8 per person in high season. Single supplement is Lm1 to Lm3.

Charian Hotel (☎ 616392, fax 616391, ✉ charian@mail.mol.net.mt) on Triq is-Salini is a modern family-run two-star hotel. All rooms have private shower, ceiling fan, heater and TV. High/low season B&B rates are Lm7/4 per person.

The four-star *Corinthia Jerma Palace Hotel* (☎ 633222, fax 639485, ✉ jerma@corinthia.com) is a vast complex dominating the southern headland of Marsaskala Bay. High/low season B&B rates begin at Lm25/15 per person twin-share.

Places to Eat

Despite its name, *Jakarta* (☎ 633993), on the square at the northern end of Triq ix-Xatt, offers mostly Malaysian and Chinese food at Lm2.75 to Lm4 for main courses.

Al Kafe (☎ 632528), on the promenade, is a good place to sit with a beer and just watch the world go by. Also on offer are some reasonably priced pizzas, pastas, salads and ice cream.

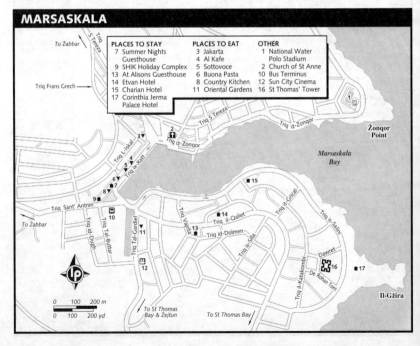

MARSASKALA

PLACES TO STAY	PLACES TO EAT	OTHER
7 Summer Nights Guesthouse	3 Jakarta	1 National Water Polo Stadium
9 SHIK Holiday Complex	4 Al Kafe	2 Church of St Anne
13 At Alisons Guesthouse	5 Sottovoce	10 Bus Terminus
14 Etvan Hotel	6 Buona Pasta	12 Sun City Cinema
15 Charian Hotel	8 Country Kitchen	16 St Thomas' Tower
17 Corinthia Jerma Palace Hotel	11 Oriental Gardens	

Maltese Boats

The brightly coloured fishing boats that crowd the harbours around the coast have become one of Malta's national symbols. Painted boldly in blue, red and yellow, with the watchful 'Eyes of Osiris' on the bows to ward off evil spirits, they are unmistakably Maltese.

There are different kinds of traditional Maltese vessel. The *luzzu* (**loots**-zoo) is a large double-ended fishing boat (for nonsailors, that means it's pointed at both ends). The *kajjik* (**ka**-yik) is similar in appearance, but has a square transom (ie, it's pointed at the front end only). The harbour at Marsaxlokk is famous for its colourful vista of moored fishing boats.

The *dghajsa* (**dye**-sa) is a smaller and racier-looking boat, with very high stem and stern-posts – a bit like a Maltese gondola. These are not solid, seaworthy fishing boats, but sleek water taxis. A flotilla of dghajsas was once used to carry passengers back and forth between Valletta and the Three Cities. They were powered by oars, but today's dghajsas – used mainly for tourist trips – generally carry an outboard engine. Local enthusiasts maintain – and race – a small fleet of oar-driven vessels. The waterfront at Vittoriosa and Senglea is the best place to admire these classic boats.

Sottovoce (☎ *632669*), a few doors down from Al Kafe, is a rather more upmarket Maltese-Italian restaurant with a wide range of pasta, seafood, steak and rabbit dishes. Expect to pay around Lm15 for dinner for two including wine.

Buona Pasta (☎ *684050*), also on the promenade, has cheap and tasty home-made pasta dishes for Lm2 to Lm3, and the coffee is good too.

Oriental Garden (☎ *632687*) on Triq Tal-Gardiel is one of several Chinese restaurants in Marsaskala. Main courses range from Lm2.25 to Lm4.50, and take-away is also available.

For fast food, try *Country Kitchen* at the southern end of the promenade. It has a selection of soups, sandwiches, doughnuts, cakes and coffee, and there's a playground outside where you can keep an eye on the kids.

Entertainment
The five-screen *Sun City Cinema Complex* (☎ *632858 or 668888*) on Triq Tal-Gardiel shows first-run films. Tickets are Lm2.40 each.

MARSAXLOKK
Marsaxlokk Bay is Malta's second natural harbour. It was here that the Turkish fleet was moored during the Great Siege of 1565, and Napoleon's army landed here during the French invasion of 1798. In the 1930s the calm waters of the bay were used as a staging post by the huge, four-engined Short C-Class flying boats of Britain's Imperial Airways as they pioneered long-distance air travel to the far-flung corners of the Empire. During WWII Marsaxlokk Bay was the base for the Fleet Air Arm, and in 1989 the famous summit meeting between Soviet and US presidents Mikhail Gorbachev and George Bush was held on board a warship anchored in Marsaxlokk Bay. Today the harbour is framed by the fuel tanks and chimney of a power station and the huge cranes of the Kalafrana Container Terminal – eyesores that will probably prevent any serious tourist development.

Despite these 20th-century encroachments, the ancient fishing village of Marsaxlokk (marsa-shlock; from *marsa scirocco,* meaning 'south-easterly harbour') at the head of the bay remains resolutely a slice of real Maltese life. Old, low-rise houses ring the waterfront, and a fleet of brightly coloured *luzzus* dance in the harbour. Men with weathered faces sit by the waterside mending nets and grumbling about the tax on diesel, while others scrape and paint and saw as they ready their boats for the sea.

The daily market on the waterfront sells mainly tourist tat aimed at the tour groups, who regularly sally forth from their buses for a lunchtime shopping break. Far more interesting is the **Sunday Fish Market**, where you can admire the riches of the Med before they're whisked off to Malta's top hotels and restaurants. It starts early in the morning and the best stuff is long gone by afternoon.

Delimara Point, south-east of Marsaxlokk, is blighted by a huge power station whose chimney can be seen for miles around, but there are a few good swimming places on the eastern side of the peninsula. **Peter's Pool** is the best, a natural lido in the rocks with large areas of flat slab for sunbathing between swims. Follow the narrow, potholed road out towards Delimara Lighthouse until you are practically under the power station chimney, and you will see a low building on the left with 'Peter's Pool' painted on it. A sump-crunchingly rough track leads down to a parking area where a cheerful young man will relieve you of 50c. Don't leave anything in your car – this is a favourite spot for thieves.

The road to Delimara passes **Tas Silġ**, where archaeologists have uncovered a Punic-Roman temple. This may be the famous Temple of Juno that was plundered by Verres, the Roman Governor of Sicily and Malta in 70 BC, as recorded in the writings of Cicero. Unfortunately the site is locked up.

South of Marsaxlokk, on the road to Birżebbuġa, is **Fort St Lucian**, built in 1610 to protect the bay. Today it houses a naval college and offices of a government fish farm.

Ir-Rizzu (☎ 651569), on Xatt is-Sajjieda on the Marsaxlokk waterfront, is the best place to enjoy fresh fish cooked in the traditional Maltese way, steamed with tomatoes, onions, garlic and herbs. The nearby *Is-Sajjied* (☎ 651593) offers similar fare.

The Hunter's Tower (☎ 651356), on Triq il-Wilga on the north side of the harbour, also specialises in seafood, but is a little more upmarket.

BIRŻEBBUĠA

Birżebbuġa (beer-zeb-**boo**-ja, meaning 'well of the olives') lies on the western shore of Marsaxlokk Bay. It began life as a fishing village, but today it's a dormitory town for workers from the nearby Malta Freeport. The misleadingly named **Pretty Bay** lies at the southern end of town. Although it has a pleasant sandy beach, it also has a wonderful view of the Kalafrana Container Terminal, only 500m away across the water.

There's nothing to see in town, but just 500m north on the road from Valletta is the cave and museum of **Għar Dalam** (aar-da-**lam**, meaning 'cave of darkness'). This

The Maltese Compass

In the Maltese language, the points of the compass are mostly named for the winds that blow from that direction. These are Maltese versions of the old Latin names used by Roman sailors.

North	Tramuntana	North-East	Grigal
East	Lvant	South-East	Xlokk
South	Nofs in-Nhar	South-West	Lbiċ
West	Punent	North-West	Majjistral

Xlokk is the Maltese equivalent of the Italian *scirocco*, both of which derive from the Arabic word *sharg*, meaning 'east.' The xlokk is a hot, humid and oppressive wind that blows from the southeast, usually in spring, bringing misty conditions to the island. It derives its heat from the Sahara Desert, and picks up its humidity passing over the sea. The Tramuntana, from the Italian for 'across the mountains', is the cold northerly wind from the direction of the Alps. The north-easterly Grigal is the typical winter wind that batters the rocky coast of Malta, and makes for an uncomfortable ferry crossing to Gozo, while the north-westerly Majjistral is the stiff sailing breeze of summer afternoons, the equivalent of the Turkish *meltem*.

145m-long cave in the Lower Coralline Limestone has yielded a magnificent harvest of fossil bones and teeth belonging to dwarf elephants, hippopotamuses and deer – an estimated total of over 7000 animals – which lived between 180,000 and 18,000 years ago. The animals are all of European type, suggesting that Malta was once joined to Italy, but not to northern Africa.

The little museum at the entrance contains display cases mounted with thousands and thousands of bones and teeth. It's not hugely interesting unless you're a palaeontologist, but impressive in terms of sheer numbers. Beyond the museum a path leads down through attractive gardens to the mouth of the cave, where a walkway leads 80m into the cavern. A pillar of sediment has been left in the middle of the excavated floor to show the stratigraphic sequence.

Għar Dalam is open 7.45 am to 2 pm daily from 16 June to 30 September, and 8.15 am to 5 pm Monday to Saturday and 8.15 am to 4 pm on Sunday from 1 October to 15 June (closed on public holidays). Admission costs Lm1, but under-19s and over-65s get in free.

On the cliff-bound coastline south of Birżebbuġa lies the cave, **Għar Ħasan**. Follow the road towards Żurrieq, then turn left on a minor road that ends at an industrial estate (there are plenty of signposts). The cave entrance is down some steps in the cliff-face to the left; admission is free. The 'Cave of Hasan' is supposed to have been used as a hideout by a 12th-century Saracen rebel. With a torch you can follow a passage off to the right to a 'window' in the cliff-face.

To get to Għar Dalam and Birżebbuġa, take bus No 11 from Valletta. The cave museum is on the right-hand side of the road at a small, semi-circular parking area 500m short of Birżebbuġa – look out for it as it's not well signposted. There is no public transport to Għar Ħasan – it's a 2.5km walk from Birżebbuġa.

ŻURRIEQ

The village of Żurrieq sprawls across a hillside on the south coast, in a sort of no-man's land to the south of the airport. This part of Malta feels cut off from the rest of the island, and although it's only 10km from Valletta as the crow flies, it seems much farther. If you come by car, be prepared to get lost – several times.

The **parish church of St Catherine** was built in the 1630s and houses a fine altarpiece of St Catherine – painted by Mattia Preti in 1675, when the artist took refuge here during a plague epidemic – and there are several 17th- and 18th-century windmills dotted about the village. On a minor road between Żurrieq and Mqabba is the **Church of the Annunciation** in the deserted medieval settlement of Ħal Millieri. This tiny, plain church, set in a pretty garden, dates from the mid-15th century and contains important 15th-century frescoes. Both church and garden are normally locked – contact the parish priest at St Catherine's (☎ 642010) to arrange a viewing.

About 2km west of Żurrieq lies the tiny harbour of **Wied iż-Żurrieq**, set in a narrow inlet in the cliffs and guarded by a watchtower. Here boats depart for 30-minute cruises to the famous **Blue Grotto**, a huge natural arch in the sea-cliffs 400m to the east. The boat trips take in about seven caves, including the Honeymoon Cave, Reflection Cave and Cat's Cave. The best time is before mid-morning, when the sun is shining into the grotto. You can see the Blue Grotto without a boat from a viewing platform beside the main road, just before the turn-off to Wied iż-Żurrieq.

There are several souvenir shops and restaurants above the harbour in Wied iż-Żurrieq. *Congreve Channel Restaurant* (☎ 647928) specialises in fresh fish (Lm3.75 to Lm4.95) and rabbit, but also offers baked potatoes (Lm1.20 to Lm1.60) and excellent bacon rolls.

Boat trips depart from 8 am to 4 pm daily in summer, weather permitting. If there is any doubt about the weather or sea conditions, call ☎ 640058 or 649925 to check. The boats take up to eight passengers each, and tickets cost Lm1.25 per person. Bus Nos 38 and 138 run from Valletta to Żurrieq and Wied iż-Żurrieq every 30 minutes or so between 9.45 am and 3.45 pm.

ĦAĠAR QIM & MNAJDRA

The megalithic temples of Ħaġar Qim and Mnajdra are the best preserved and most evocative of Malta's prehistoric sites, especially at dawn or sunset when the ancient stones are tinged pink and gold by the rising or setting sun. The temples are fenced off and the gates will be locked at these times but it's worth the effort, especially around the time of the winter solstice (21 December) when you can check out some of the supposed solar alignments.

Ħaġar Qim (adge-ar eem, the name means 'standing stones') is right next to the parking area. The facade, with its trilithon entrance, has been restored, rather too obviously, but gives an idea of what it may once have looked like. The temples were originally roofed over, but the wooden structures have long since rotted away.

Before going in, look round the corner to the right – the megalith here is the largest in the temple, and weighs more than 20 tonnes.

The temple consists of a series of interconnected, oval chambers with no uniform arrangement, and differs from other Maltese temples in lacking a regular trefoil plan. In the first chamber on the left you will see a little altar post decorated with plant motifs, and in the second there are a couple of pedestal altars. The 'fat lady' statuettes and the so-called 'Venus of Malta' figurine that were found here are on display in the National Museum of Archaeology in Valletta.

Mnajdra (mm-**nigh**-dra), a 500m walk downhill from Ħaġar Qim, is more interesting. Sadly, it has been defaced by vandals who have painted crosses and letters on the stone. There are three temples side by side, each with a trefoil plan and each with a different orientation. The oldest temple is the small one on the right, which is aligned towards the south-west and Filfla Island. The central temple, pointing towards the southeast, is the youngest. All date from between 3600 and 3000 BC.

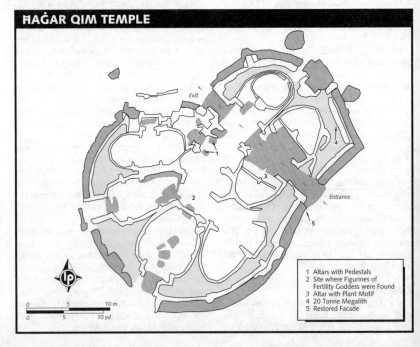

ĦAĠAR QIM TEMPLE

Exit

Entrance

0   5   10 m
0   5   10 yd

1 Altars with Pedestals
2 Site where Figurines of Fertility Goddess were Found
3 Altar with Plant Motif
4 20 Tonne Megalith
5 Restored Facade

Gozo, the perfect place to get away from it all

When in Gozo, guzzle the local vintage.

The imposing bulk of Fungus Rock with the Azure Window in the background, near Gharb, Gozo

Fossil 'sand dollar' *Scutella subrotunda*, found at an inlet at Wied il-Għasri, Gozo

Gozo's Ta'Ċenċ cliffs are the highest in Malta.

Home from school in Mġarr, Gozo

Clay bottles, Folklore Museum, Għarb, Gozo

Megalithic Temples

The megalithic temples of Malta, which date mainly from the period 3600 to 3000 BC, are the oldest freestanding stone structures in the world. They pre-date the Pyramids of Egypt by more than 500 years.

The oldest surviving temples are thought to be those of Ta'Ħaġrat and Skorba near the village of Mġarr on Malta. Ġgantija on Gozo, and Ħagar Qim and Mnajdra on Malta are among the best preserved. Tarxien is the most developed, its last phase dating from 3000 to 2500 BC. The subterranean tombs of the Hypogeum date from the same period as the temples, and mimic many of their architectural features.

The purpose of these mysterious structures is the subject of much debate. They all share certain features in common – a site on a south-easterly slope, near to caves, a spring and fertile farmland; a trefoil or clover-leaf plan with three or five rounded chambers (often referred to as apses) opening off the central axis, which usually faces between south and east; megalithic construction, using blocks of stone weighing up to 20 tonnes; and holes and sockets drilled into the stones, perhaps to hold wooden doors or curtains. Most temple sites have also revealed spherical stones, about the size of cannonballs – it has been suggested that these were used like ball bearings so that the heavy megaliths could be more easily moved over the ground.

An oracle hole clearly displayed at the ancient Ġgantija temples, Gozo

NEIL WILSON

No burials have been found in any of the temples, but most have yielded statues and figurines of so-called 'fat ladies' – possibly fertility goddesses. Most have some form of decoration on the stone, ranging from simple pitting to the elaborate spirals and carved animals seen at Tarxien. There are also 'oracle holes' – small apertures in the chamber walls which may have been used by priests or priestesses to issue divinations. The temples' south-easterly orientation has suggested a relationship to the winter solstice sunrise, and one amateur investigator has recently put forward a convincing theory of solar alignment (see the Web site www.geocities.com/maltatemples/).

It has been claimed that the southern temple is full of significant solar alignments. At sunrise during the winter solstice, a beam of sunlight illuminates the altar to the right of the inner doorway. At sunrise during the summer solstice, a sunbeam penetrates through the window in the back of the left-hand apse into the pedestal altar in the left rear chamber. In the right-hand apse there is a separate chamber entered through a small doorway, with a so-called 'oracle hole' to its left. The function of this is unknown.

The temples are open 7.45 am to 2 pm daily from 16 June to 30 September, and 8.15 am to 5 pm Monday to Saturday and 8.15 am to 4 pm on Sunday from 1 October to 15 June (closed on public holidays). Admission costs Lm1, but under-19s and over-65s get in free.

On the clifftop to the south-east of Mnajdra is a 17th-century watchtower and a memorial to Sir Walter Congreve (Governor of Malta 1924-27) who was buried at sea off this point. You can hike east along the cliffs towards Wied iż-Żurrieq and the Blue Grotto, or west to Għar Lapsi (see Central Malta). The tiny uninhabited island of **Filfla**, 10km offshore, is clearly visible. It suffered the ignominy of being used for target practice by the British armed forces until it was declared a nature reserve in 1970. It supports important breeding colonies of sea birds, including an estimated 10,000 pairs of storm petrels, and a unique species of lizard. Landing on the island is forbidden.

Ħaġar Qim Restaurant (☎ 0949 7329), above the car park, serves Maltese specialities. It's open 10 am to 4 pm and 7 pm till late from Tuesday to Saturday, and all day on Sunday.

Bus Nos 38 and 138 run from Valletta to Ħaġar Qim every 30 minutes or so between 9.45 am and 3.45 pm.

Gozo & Comino

If the crowded resorts and manic drivers of Malta get to be too much for you, then you can escape to the quieter islands to the north of Malta.

Gozo

Gozo, called Għawdex (**aow**-desh) in Malti, is quite different to the island of Malta. Although it is more than one-third the size, it has less than one-tenth of the population. Farming and fishing are the main activities. The land is more fertile, the scenery is greener, and the pace of life much slower. It offers good walking, superb coastal scenery and some of the best scuba-diving in Europe, plus the megalithic temple of Ġgantija and Victoria's medieval citadel.

In this chapter the main town, Victoria, is described first, then Mġarr, the main harbour. The rest of the island is covered in a clockwise direction from Mġarr.

VICTORIA (RABAT)

Victoria, the chief town of Gozo, was named for the Diamond Jubilee of Queen Victoria in 1897. It was originally known as Rabat, and is still called that by many of the islanders (and by several road signs). The town sits in the centre of the island, 6km from the ferry terminal at Mġarr, and 4km from the resort town of Marsalforn. Victoria's main attraction is the compact citadel, Il-Kastell, with its cathedral and museums. It is also Gozo's main source of shops and services.

Orientation

Victoria is built on a hill crowned by the ramparts of Il-Kastell (the Citadel, also known by its Italian names, Gran Castello or the Cittadella). Telgħa Tal-Belt (Castle Hill) runs downhill from Il-Kastell to Pjazza Indipendenza, where you will find the Tourist Information Office. Triq ir-Repubblika, Victoria's main street, runs east (downhill) from Pjazza Indipendenza.

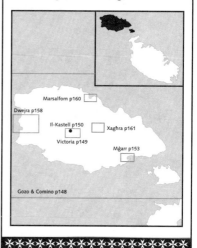

Marsalforn p160
Dwejra p158
Il-Kastell p150
Xagħra p161
Victoria p149
Mġarr p153
Gozo & Comino p148

GOZO & COMINO

The bus station and main car park are on Triq Putirjal, south of Triq ir-Repubblika.

Victoria's narrow streets are locked into a labyrinthine one-way system – it may take several circuits of the town and one or two unintentional trips to the towns of Kerċem or Sannat before you find your way around.

Information

Tourist Office Victoria's Tourist Information Office (☎ 558106) is in the Banca Giuratale building on Pjazza Indipendenza.

Money You can cash travellers cheques and change money at the Thomas Cook office on the corner of Triq ir-Repubblika and Telgħa Tal-Belt (Castle Hill). There's a Bank of

GOZO & COMINO

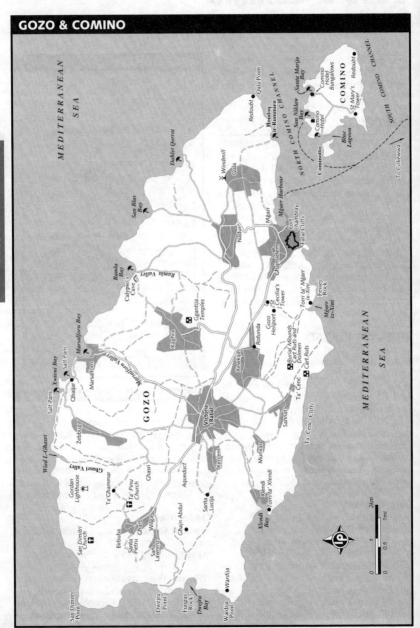

Valletta with ATM on Triq ir-Repubblika, and a foreign exchange bureau on Pjazza Savina that's open 9.30 am to 6 pm daily.

Post & Communications The island's main post office is on Triq ir-Repubblika. You can check your email at the Maltanet Internet Zone (☎ 489600, @ info@malta .net) on the ground floor of the Arkadia Shopping Centre on Triq Fortunato Mizzi. You'll need a smartcard (Lm2.50 deposit) – available from the nearby Things Plus shop – to activate the machines. Internet access costs 35c for 30 minutes.

Bookshops Books and newspapers, both local and British, can be found at Book-point News, opposite the bus station, and at Bookworm, on Triq ir-Repubblika.

Walking Tour of Il-Kastell

From the Tourist Information Office in Pjazza Indipendenza, cross the main street and climb up Telgħa Tal-Belt to the Citadel's main gate. On the way you'll pass the entrance to the Citadel Theatre, which houses **Gozo 360°**, a 30-minute audiovisual show on the history of Gozo, along the lines of the

Malta Experience in Valletta. There are two gates into Il-Kastell – enter through the **Old Main Gate** on the right (the larger new gate was opened in 1957), noting the Roman inscription on the left-hand inner wall.

Past the Museum of Archaeology (see under Museums later in this section) go up the stairs on the right into **St Michael's Bastion** and continue along the top of the city wall to **St John's Demi-Bastion**. There is a good **view** from here – the huge dome of the Rotunda at Xewkija, with Comino and Malta in the background; the distant Gothic spire of the church above Mġarr harbour; the watchtower of Nadur, and the dome and twin clock-towers of its parish church; and Xagħra on its hilltop to the east, capped by Ta' Kola windmill and the Church of Our Lady of Victory. Off to the left you can see the white apartment blocks around Marsalforn Bay. The **Gozo Craft Centre** is in the old prison building behind the bastion.

Climb the stairs below St John's Cavalier to reach the upper battlements, with more good views to the north and west. The **fortifications** were built at the beginning of the 17th century to guard against further Turkish

GOZO & COMINO

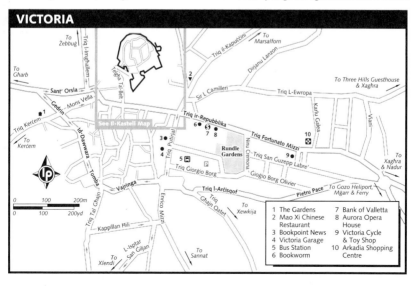

VICTORIA

1 The Gardens
2 Mao Xi Chinese Restaurant
3 Bookpoint News
4 Victoria Garage
5 Bus Station
6 Bookworm
7 Bank of Valletta
8 Aurora Opera House
9 Victoria Cycle & Toy Shop
10 Arkadia Shopping Centre

IL-KASTELL (ĊITTADELLA)

PLACES TO EAT
12 Cittadella Restaurant
15 Castle Bar
19 Cafe Jubilee

THINGS TO SEE & DO
1 Natural Science Museum
2 Chapel of St Joseph
3 Archway
4 Folklore Museum
5 Cathedral Museum
6 St John's Cavalier
8 Cathedral of the Assumption
9 Main Gate
10 Old Main Gate
11 Museum of Archaeology
14 Church of St Ursula
16 Citadel Theatre & Gozo 360
21 Church of St James
22 Astra Theatre
24 Basilica of St George

OTHER
7 Gozo Crafts Centre
13 Exchange Bureau
17 Thomas Cook
18 Tourist Information Office
20 Air Malta
23 Post Office

attacks following the Great Siege of 1565. Until 1637, when the Turkish threat receded, all Gozitans were bound by law to spend each night within the city walls. After that date, people drifted back to the countryside, and many of the abandoned houses were ruined in the earthquake of 1693 – their tumbled remains can still be seen.

Walk down Triq il-Kwartier San Ġwann. Beyond the archway, at the little **Chapel of St Joseph**, turn left down Triq Bernardo de Opuo, past a beautifully restored medieval building that houses the Folklore Museum (see under Museums), and then right on Triq il-Fossos to arrive in the little square in front of the cathedral.

Cathedral of the Assumption

The Cathedral of the Assumption was built between 1697 and 1711 to replace the church that had been destroyed in the earthquake of 1693. It was designed by Lorenzo Gafa, who was also responsible for the Cathedral of St Paul at Mdina. The elegant facade is adorned with the escutcheons of Grand Master Ramon de Perellos and Bishop Palmieri. Due to lack of money the dome was never completed, but the impression of

NEIL WILSON

The escutcheon of Grand Master Perellos adorns the Cathedral of the Assumption.

one was maintained inside by way of a clever trompe l'oeil painting.

The **Cathedral Museum** is along Triq il-Fossos. The downstairs vault contains church gold and silver, while the upstairs gallery is devoted to religious art. The ground floor houses various items including a 19th-century bishop's carriage and an altar with a wax model of the Last Supper. The cathedral and museum are open 9 am to 4.30 pm (closed 12.55 to 1.30 pm) from Monday to Saturday. The 15c ticket covers admission to both.

Museums
Three other museums are within the Citadel. The **Museum of Archaeology** (☎ 556144) contains finds from the prehistoric temples at Ġgantija, though the model of the temple is more interesting than the array of pottery shards. Finds from the Punic and Roman periods are displayed upstairs, including terracotta cremation urns, lots of amphorae and anchors, and some fascinating jewellery and amulets in the form of the Eye of Osiris – an ancient link to the symbols found on Maltese fishing boats of today.

The **Folklore Museum** (☎ 556144) is in a lovely old building that dates from around 1500, and shows Sicilian and Catalan influ-

ence – note the beautiful arched windows overlooking Triq Bernardo de Opuo. The museum houses a large and interesting collection of domestic, trade and farming implements that give a good insight into rural life in Gozo.

The **Natural Science Museum** (☎ 556153) on Triq il-Kwartier explains the geology of the island and its water supply. Also on display is a rather sad collection of stuffed birds upstairs.

The museums are open 7.45 am to 2 pm daily from 16 June to 30 September, and 8.15 am to 5 pm Monday to Saturday and 8.15 am to 4 pm on Sunday from 1 October to 15 June (closed on public holidays). Entry costs Lm1, but under-19s and over-65s get in free. A combined ticket, giving entry to all three museums, costs Lm1.50.

The Town
Pjazza Indipendenza, the main square of Victoria, hosts a daily market known throughout the island as **It-Tokk** (meaning 'the meeting place'). The semi-circular baroque building at the west end of the square is the **Banca Giuratale**, built in 1733 to house the city council; today it contains the Tourist Information Office and other government offices.

A narrow lane behind the Banca Giuratale leads to Pjazza San Ġorġ and the **Basilica of St George**, the original parish church of Rabat dating from 1678. The lavish interior contains a fine altarpiece of *St George and the Dragon* by Mattia Preti. The old town, known as Il-Borgo, is a maze of narrow alleys around Pjazza San Ġorġ, and is an interesting place to wander.

Rundle Gardens, south of Triq Repubblika, were laid out by General Sir Leslie Rundle (Governor of Malta 1909-15) in around 1914. On the *festa* of the Assumption (15 August) the gardens host a lively agricultural fair.

Places to Stay & Eat
Since the closure of the Duke of Edinburgh in Triq ir-Repubblika, Victoria has been without a hotel. The only accommodation options presently available are rooms at

GOZO & COMINO

The 1693 Earthquake

On 11 January 1693 an earthquake of magnitude 6.8 on the Richter scale struck southern Italy. The epicentre was in the Val di Noto region of eastern Sicily, and several towns and villages were destroyed. Two-thirds of the population of Catania were killed, and the total death toll came to around 70,000. In Malta, the quake damaged many buildings including the cathedrals of Mdina and Victoria, both of which were built anew.

****

The Gardens (☎ 557737 or 553723) in Triq Kerċem, for Lm5 per person B&B, or the *Three Hills Guest House* (☎ 551895) on Triq Xagħra.

Cittadella Restaurant (☎ 556628), on Telgħa Tal-Belt, is a bit of a tourist trap, but it has a pleasant garden courtyard and good pasta dishes – a platter of lasagne, ricotta ravioli and timpana costs Lm2.85 including a glass of local wine.

Castle Bar, across the street, is a more down-to-earth alternative, offering a lunch of toasties, sandwiches or pastizzi washed down with a beer for around Lm1.

Cafe Jubilee on Triq Repubblika is a lovely old-fashioned bar with a marble counter, brass rails, lots of dark wood and waiters in black waistcoats and white aprons. As well as drinks and coffee, it serves soup, salad, baguettes, sandwiches and delicious *ftira* – local bread flavoured with olive oil and tomatoes.

For a change of cuisine, try the *Mao Xi Chinese Restaurant* (☎ 561820) on Triq il-Kapuċċini. Main courses cost Lm2.50 to Lm4, and they offer takeaway meals too. It's open from noon to 2.30 pm and 6 to 11 pm daily.

Even Gozo has not managed to avoid the Big Mac attack. If you must have a burger, there's a *McDonalds* in the Arkadia shopping centre on Triq Fortunato Mizzi (the continuation of Triq ir-Repubblika) at the east end of town.

For picnics, you can buy Gozitan wine, cheese, bread, tomatoes and other local products at the *food shop* at 4 Triq il-Fossos in the Citadel, across from the Cathedral Museum. There are *fruit and vegetable vendors* around It-Tokk and at the car park beside the bus station, and a *supermarket* at the Arkadia shopping centre.

Entertainment

Despite its diminutive size, Victoria has two theatres to Valletta's one, a consequence of rivalry between two local band clubs. The *Aurora Opera House* (☎ 562974), home of the Leone Philharmonic Society, and the *Astra Theatre* (☎ 556256), are both on Triq ir-Repubblika, and stage opera, ballet, comedies, drama, cabaret, pantomime and celebrity concerts. Check the local press for details of performances.

Victoria also has the two-screen *Citadel Cinema* (☎ 559955) on Telgħa Tal-Belt which shows mainstream films; film tickets cost Lm1.75 for adults and Lm1.25 for children. Check the *Times* newspaper to see what's on.

Getting There & Away

For details on ferry and helicopter services to Gozo see the Getting Around chapter.

Getting Around

To/From the Heliport Gozo's heliport is just south of St Cecilia's Tower, about 3.5km south-east of Victoria on the main road to Mġarr. Most hotels will offer to pick you up from the heliport; otherwise, you could phone and arrange for a taxi to meet your flight. Alternatively, you can walk 200m up to the main road and catch bus No 25 into Victoria.

Bus Victoria's bus station is just south of Triq ir-Repubblika on Triq Putirjal, about 10 minutes' walk from the Citadel. All the bus routes are circular, starting and finishing at Victoria. Except for bus No 25, which shuttles regularly between Victoria and Mġarr and connects with the ferries to Malta, the buses are slow and run according to the needs of the local schools and shoppers, so the schedule is rarely convenient for sightseeing. There's a flat fare of 10c.

Taxi Taxis hang around at the bus station and at Pjazza Indipendenza, or you can try phoning Belmont Garage (☎ 556962) or Mario's Taxis (☎ 557242).

Car & Bicycle If you want to see as much of the island as possible, then it makes sense to rent a car. It's also very cheap – even cheaper than on Malta. You'll also find that the quieter roads and shorter distances make cycling a more attractive option on Gozo than on Malta.

Both Victoria Garage (☎ 556414, 553741 or 553758), on Triq Putirjal opposite the bus station, and the Victoria Cycle & Toy Shop (☎ 553741), on Pjazza J F Kennedy opposite the Arkadia shopping centre, hire out cars/motorbikes/bicycles for around Lm7/3.50/1.50 a day.

The only petrol stations on Gozo are in Mġarr and Victoria.

Walking Gozo is so small that you could walk from Mġarr to Marsalforn in two hours. Away from the relatively busy road between Mġarr and Victoria the roads are pretty quiet and there are lots of attractive hikes around the coast.

MĠARR

Mġarr is Gozo's main harbour and the point of arrival for ferries from Malta. The row of buildings beside the harbour car park includes a helpful Tourist Information Office (☎ 553343), open 9 am to 12.30 pm and 1 to 5 pm Monday to Friday, and 9 am to 12.30 pm on Sunday and public holidays. In the same block you will also find public toilets, a post office and a bank.

The 20th-century neogothic **Church of Our Lady of Lourdes** appears almost to hang over the village. Begun in 1924, lack of funds meant that its construction was not finally completed until the 1970s. The hilltop above it is capped by the ramparts of **Fort Chambray**, built by the Knights of St John in the early 18th century. It was originally intended to supplant the Citadel as Gozo's main fortified town, and the area within the walls was laid out with a grid of streets similar to Valletta. But with the decline of the Order in the late 18th century the plan ended up coming to naught. Instead, the fort served as a garrison and later as a mental hospital, and is currently being developed as a four-star hotel and residential development.

GOZO & COMINO

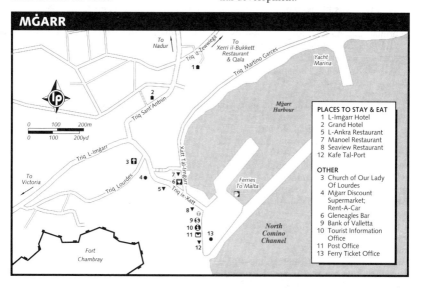

MĠARR

To Nadur

To Xerri il-Bukkett Restaurant & Qala

Triq iz-Zewwieqa

Triq Martino Garces

Yacht Marina

Triq Sant'Antnin

Mġarr Harbour

Triq L-Imġarr

Xatt Tal-Imġarr

To Victoria

Triq Lourdes

Triq ix-Xatt

Ferries To Malta

North Comino Channel

Fort Chambray

0   100   200m
0   100   200yd

PLACES TO STAY & EAT
1 L-Imġarr Hotel
2 Grand Hotel
5 L-Ankra Restaurant
7 Manoel Restaurant
8 Seaview Restaurant
12 Kafe Tal-Port

OTHER
3 Church of Our Lady Of Lourdes
4 Mġarr Discount Supermarket; Rent-A-Car
6 Gleneagles Bar
9 Bank of Valletta
10 Tourist Information Office
11 Post Office
13 Ferry Ticket Office

A right turn at the top of the harbour hill leads along a **belvedere** with a grand view over the harbour to Comino and northern Malta. Triq iż-Żewwieqa (near the L-Imġarr Hotel) leads in 1.5km to an even better **viewpoint** just south of Qala.

Places to Stay & Eat

Both of Mġarr's accommodation options are decidedly upmarket. The five-star **L-Imġarr Hotel** (☎ 560455 or 560457, fax 557589, ✉ mgarrhtl@mbox.vol.net.mt) is perched high above the marina, and is not bad value at Lm22/12 per person for B&B in high/low season for a suite with an inland view.

The four-star **Grand Hotel** (☎ 556183, fax 559744, ✉ belmont@waldonet.net.mt) on Triq Sant'Antnin also has a fine position overlooking the harbour. Its least expensive rooms (no view) go for Lm13.50/6.50 per person in high/low season, while rooms with a balcony overlooking the harbour cost Lm21.50/13.50. Prices include a buffet breakfast. The single occupancy supplement is Lm5, and there's an additional surcharge of Lm3 per person if you stay for only one night.

Seaview Restaurant (☎ 553985), at the foot of Triq ix-Xatt, has a pleasant outdoor terrace and serves steaks and seafood dishes at around Lm3 to Lm5 for main courses.

L-Ankra Restaurant (☎ 555656), a bit farther up the hill on Triq ix-Xatt, has a good seafood menu, including crab cakes (Lm1.90), calamari (Lm3.40) and grilled swordfish (Lm3.50).

Across the street and down the stairs you will find **Manoel Restaurant** (☎ 563588), housed in the vaults of an old fort.

Kafe Tal-Port, beside the harbour car park, serves cheap coffee (30c), burgers, sandwiches, salads, cakes and doughnuts.

Xerri Il-Bukkett Restaurant (☎ 553500) on Triq iż-Żewwieqa (about 1.5km east of Mgarr, just south of Qala) has a terrace with a stupendous view across the channel to Comino and northern Malta. It serves pizzas (Lm1 to Lm1.50), pastas (Lm2.30) and rabbit stew (Lm3.95).

For picnics and self-caterers, the **Mġarr Discount Supermarket** is just a few min-utes' walk uphill from the harbour. It's open 8 am to 8 pm daily except Sunday (to 9.30 pm on Saturday).

Gleneagles Bar, above the Manoel Restaurant, is the place to head for a cold beer at the end of the day. It commands a view over the harbour, and is the social hub of the village, filling up in the early evening with a lively mix of locals, fishermen, yachties and tourists.

Getting There & Around

The car ferry from Ċirkewwa in Malta shuttles back and forth to Mġarr every 45 to 60 minutes (and every two hours through the night in the peak summer months). There is also a once-daily car ferry from Sa Maison in Floriana. The Gozo Channel Co ticket office (☎ 556114 or 561622 for timetable info) is near Kafe Tal-Port in the harbour car park. For more information on ferry services see the Getting Around chapter earlier in the book.

Bus No 25 runs from the harbour to Victoria, and taxi drivers tout for business among the crowds disembarking from the ferry. There are a couple of car hire agencies near the harbour. Mġarr Rent-A-Car (☎ 564986 or 556098), above the supermarket a few minutes' walk uphill from the harbour, is good value, with low season rates beginning at Lm6 a day.

GĦAJNSIELEM

Mġarr merges uphill into the town of Għajnsielem (ayn-**see**-lem, meaning 'spring of peace'). The huge, modern **Church of Our Lady of Loreto**, built in neogothic style, looms over the village square.

On the western edge of the village, on the main road from Mġarr to Victoria, is **Gozo Heritage** (☎ 551475), which advertises itself as 'a walk through 7000 years of living history'. It's a series of historical tableaux – the legend of Calypso, Ġgantija temple, the Romans, the Great Siege, WWII – accompanied by special light and sound effects. It's open 9 am to 5 pm Monday to Saturday, and costs Lm1.75.

Another 500m along the road to Victoria is St Cecilia's Tower. The level area around the tower served as a temporary airfield during the invasion of Sicily in 1943. A left turn at the tower leads to Gozo heliport (see the Getting Around chapter for details on the Malta-Gozo helicopter service).

XEWKIJA

The village of Xewkija – and most of southern Gozo – is dominated by the vast dome of the Parish Church of St John the Baptist, better known as the **Rotunda**. Work on the new church began in 1951 and it was finally completed in 1971. It was built mainly with the volunteer labour of the parishioners, and paid for by local donations. Its vast size – the dome is higher than St Paul's Cathedral in London, and the nave can seat 4000 people – is said to be due to rivalry with Mosta on Malta, whose rotunda was also funded by the local people.

The rotunda was built around the old 17th-century church, which was too small for the community's needs – the new one can seat around three times the village's population. The interior is plain, but impresses through sheer size. Paintings of scenes from the life of St John the Baptist adorn the six side-chapels. To the left of the altar is a **museum** where baroque sculpture and other relics salvaged from the old church are displayed. The wooden statue of St John was fashioned in 1845 by Maltese sculptor Paul Azzopardi.

TA'ĊENĊ

The quiet village of Sannat, once famed for its lace-making, lies 2km south of Victoria, near the Ta'Ċenċ plateau. Signs from the village square point the way to the Hotel Ta'Ċenċ, one of Gozo's best. The track to the left of the entrance to the walled hotel grounds gives access to the high plateau of Ta'Ċenċ – the **views** north to Victoria, Xewkija and Xagħra are good, especially towards sunset. Wander off to the left of the track, near the edge of the limestone crag, and you will find a prehistoric **dolmen** – a large slab propped up on three smaller stones like a table.

But the best walking is off to the right, along the top of the huge Ta'Ċenċ **seacliffs**. These spectacular limestone crags, more than 130m high, were once the breeding ground of the Maltese peregrine falcon (see boxed text 'The Maltese Falcon'). Near the clifftop you can see traces of prehistoric 'cart ruts' (see boxed text 'Riddle of the Ruts' in the Central Malta chapter).

The five-star **Hotel Ta'Ċenċ** (☎ 556819 or 561522/3, fax 558199, @ vjbgozo@ maltanet.net) has a fine, remote setting on the clifftop plateau just east of the village of Sannat. It was ranked No 25 in the world by Conde Nast Traveller magazine, and its attractive, low-rise design and use of local stone have made it one of the most desirable hotels in the Maltese Islands.

The Maltese Falcon

Falconry was the great passion of the Holy Roman Emperor Frederick II (1194-1250) – he wrote a famous treatise on the subject, De arte venandi cum avibus, and chose as his emblem a peregrine falcon, the king of birds. He grew up in Sicily, and learned from his own experience that the finest peregrines came from Malta (the Maltese falcon is a sub-species of peregrine, Falco peregrinus brookei).

When Malta was gifted to the Knights of St John in 1530, the only condition attached was an annual rent of two Maltese falcons – one for the Spanish emperor and one for the viceroy of Sicily. Sadly, by the 1970s trapping and shooting had reduced these magnificent raptors to just one or two breeding pairs. There are occasional reports of peregrines – known as bies in Malti – being seen on the remote south-western cliffs of Malta and Gozo, but there have been no confirmed sightings since the mid-1980s.

All this, of course, has nothing to do with Dashiell Hammett's famous detective story, The Maltese Falcon. If you've read the book you'll know that the eponymous black bird is actually a red herring.

MĠARR IX-XINI

The narrow, cliff-bound inlet of Mġarr ix-Xini (Port of the Galleys) was once used by the Knights of St John as their main harbour on Gozo – one of their watchtowers still guards the entrance. It was also used by the Turkish admiral Dragut Reis, who raided Gozo in 1551 and took most of the island's population into slavery.

There's a tiny shingle beach at the head of the inlet, and a paved area where tourists and locals stake out their sunbathing territories. The swimming and snorkelling along the rocks is very good, and the little cove near the western headland of the bay is a private lido that belongs to the Hotel Ta'Ċenċ.

The road from Sannat and Xewkija down to Mġarr ix-Xini is alarmingly steep and narrow – not recommended for timid drivers. You can walk there from Victoria in just over an hour.

XLENDI

Xlendi was once one of the most beautiful fishing villages on Gozo, but unregulated building on the south side of scenic Xlendi Bay has turned it into just another resort town. That said, it's a pleasant enough place to chill out by the sea, with good swimming, snorkelling and diving, and plenty of rocks for sunbathing.

Steps lead up the cliff above the little fishing boat harbour at the head of the bay, leading to a little cove in the rocks where you can swim. Alternatively you can keep walking up the hillside above and then hike over to Wardija Point and Dwejra Bay. On the south side of the bay a footpath winds around to the 17th-century **watchtower** on Ras il-Bajda. From here you can hike east to the Sanap cliffs, and on towards Ta'Ċenċ.

St Andrews Divers Cove (☎ 561548), between the car park and the promontory, offers a range of beginner's dives, escorted dives, diving courses and equipment hire.

Xlendi Pleasure Cruises (☎ 559967) offers boat trips to Comino and around Gozo. Cruises depart at 10 am and return at 4.30 pm; tickets cost Lm8.

Places to Stay & Eat

The *San Antonio Guesthouse* (☎ 563555, fax 555587, ✉ cgmail@clubgozo.com.mt) is on Triq it-Torri, a fair climb up the hill on the south side of the bay. A double room costs Lm12/6 per person in high/low season including breakfast. A two-person self-catering apartment costs Lm12/8 per night.

Serena Aparthotel (☎ 553719, fax 557452, ✉ serena@vol.net.mt) is on Triq Puniċi, above the south side of the bay. The two-star hotel has a swimming pool and roof-top sun terrace, and all rooms have private bathroom, air-con and TV. Prices range from Lm8/5 per person in high/low season for a landward-facing twin room, to Lm18/12 per person for a luxury suite with sea view.

St Patrick's Hotel (☎ 562951, fax 556598), bang in the middle of the Xlendi waterfront, has attractive air-con rooms with satellite TV overlooking the harbour for Lm22.50/12.50 per person in high/low season. The price includes a buffet breakfast. Rooms that face up the valley are Lm18.50/11.

Iċ-Ċima Restaurant (☎ 558407 or 559032) on Triq San Xmun has a wooden terrace with a great view over the bay. The menu is Italian and Maltese, with the emphasis on seafood. It's open daily for lunch and dinner.

Huang Fong (☎ 561518), at the north end of the promontory, offers Chinese food with a view from its third-floor balcony. There's also a roof-top garden restaurant serving Maltese specialities.

The *Churchill Restaurant* (☎ 563503) is set right on the water's edge on the north side of the bay. It's a pizza and pasta place – the home-made fish ravioli is worth trying (Lm3.75).

Entertainment

La Grotta (☎ 551149), on the road to Victoria about 1km east of Xlendi, is the best nightclub in the Maltese Islands. Part open-air and part housed in a limestone cave in the cliffs above the valley, it's open from 10 pm until dawn on Friday and Saturday throughout summer. Entry costs Lm2.

Getting There & Away
Bus No 87 goes to Xlendi. By car, follow signs from the roundabout at the south end of Triq Putirjal in Victoria. Otherwise, it's a 40-minute walk from Victoria bus station.

Xlendi Tourist Services (☎ 560683) on the main street hire out cars, jeeps, motorbikes and mountain bikes.

GĦARB
The village of Għarb (pronounced aarb, meaning 'west') in the north-west of Gozo has one of the most beautiful churches in the Maltese Islands. The baroque **Church of the Visitation** was built between 1699 and 1729, with an elegant curved facade and twin bell-towers. Three female figures adorn the front: Faith, above the door; Hope, with her anchor, to the right; and Charity. Inside, there is an altarpiece of *The Visitation of Our Lady to St Elizabeth*, which was gifted to the church by Grand Master de Vilhena.

The attractive village square was the location for the classic postcard, on sale throughout Malta and Gozo, showing a traditional British red telephone box beside a red letter box and a blue police station lamp. Next door to the police station is **Għarb Folklore Museum** (☎ 561929). This early 18th-century house has 28 rooms crammed with a fascinating private collection of folk artefacts that rivals the Folklore Museum in Victoria. The exhibits, assembled by the owner over the past 20 years, include an early 18th-century printing press, a child's hearse, farming implements, fishing gear, jam-making equipment and much more. The museum is open 9 am to 4 pm Monday to Saturday, and 9 am to 1 pm on Sunday; entry is Lm1.25.

A pleasant walk of about 30 minutes from Għarb leads to the tiny **Chapel of San Dimitri** (signposted on the road to the left of the church). This small, square church with its baroque cupola dates originally from the 15th century, though it was rebuilt in the 1730s. It stands in splendid isolation amid terraced fields. You can continue the walk down to the coast, and return via the hilltop of **Ġordan Lighthouse**, or the church of Ta'Pinu.

The **Basilica of Ta'Pinu** is Malta's national shrine to the Virgin Mary and an important centre of pilgrimage. It was built in the 1920s on the site of a chapel where a local woman, Carmela Grima, heard the Virgin speak to her in 1883. Thereafter, numerous miracles were attributed to the intercession of Our Lady of Pinu, and it was decided to replace the old church with a grand new one. Built in a Romanesque style, with an Italianate campanile, the interior of pale golden stone is calming and peaceful. Part of the original chapel, with Carmela Grima's tomb, is incorporated behind the altar. The basilica's name comes from the man, Filippino Gauci, who used to tend the old church – Pinu is the Maltese diminutive for Filippino.

The basilica is open 7 am to 6 pm daily, and closes from 12.30 to 1 pm during Mass. No shorts, mini-skirts or sleeveless dresses are allowed. The track to the top of the hill of Ta'Għammar opposite the church is punctuated by marble statues marking the Stations of the Cross.

Where the road to Għarb from Victoria forks (400m after the turning to Ta'Pinu) is *Jeffrey's Restaurant (☎ 561006)*. Set in a converted farmhouse with a courtyard out the back, it offers rabbit, seafood and vegetarian dishes using fresh produce from the owner's farm. Expect to pay around Lm18 for a meal for two including wine. It's open for dinner only, and closes from November to March.

Bus Nos 2 and 91 go to Għarb; No 61 will take you to Ta'Pinu.

DWEJRA
The village of San Lawrenz, 1km southwest of Għarb, was where the novelist Nicholas Monsarrat (1910-79) lived and worked for four years in the early 1970s. His love for the Maltese Islands is reflected in his novel *The Kappillan of Malta,* which grew out of his experiences here.

A left turn at San Lawrenz leads past the **Ta'Xbiegi Crafts Village** – a miniature clone of Malta's Ta'Qali – and down to Dwejra, where geology and the sea have conspired to produce some of Gozo's most spectacular

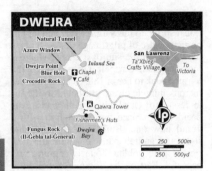

DWEJRA

Natural Tunnel
Azure Window
Dwejra Point
Blue Hole
Crocodile Rock
San Lawrenz
Inland Sea
Ta'Xbiegi Crafts Village
To Victoria
Chapel
Café
Qawra Tower
Fishermen's Huts
Fungus Rock (Il-Gebla tal-General)
Dwejra Bay

0   250   500m
0   250   500yd

coastal scenery. Two vast, underground caverns in the limestone have collapsed to create two circular depressions now occupied by Dwejra Bay and the Inland Sea.

The **Inland Sea** is a cliff-bound lagoon connected to the open sea by a cave that runs for 100m through the headland of Dwejra Point. The cave is big enough for small boats to sail through in calm weather, and the Inland Sea has been used as a fisherman's haven for centuries. Today the fishermen supplement their income by taking tourists on boat trips through the cave.

A few minutes' walk from the Inland Sea is a huge natural arch in the sea-cliffs, known as the **Azure Window**. In the rocks in front of it is another geological freak called the **Blue Hole** – a natural vertical chimney in the limestone, about 10m in diameter and 25m deep, that connects with the open sea through an underwater arch about 8m down. Understandably, it's a very popular dive site. The snorkelling here is excellent too. Between the Inland Sea and the Azure Window is the little **Chapel of St Anne**, built in 1963 on the site of a much older church.

The broad horizontal shelf of rock to the south

of Dwejra Point has been eroded along the geological boundary between the Globigerina Limestone and the Lower Coralline Limestone – the boundary is marked by a layer of many thousands of fossil scallop shells and sand dollars (a kind of flattened, disc-shaped sea-urchin). Just offshore is **Crocodile Rock**. No, nothing to do with Elton John – seen from near Qawra Tower, it looks like a crocodile's head.

Qawra Tower overlooks **Dwejra Bay**. This collapsed cavern has been completely invaded by the sea, and is guarded by the brooding bulk of **Fungus Rock** (see the boxed text). A path below the tower leads to a flight of steps cut into the rock which leads down to some boathouses and a little slipway on the edge of the bay. There is good swimming and sunbathing here, away from the crowd of day trippers who throng the rocks around the Azure Window. For even more peace you can hike right around to the clifftop on the far side of the bay, where the view back over Fungus Rock to Dwejra Point is spectacular.

To get to Dwejra, take bus No 2 or 91 to San Lawrenz, then walk down to the bay (15 to 20 minutes). Bus 91 also goes down to the car park at Dwejra.

MARSALFORN

Marsalforn is Gozo's main holiday resort. The bay of this former fishing village (the name is possibly derived from the Arabic for 'bay of ships') is now lined with an ugly sprawl of hotels and apartment buildings, which is gradually spreading north along the coast towards Qbaijar. Still, it's a low-key resort compared to the fleshpots of Sliema and St Paul's Bay in Malta, and offers some good out-of-season deals on accommodation.

ADRIANA MAMMARELLA

The common dolphin is occasionally sighted from cruise and dive boats off the Gozo coastline.

Fungus Rock

Known in Malti as Il-Ġebla Tal-Ġeneral (The General's Rock), Fungus Rock takes both of its names from the fact that the Knights of St John used to collect a rare plant from the rock's summit. The plant *(Cynomorium coccineus)* is dark brown and club-shaped, and grows to about 18cm in height. It is parasitic and has no green leaves, which is why it was called a fungus or, in Malti, *gherq tal-Ġeneral* (the General's root). It is native to North Africa, and Fungus Rock is the only place in Europe that it is found.

Extracts made from the plant had powerful pharmaceutical qualities, and were said to staunch bleeding and prevent infection when used to dress wounds. It cured dysentery and ulcers, and was also used to treat apoplexy and venereal diseases. It was long known to the Arabs as 'the treasure among drugs', and when a general of the Knights of St John discovered it growing on a rock on Gozo, he knew he had struck gold. A rope was strung between the mainland and the rock, and harvesters were shuttled back and forth in a miniature, one-man cable car. Qawra Tower was built to guard the precious resource. The plant extract was much in demand in the Knights' hospitals, and was sold at a high price to the various courts of Europe.

❋❋

Orientation & Information

Most of the restaurants, hotels and guesthouses are clustered around the waterfront. You can change money at the Bank of Valletta on the promenade and the HSBC bank near the Calypso Hotel – both have ATMs and 24-hour money-changing machines.

Things to See & Do

There is absolutely nothing to see in the town itself. At the head of the bay is a tiny scrap of sand, but better swimming and sunbathing can be found on the rocks out to the west. You can hike eastward over the hill to Calypso's Cave and Ir-Ramla in about 45 minutes.

Xwieni Bay, a 15-minute walk to the west, has a sandy beach beneath a headland with a small fort. Beyond Xwieni the rocky shore has been carved into a patchwork of **salt pans** which are still worked in summer.

Another 20-minute hike beyond the salt pans will bring you to the narrow, cliff-bound inlet of **Wied il-Għasri**. Here a narrow staircase cut into the rock leads down to a tiny shingle beach at the head of the inlet. There is good swimming and snorkelling here when the sea is calm. The beach is best avoided in rough weather when the waves come crashing up the narrow defile.

Places to Stay

Lantern Guesthouse (☎ 562365 or 554186, fax 556285) on Triq il-Munġbell has a lively bar and restaurant on the ground floor, and rooms upstairs for Lm6/4 per person in high/low season. There's also a self-catering flat for up to four people for Lm8 per night.

Marsalforn Hotel (☎ 556147) occupies its own little traffic island at the end of Triq ir-Rabat. B&B is Lm6 per person and self-catering flats for four are Lm10 to Lm12 per day. The hotel also hires out bicycles.

The *Atlantis Hotel (☎ 554685, fax 555661, @ atlantis@digigate.net)* is above the west side of the bay on Triq il-Qolla. It extends to both sides of the street, has indoor and outdoor pools, a fitness centre and a diving school and shop. The well-appointed rooms are excellent value in winter at only Lm8 per person B&B for a room with en suite bath, balcony and satellite TV, rising to Lm16.50 in high season.

Calypso Hotel (☎ 562000, fax 562012), down by the harbour, has rooms overlooking the bay for Lm14.50/6.50 per person B&B in high/low season. Rooms facing inland are Lm12/5.50. The hotel has many facilities, including three restaurants and a diving school.

GOZO & COMINO

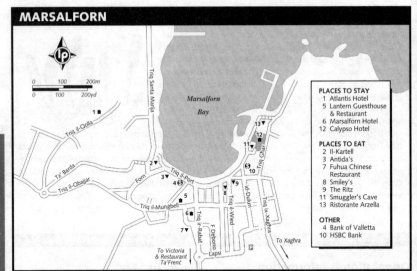

MARSALFORN

PLACES TO STAY
1 Atlantis Hotel
5 Lantern Guesthouse & Restaurant
6 Marsalforn Hotel
12 Calypso Hotel

PLACES TO EAT
2 Il-Kartell
3 Antida's
7 Fuhua Chinese Restaurant
8 Smiley's
9 The Ritz
11 Smuggler's Cave
13 Ristorante Arzella

OTHER
4 Bank of Valletta
10 HSBC Bank

Places to Eat

The restaurants are clustered around the harbour, and there's not really a great deal to distinguish between them all. *Smiley's* (☎ 553096), on the square by the waterfront, is the cheapest, but it's pretty basic – burgers cost 60c, fish and chips Lm1.30. *Ristorante Arzella*, on a terrace suspended over the east side of the bay, is similarly priced but also has Maltese specialities like timpana (Lm1.50) and braġioli (Lm3.20).

The *Smuggler's Cave* (☎ 551005 or 551983), under the Calypso Hotel, has cheap pizzas (Lm1.15 to Lm2) and burgers (55c), but feels more like a British seaside restaurant than a Maltese one.

The Ritz (☎ 558392) on Triq il-Wied is a cafe-bar that sells snacks and sandwiches, while the *Italian Pizza Co* next door offers takeaway pizzas. *Antida's* on the promenade has a nice little dining room and has fresh fish and pasta dishes available for Lm2 to Lm4.50.

Il-Kartell (☎ 556918) is housed in a couple of old boathouses in the south-west corner of the bay. The menu is mostly pizza and pasta in the Lm1.30 to Lm1.60 range, along with fresh fish and daily specials

chalked up on the blackboard. *Coniglio Alla Gozitana* (Gozo-style rabbit braised with red wine and peas) is Lm3.10.

Dragon Chinese Restaurant (☎ 562000) in the Calypso Hotel and the *Fuhua Chinese Restaurant* on Triq ir-Rabat both offer a choice of sit-down or takeaway meals, with main courses priced from Lm2.80 to Lm3.20.

Restaurant Ta'Frenċ (☎ 553888) is about 1.5km south of Marsalforn on the road to Victoria. It's set in a lovely old farmhouse and has an impressive menu of French, Italian and Maltese dishes, but at Lm12 to Lm15 a head it's best saved for special occasions.

XAGĦRA

The pretty village of Xagħra (**shaa**-ra) spreads across the flat summit of the hill east of Victoria, seemingly lost in a dream of times past. The early-19th-century Church of Our Lady of Victory looks down benignly on the tree-lined village square, where a farmer trundles through on his miniature tractor, a woman pushes a pram loaded with a bale of hay, and old men sit and chat in the shade of the oleanders.

Orientation & Information

The main road from Mġarr and Victoria zigzags up the hill from the south and passes the site of the temples of Ġgantija before joining the village square in front of the church. A left turn here leads back towards Victoria on a rough, minor road. A right turn leads past the school and post office to the Marsalforn road. The Bank of Valletta is at the west end of the square, and there are public toilets beside the police station just south of the church on Vjal it-18 Ta'Settembru.

Things to See

A narrow lane beside the school leads to the restored **Ta'Kola Windmill**. Built in 1725, the windmill is now somewhat of a tourist attraction, housing an interesting museum of country life, with exhibits of woodworking tools, farm equipment and period bedroom and living quarters. Best of all is the climb up the narrow stairs to see the original milling gear complete with millstones. The windmill is open 7.45 am to 2 pm daily from 16 June to 30 September, and 8.15 am to 5 pm Monday to Saturday and 8.15 am to 4 pm on Sunday from 1 October to 15 June. It's closed on public holidays. The admission price is Lm1, but under-19s and over-65s get in free. The ticket also includes admission to the megalithic temples of Ġgantija.

In the back streets to the north of the village square lie **Xerri's Grotto** (☎ 552733) and **Nino's Cave**. These underground caverns, complete with stalactites and stalagmites, are unusual in that they are both entered through private houses. Having discovered the caves beneath their homes, the owners decided to cash in on the tourist potential.

Xerri's Grotto was discovered in 1923 when Antonio Xerri was digging a well. It's the bigger, deeper and more interesting of the two. Opening times are at the discretion

GOZO & COMINO

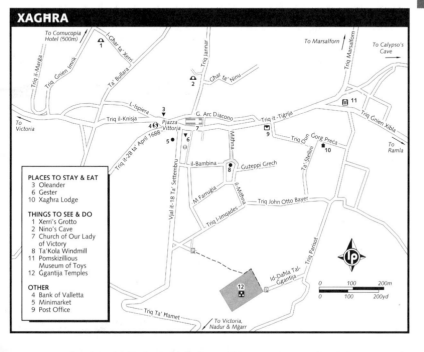

XAGHRA

PLACES TO STAY & EAT
3 Oleander
6 Gester
10 Xaghra Lodge

THINGS TO SEE & DO
1 Xerri's Grotto
2 Nino's Cave
7 Church of Our Lady of Victory
8 Ta'Kola Windmill
11 Pomskizillious Museum of Toys
12 Ġgantija Temples

OTHER
4 Bank of Valletta
5 Minimarket
9 Post Office

Edward Lear in Gozo

Edward Lear (1812-1888), the English landscape painter and nonsense poet (Lear popularised the limerick as a form of comic verse), spent much of his life travelling around the Mediterranean. He visited Gozo in 1866, and described the scenery as 'pomskizillious and gromphiberous, being as no words can describe its magnificence'.

The Pomskizillious Museum of Toys in Xagħra has a life-size wax effigy of Lear with his cat, Foss.

✳✳✳✳✳✳✳✳✳✳✳✳✳✳✳✳✳✳✳

of the owners, but are generally 9 am to 5 pm in summer. Entry costs 50c at Xerri's and 35c at Nino's.

At the east end of town the road forks – left for Marsalforn, right for Ir-Ramla. A few metres along the Ramla road on the left is the **Pomskizillious Museum of Toys** (☎ 562489). Popular with kids, it's open 10 am to noon and 3 to 6 pm Monday to Saturday from May till mid-October; 10 am to 1 pm Thursday to Saturday in April; and 10 am to 1 pm on Saturday and public holidays only in winter. The admission cost is 85c for adults and 35c for children aged six to 12; children under six get in free.

Signposts near the Pomskizillious Museum of Toys point the way through the maze of minor roads east of Xagħra down to **Calypso's Cave** overlooking the sandy beach of Ir-Ramla – it's a 30-minute walk from the village square.

The cave itself is hardly worth the hike – it's just a hollow under an overhang at the top of the cliff – but the view over Ir-Ramla is lovely. On a calm day visitors can usually see the remains of an artificial reef extending into the sea off the eastern headland of the bay. This was part of the defences built by the Knights of St John to prevent attackers landing on the beach. In theory, the enemy ships would run aground on the reef, where they would be attacked using a couple of fougasses (see the boxed text 'The Fougasse' in the North-West Malta chapter).

Ġgantija

Located on the crest of the hill to the south of Xagħra, the megalithic temples of Ġgantija (dje-**gant**-ee-ya) command a splendid view over most of southern Gozo and beyond to Comino and Malta. As the name implies (ġgantija means 'giantess') these are the largest of the megalithic temples found in the Maltese Islands – the walls stand over 6m high, and the two temples together span over 40m.

Along with Ta'Ħaġrat and Skorba on Malta, Ġgantija is thought to be the oldest of Malta's temples, dating from the period 3600 to 3000 BC. Both temples face towards the south-east, and both have five semi-circular niches within. The south temple (on the left) is the older, and is entered across a huge threshold slab with four holes at each side, thought to be for libations. The first niche on the right contains an altar with some spiral decoration – a pillar with a snake carved on it is now in the Archaeological Museum in Victoria. The left-hand niche in the inner chamber has a well-preserved trilithon altar; on the right is a circular hearth stone and a bench altar.

There is little of interest in the north temple. The outer wall of the temple complex

Calypso's Isle

Gozo is one of the half dozen or so contenders for the title of Calypso's Isle – the mythical island of Ogygia described in Homer's *Odyssey* where the nymph Calypso seduced the hero Odysseus and kept him captive for seven years. But she could not overcome his longing for his home in Ithaca, and Zeus eventually sent Hermes to command her to release him.

If the cave above Ir-Ramla on Gozo was really Calypso's hideaway, then it's no wonder that Odysseus was keen to get home. The view may be pretty and the island delightful, but it's a long, hot and scratchy climb up from the beach, and the cramped living quarters leave a lot to be desired.

✳✳✳✳✳✳✳✳✳✳✳✳✳✳✳✳✳✳✳

is impressive in scale. The largest of the megaliths measures 6m by 4m and weighs around 57 tonnes, and the wall may originally have stood up to 16m tall.

Ġgantija is open 7.45 am to 2 pm daily from 16 June to 30 September, and 8.15 am to 5 pm Monday to Saturday and 8.15 am to 4 pm on Sunday from 1 October to 15 June (closed on public holidays). Entry costs Lm1; under-19s and over-65s get in free. The ticket includes admission to Ta'Kola Windmill in Xagħra.

Places to Stay & Eat

Xagħra Lodge (*☎/fax 562362, ✆ xaghra lodge@waldonet.net.mt*) in Triq Dun Ġorġ Preċa is a cosy little guesthouse run by an English couple. All rooms have en suite bathroom and balcony, and there's a fair-sized pool out the back. A twin or double costs Lm8/10 per person B&B in low/high season, with a Lm4/5 single supplement.

The *Cornucopia Hotel* (*☎ 556486, 553866 or 552633, fax 552910*) is set in and around a converted farmhouse at the far end of Triq Ġnien Imrik, about 1km north of the village square. Four-star accommodation is available in hotel rooms, villas, bungalows and apartments. The rates for B&B in a twin room range from Lm11.25 per person in winter, to Lm16.50 per person in high season.

Both hotels have restaurants, but there are two good eating places in the village centre. *Oleander* (*☎ 557230*), on the village square, has fresh pastas for Lm2.50, Maltese braġioli or rabbit in garlic and wine for Lm3.30, and steak and seafood dishes for Lm4 to Lm5. Service can be slow, but it's a pleasant place to while away an evening. It's open 7 to 11 pm Monday to Saturday.

Gester (*☎ 556621*) is just off the square on Vjal it-18 Ta'Settembru. This little restaurant, run by two sisters, is very basic, but the cooking is authentic home-made Gozitan and the prices are a bargain. You can fill up on braġioli for around Lm2.50.

For those who prefer to picnic or self-cater, there's a handy *mini-market* across the street from Gester.

Getting There & Away

Bus Nos 64 and 65 run between Victoria and Xagħra.

NADUR

With a population of 3500, Nadur is Gozo's 'second city', spreading along a high ridge to the east of Victoria. In Malti, Nadur means 'look-out', and a 17th-century watchtower overlooks the Comino sea lanes from the western end of the ridge.

Nadur's ornate **Church of Sts Peter & Paul** was built in the late 18th century – the entrance is framed between white statues of the two saints, giving the church its local nickname of *iż Żewġ* (the pair). The interior is richly decorated with marble sculptures, and the vault is covered with 150 paintings.

In Triq il-Kappillan, a block south of the church, is the **Kelinu Grima Maritime Museum** (*☎ 565226*), a private collection of ship models, relics and maritime memorabilia. It's open 9 am to 4.45 pm Monday to Saturday, and entry is Lm1, or 50c for kids.

If you're peckish, you can grab a pizza from *Rabokk Snack Bar* on the square opposite the church, or head to *Martin's Diner* (*☎ 558974*), beside the football pitch on the road that zig-zags down towards Mġarr.

To get to Nadur, take Bus Nos 42 and 43 from Victoria.

AROUND NADUR

Narrow country roads radiate northward from Nadur to three beaches, all signposted. **Ir-Ramla** is the biggest and best sandy beach on Gozo, and one of the prettiest in the islands – the strand of reddish-gold contrasts picturesquely with the blue of the sea and white statue of the Virgin Mary. As such, it is usually heaving with people in summer, when cafes, souvenir stalls and water-sports facilities abound. It's much quieter and more pleasant in spring and autumn, and in winter you can have the place almost to your (goose-pimpled) self. The minimal remains of a **Roman villa** are hidden among the bamboo behind the beach, and Calypso's Cave (see the Xagħra section earlier in this chapter) looks down from the hilltop to the west.

The next beach to the east is **San Blas**, a tiny, rock-strewn bay with some patches of coarse sand backed by steep, terraced fields with prickly pear hedges. It's a place to take a picnic lunch and a good book, and perhaps a mask and fins for snorkelling. There are no facilities, and parking space for only one or two cars on the very narrow track above the bay. You can walk there from Nadur in 20 to 30 minutes.

Dahlet Qorrot, the third bay, is popular with local weekenders. There's a small sandy beach, but most of the swimming is off the rocks beside the rows of little boathouses. There's usually plenty of space to park, and you can buy drinks and snacks in summer only.

QALA

The village of Qala (a-la) has little to see except for a couple of 18th-century **windmills**. The road east of the village square leads down to the coast at **Hondoq ir-Rummien**, a little cove with a scrap of sand, bathing ladders on the rocks, and benches with a view across the water to Comino.

St Joseph Guesthouse and Restaurant (☎ 556573), just past the village square on the road to Hondoq ir-Rummien, is open for lunch and dinner and has rooms to let for Lm5 per person.

Comino

Comino (or Kemmuna in Malti) is a small and barren chunk of limestone wedged between Malta and Gozo. The only inhabitants are the guests and staff of the island's single hotel, though they are joined in summer by hordes of day-trippers from Malta. In winter, when the hotel is closed, only a handful people remain on the island.

ORIENTATION & INFORMATION

Comino is only 2.5km by 1.5km in size, so it's difficult to get lost. St Mary's Tower, the only landmark of note, is visible from almost everywhere on the island. The main part of the Comino Hotel is on San Niklaw Bay, and the Comino Bungalows are on Santa Marija Bay, 500m to the west. A

Spice Island

Comino is named after the herb cumin (*Cuminum cyminum*), which was once cultivated on the island and harvested for its seeds. Cumin seeds, roasted and ground, are much used in North African, Middle Eastern, Asian and Latin American cuisines, and are an essential flavouring for many curries, mixed spices and chutneys.

✳✳✳✳✳✳✳✳✳✳✳✳✳✳✳✳✳✳✳✳

---

rough track lined with oleander trees, rather grandly named Triq Congreve, runs from Santa Marija Bay south to St Mary's Tower. Side tracks lead to the Blue Lagoon and San Niklaw Bay.

Apart from the public toilets above the Blue Lagoon, all facilities on the island – including telephones and currency exchange – belong to the hotel, and they aren't too keen on nonresidents using them.

THINGS TO SEE & DO

The only sights to see on Comino are the little **Chapel of Our Lady's Return from Egypt** at Santa Marija Bay and **St Mary's Tower**, built by the Knights in 1618. It was once part of the chain of signal towers between Gozo and Mdina but today it is just an observation post used by the Maltese military.

The island's main attraction is the **Blue Lagoon**, a sheltered cove between the west end of the island and the uninhabited islet of Cominotto (Kemmunett in Malti). The cove has a white-sand sea-bed and beautifully clear turquoise waters. In summer the bay is inundated with people each day between around 10 am and 4 pm, which detracts a little from the desert island atmosphere. The southern end of the lagoon is roped off to keep boats out, and there is excellent swimming and snorkelling here. If you are staying at the hotel, of course, you can enjoy the lagoon in relative peace in the early morning and late afternoon.

PLACES TO STAY & EAT

Comino Hotel & Bungalows (☎ 529821, fax 529826, ✉ cominohtl@digigate.net) is the only place to stay on the island, and it is only open from April to October. The four-star hotel has 150 rooms at San Niklaw Bay and 45 self-catering bungalows at Santa Marija Bay. A garden view room costs Lm28 per person per night for half board, and a sea view room is Lm32 per person. The single room supplement is Lm8, and full board costs Lm6 extra.

The hotel has a private beach (in San Niklaw Bay), swimming pools, tennis courts, water-sports facilities and a diving school. Day-trippers can use the hotel facilities for a stiff fee of Lm10 a day (Lm12 at weekends), but this must be arranged in advance through a travel agent or by phoning ☎ 529827. The price includes lunch, but not the ferry ticket.

GETTING THERE & AWAY

The Comino Hotel runs its own ferry service, with eight crossings a day from Ċirkewwa in Malta (between 7.30 am and 6.30 pm) and Mġarr in Gozo (between 6.30 am and 11 pm). The ferry is free to hotel guests, but costs Lm2 return for nonresidents. The ferry does not run from November to March when the hotel is closed.

You can also make a day trip from Sliema and Buġibba in Malta, and Xlendi in Gozo.

Language

Malti – the native language of Malta – is a member of the Semitic language group, which also includes Arabic, Hebrew and Amharic. It's thought by some to be a direct descendant of the language spoken by the Phoenicians, but most linguists consider it to be related to the Arabic dialects of western North Africa. Malti is the only Semitic language that is written in a Latin script.

Both Malti and English are official languages in Malta, and almost everyone is bilingual. Travellers will have no trouble at all getting by in English at all times. However, it's always good to learn at least a few words of the native language, and the sections that follow will provide a basic introduction to Malti.

If you want to learn more about Malti, look out for *Teach Yourself Maltese* by Joseph Aquilina or *Learn Maltese – Why Not?* by Joseph Vella. There is a small range of pocket dictionaries and phrasebooks available in bookshops in Malta. They are of variable quality and usefulness – check the content carefully before buying.

Pronunciation

There are 29 letters in the Maltese alphabet. Individual letters in Malti aren't too diffcult to pronounce once you learn the rules, but putting them together to make any kind of sense is a major achievement. Most are pronounced as they are in English. The exceptions are:

ċ   as the 'ch' in child
g   as in 'good'
ġ   'soft' as the 'j' in 'job'
għ   silent; lengthens the preceding or following vowel
h   silent, as in 'hour'
ħ   as the 'h' in 'hand'
j   as the 'y' in 'yellow'
ij   as the 'igh' in 'high'
ej   as the 'ay' in 'day'

Signs

Miftuħ	Open
Magħluq	Closed
Dħul	Entrance
Ħruġ	Exit
Triq	Street
Vjalq	Avenue
Misraħ	Square
Sqaq	Lane/Alley
Pulizija	Police
Twaletta	Toilet
Rġiel	Men
Nisa	Women

q   a glottal stop; like the missing 't' in the Cockney pronunciation of 'that' or between the two syllables in 'bottle'
x   as the 'sh' in 'shop'
z   as the 'ts' in 'bits'
ż   soft as in 'buzz'

Basics

Hello.	*Merħba.*
Good morning/ Good day.	*Bonġu.*
Good evening.	*Bonswa.*
Goodbye.	*Saħħa.*
Yes/No.	*Iva/Le.*
Please.	*Jekk jogħġbok.*
Thank you.	*Grazzi.*
Excuse me.	*Skużani.*
Do you speak English?	*Titkellem bl-ingliż?* (informal)
How much is it?	*Kemm?*
What's your name?	*X'ismek?*
My name is ...	*Jisimni ...*

Getting Around

When does the boat leave/arrive?
Meta jitlaq/jasal il-vapur?
When does the bus leave/arrive?
Meta titlaq/jasal il-karozza?
I'd like to hire a car/bicycle.
Nixtieq nikri karozza/rota.
left luggage
ħallejt il-bagalji

I'd like a ... ticket. *Nixtieq biljett ...*
  one-way   *'one-way'*
  return   *'return'*
  1st class   *'1st class'*
  2nd class   *'2nd class'*

Where is a/the ...? *Fejn hu ...?*
Go straight ahead. *Mur dritt.*
Turn left.   *Dur fuq il-lemin.*
Turn right.   *Dur fuq ix-xellug.*
near   *il-viċin*
far   *il-boghod*

Around Town

... embassy   *ambaxxata ...*
bank   *bank*
castle   *kastell*
chemist/pharmacy   *ispiżerija*
church   *knisja*
hotel   *hotel/il-lukanda*
market   *suq*
museum   *mużew*
post office   *posta*
public telephone   *telefon pubbliku*
shop   *hanut*
stamp   *timbru*

What time does it   *Fix'hin jiftah/jaghlaq?*
  open/close?

Time & Days

What's the time?   *X'hin hu?*
today   *illum*
tomorrow   *ghada*
yesterday   *il-bierah*
morning   *fil-ghodu*
afternoon   *wara nofs in-nhar*

Monday   *it-tnejn*
Tuesday   *it-tlieta*
Wednesday   *l-erbgha*
Thursday   *il-hamis*
Friday   *il-gimgha*
Saturday   *is-sibt*
Sunday   *il-hadd*

Emergencies

Help!   *Ajjut!*
Call a doctor!   *Qibghad ghat-tabib!*
Police!   *Pulizija!*
I'm lost.   *Ninsab mitluf.*
hospital   *sptar*
ambulance   *ambulans*

Numbers

0	*xejn*
1	*wiehed*
2	*tnejn*
3	*tlieta*
4	*erbgha*
5	*hamsa*
6	*sitta*
7	*sebgha*
8	*tmienja*
9	*disgha*
10	*ghaxra*
11	*hdax*
12	*tnax*
13	*tlettax*
14	*erbatax*
15	*hmistax*
16	*sittax*
17	*sbatax*
18	*tmintax*
19	*dsatax*
20	*ghoxrin*
30	*tletin*
40	*erbghin*
50	*hamsin*
60	*sittin*
70	*sebghin*
80	*tmienin*
90	*disghin*
100	*mija*
1000	*elf*

one million   *miljun*

Glossary

auberge – the residence of an individual langue of the Knights of St John

bajja – bay
bieb – gate
belt – city

ċimiterju – cemetery

daħla – creek
dawret – bypass
dgħajsa – a traditional oar-powered ferry boat

festa, festi (pl) - feast day
foss – ditch

ġnien – garden
għajn – spring (of water)
għar – cave

kajjik - fishing boat
kappillan – parish priest
knisja – church
kbira – big, main
kortin – court
kwartiet – quarter, neighbourhood

langue – a division of the Knights of St John, based on nationality
luzzu - fishing boat

marsa – harbour
mdina – fortified town, citadel
mina – arch, gate
misraħ – square
mitħna – windmill
mużew – museum

parroċċa – parish
passeggiata - evening stroll
pjazza – square

plajja – beach, seashore
pont – bridge
pulizija – police

rabat – town outside the walls of a citadel
ramla – bay, beach
ras – point, headland
rdum – cliff

sqaq – alley, lane
suq – market
sur – bastion

telgħa – hill
torri – tower, castle
trejqa – junction
triq – street, road

vjal – avenue

wied – valley

xatt – wharf, waterfront

żebbuġa – olive

Terms used to describe fortifications:

bastion – a defensive work with two faces and two flanks, projecting from the line of the rampart
cavalier – a defensive work inside the main fortification, rising above the level of the main rampart to give covering fire
curtain – a stretch of rampart linking two bastions, with a parapet along the top
demi-bastion – a half-bastion with only one face and one flank
ravelin – a defensive work outside the main rampart, usually with two faces meeting at an angle and open to the rear
vedette – a look-out point

LONELY PLANET

You already know that Lonely Planet produces more than this one guidebook, but you might not be aware of the other products we have on this region. Here is a selection of titles which you may want to check out as well:

Read this First: Europe
ISBN 1 86450 136 7
US$14.99 • UK£8.99

Europe phrasebook
ISBN 1 86450 224 X
US$8.99 • UK£4.99

Europe on a shoestring
ISBN 1 86450 150 2
US$24.99 • UK£14.99

Mediterranean Europe
ISBN 1 86450 154 5
US$27.99 • UK£15.99

Italy
ISBN 1 86450 352 1
US$24.99 • UK£14.99

Sicily
ISBN 1 86450 099 9
US$15.99 • UK£9.99

Available wherever books are sold.

Lonely Planet Guides by Region

Lonely Planet is known worldwide for publishing practical, reliable and no-nonsense travel information in our guides and on our Web site. The Lonely Planet list covers just about every accessible part of the world. Currently there are 16 series: Travel guides, Shoestring guides, Condensed guides, Phrasebooks, Read This First, Healthy Travel, Walking guides, Cycling guides, Watching Wildlife guides, Pisces Diving & Snorkeling guides, City Maps, Road Atlases, Out to Eat, World Food, Journeys travel literature and Pictorials.

AFRICA Africa on a shoestring • Botswana • Cairo • Cairo City Map • Cape Town • Cape Town City Map • East Africa • Egypt • Egyptian Arabic phrasebook • Ethiopia, Eritrea & Djibouti • Ethiopian Amharic phrasebook • The Gambia & Senegal • Healthy Travel Africa • Kenya • Malawi • Morocco • Moroccan Arabic phrasebook • Mozambique • Namibia • Read This First: Africa • South Africa, Lesotho & Swaziland • Southern Africa • Southern Africa Road Atlas • Swahili phrasebook • Tanzania, Zanzibar & Pemba • Trekking in East Africa • Tunisia • Watching Wildlife East Africa • Watching Wildlife Southern Africa • West Africa • World Food Morocco • Zambia • Zimbabwe, Botswana & Namibia
Travel Literature: Mali Blues: Traveling to an African Beat • The Rainbird: A Central African Journey • Songs to an African Sunset: A Zimbabwean Story

AUSTRALIA & THE PACIFIC Aboriginal Australia & the Torres Strait Islands •Auckland • Australia • Australian phrasebook • Australia Road Atlas • Cycling Australia • Cycling New Zealand • Fiji • Fijian phrasebook • Healthy Travel Australia, NZ & the Pacific • Islands of Australia's Great Barrier Reef • Melbourne • Melbourne City Map • Micronesia • New Caledonia • New South Wales • New Zealand • Northern Territory • Outback Australia • Out to Eat – Melbourne • Out to Eat – Sydney • Papua New Guinea • Pidgin phrasebook • Queensland • Rarotonga & the Cook Islands • Samoa • Solomon Islands • South Australia • South Pacific • South Pacific phrasebook • Sydney • Sydney City Map • Sydney Condensed • Tahiti & French Polynesia • Tasmania • Tonga • Tramping in New Zealand • Vanuatu • Victoria • Walking in Australia • Watching Wildlife Australia • Western Australia
Travel Literature: Islands in the Clouds: Travels in the Highlands of New Guinea • Kiwi Tracks: A New Zealand Journey • Sean & David's Long Drive

CENTRAL AMERICA & THE CARIBBEAN Bahamas, Turks & Caicos • Baja California • Belize, Guatemala & Yucatán • Bermuda • Central America on a shoestring • Costa Rica • Costa Rica Spanish phrasebook • Cuba • Cycling Cuba • Dominican Republic & Haiti • Eastern Caribbean • Guatemala • Havana • Healthy Travel Central & South America • Jamaica • Mexico • Mexico City • Panama • Puerto Rico • Read This First: Central & South America • Virgin Islands • World Food Caribbean • World Food Mexico • Yucatán
Travel Literature: Green Dreams: Travels in Central America

EUROPE Amsterdam • Amsterdam City Map • Amsterdam Condensed • Andalucía • Athens • Austria • Baltic States phrasebook • Barcelona • Barcelona City Map • Belgium & Luxembourg • Berlin • Berlin City Map • Britain • British phrasebook • Brussels, Bruges & Antwerp • Brussels City Map • Budapest • Budapest City Map • Canary Islands • Catalunya & the Costa Brava • Central Europe • Central Europe phrasebook • Copenhagen • Corfu & the Ionians • Corsica • Crete • Crete Condensed • Croatia • Cycling Britain • Cycling France • Cyprus • Czech & Slovak Republics • Czech phrasebook • Denmark • Dublin • Dublin City Map • Dublin Condensed • Eastern Europe • Eastern Europe phrasebook • Edinburgh • Edinburgh City Map • England • Estonia, Latvia & Lithuania • Europe on a shoestring • Europe phrasebook • Finland • Florence • Florence City Map • France • Frankfurt City Map • Frankfurt Condensed • French phrasebook • Georgia, Armenia & Azerbaijan • Germany • German phrasebook • Greece • Greek Islands • Greek phrasebook • Hungary • Iceland, Greenland & the Faroe Islands • Ireland • Italian phrasebook • Italy • Kraków • Lisbon • The Loire • London • London City Map • London Condensed • Madrid • Madrid City Map • Malta • Mediterranean Europe • Milan, Turin & Genoa • Moscow • Munich • Netherlands • Normandy • Norway • Out to Eat – London • Out to Eat – Paris • Paris • Paris City Map • Paris Condensed • Poland • Polish phrasebook • Portugal • Portuguese phrasebook • Prague • Prague City Map • Provence & the Côte d'Azur • Read This First: Europe • Rhodes & the Dodecanese • Romania & Moldova • Rome • Rome City Map • Rome Condensed • Russia, Ukraine & Belarus • Russian phrasebook • Scandinavian & Baltic Europe • Scandinavian phrasebook • Scotland • Sicily • Slovenia • South-West France • Spain • Spanish phrasebook • Stockholm • St Petersburg • St Petersburg City Map • Sweden • Switzerland • Tuscany • Ukrainian phrasebook • Venice • Vienna • Wales • Walking in Britain • Walking in France • Walking in Ireland • Walking in Italy • Walking in Scotland • Walking in Spain • Walking in Switzerland • Western Europe • World Food France • World Food Greece • World Food Ireland • World Food Italy • World Food Spain **Travel Literature:** After Yugoslavia • Love and War in the Apennines • The Olive Grove: Travels in Greece • On the Shores of the Mediterranean • Round Ireland in Low Gear • A Small Place in Italy

Lonely Planet Mail Order

L onely Planet products are distributed worldwide. They are also available by mail order from Lonely Planet, so if you have difficulty finding a title please write to us. North and South American residents should write to 150 Linden St, Oakland, CA 94607, USA; European and African residents should write to 10a Spring Place, London NW5 3BH, UK; and residents of other countries to Locked Bag 1, Footscray, Victoria 3011, Australia.

INDIAN SUBCONTINENT & THE INDIAN OCEAN Bangladesh • Bengali phrasebook • Bhutan • Delhi • Goa • Healthy Travel Asia & India • Hindi & Urdu phrasebook • India • India & Bangladesh City Map • Indian Himalaya • Karakoram Highway • Kathmandu City Map • Kerala • Madagascar • Maldives • Mauritius, Réunion & Seychelles • Mumbai (Bombay) • Nepal • Nepali phrasebook • North India • Pakistan • Rajasthan • Read This First: Asia & India • South India • Sri Lanka • Sri Lanka phrasebook • Tibet • Tibetan phrasebook • Trekking in the Indian Himalaya • Trekking in the Karakoram & Hindukush • Trekking in the Nepal Himalaya • World Food India **Travel Literature:** The Age of Kali: Indian Travels and Encounters • Hello Goodnight: A Life of Goa • In Rajasthan • Maverick in Madagascar • A Season in Heaven: True Tales from the Road to Kathmandu • Shopping for Buddhas • A Short Walk in the Hindu Kush • Slowly Down the Ganges

MIDDLE EAST & CENTRAL ASIA Bahrain, Kuwait & Qatar • Central Asia • Central Asia phrasebook • Dubai • Farsi (Persian) phrasebook • Hebrew phrasebook • Iran • Israel & the Palestinian Territories • Istanbul • Istanbul City Map • Istanbul to Cairo • Istanbul to Kathmandu • Jerusalem • Jerusalem City Map • Jordan • Lebanon • Middle East • Oman & the United Arab Emirates • Syria • Turkey • Turkish phrasebook • World Food Turkey • Yemen **Travel Literature:** Black on Black: Iran Revisited • Breaking Ranks: Turbulent Travels in the Promised Land • The Gates of Damascus • Kingdom of the Film Stars: Journey into Jordan

NORTH AMERICA Alaska • Boston • Boston City Map • Boston Condensed • British Columbia • California & Nevada • California Condensed • Canada • Chicago • Chicago City Map • Chicago Condensed • Florida • Georgia & the Carolinas • Great Lakes • Hawaii • Hiking in Alaska • Hiking in the USA • Honolulu & Oahu City Map • Las Vegas • Los Angeles • Los Angeles City Map • Louisiana & the Deep South • Miami • Miami City Map • Montreal • New England • New Orleans • New Orleans City Map • New York City • New York City City Map • New York City Condensed • New York, New Jersey & Pennsylvania • Oahu • Out to Eat – San Francisco • Pacific Northwest • Rocky Mountains • San Diego & Tijuana • San Francisco • San Francisco City Map • Seattle • Seattle City Map • Southwest • Texas • Toronto • USA • USA phrasebook • Vancouver • Vancouver City Map • Virginia & the Capital Region • Washington, DC • Washington, DC City Map • World Food New Orleans **Travel Literature:** Caught Inside: A Surfer's Year on the California Coast • Drive Thru America

NORTH-EAST ASIA Beijing • Beijing City Map • Cantonese phrasebook • China • Hiking in Japan • Hong Kong & Macau • Hong Kong City Map • Hong Kong Condensed • Japan • Japanese phrasebook • Korea • Korean phrasebook • Kyoto • Mandarin phrasebook • Mongolia • Mongolian phrasebook • Seoul • Shanghai • South-West China • Taiwan • Tokyo • Tokyo Condensed • World Food Hong Kong • World Food Japan **Travel Literature:** In Xanadu: A Quest • Lost Japan

SOUTH AMERICA Argentina, Uruguay & Paraguay • Bolivia • Brazil • Brazilian phrasebook • Buenos Aires • Buenos Aires City Map • Chile & Easter Island • Colombia • Ecuador & the Galapagos Islands • Healthy Travel Central & South America • Latin American Spanish phrasebook • Peru • Quechua phrasebook • Read This First: Central & South America • Rio de Janeiro • Rio de Janeiro City Map • Santiago de Chile • South America on a shoestring • Trekking in the Patagonian Andes • Venezuela **Travel Literature:** Full Circle: A South American Journey

SOUTH-EAST ASIA Bali & Lombok • Bangkok • Bangkok City Map • Burmese phrasebook • Cambodia • Cycling Vietnam, Laos & Cambodia • East Timor phrasebook • Hanoi • Healthy Travel Asia & India • Hill Tribes phrasebook • Ho Chi Minh City (Saigon) • Indonesia • Indonesian phrasebook • Indonesia's Eastern Islands • Java • Lao phrasebook • Laos • Malay phrasebook • Malaysia, Singapore & Brunei • Myanmar (Burma) • Philippines • Pilipino (Tagalog) phrasebook • Read This First: Asia & India • Singapore • Singapore City Map • South-East Asia on a shoestring • South-East Asia phrasebook • Thailand • Thailand's Islands & Beaches • Thailand, Vietnam, Laos & Cambodia Road Atlas • Thai phrasebook • Vietnam • Vietnamese phrasebook • World Food Indonesia • World Food Thailand • World Food Vietnam

ALSO AVAILABLE: Antarctica • The Arctic • The Blue Man: Tales of Travel, Love and Coffee • Brief Encounters: Stories of Love, Sex & Travel • Buddhist Stupas in Asia: The Shape of Perfection • Chasing Rickshaws • The Last Grain Race • Lonely Planet ... On the Edge: Adventurous Escapades from Around the World • Lonely Planet Unpacked • Lonely Planet Unpacked Again • Not the Only Planet: Science Fiction Travel Stories • Ports of Call: A Journey by Sea • Sacred India • Travel Photography: A Guide to Taking Better Pictures • Travel with Children • Tuvalu: Portrait of an Island Nation

Index

Text

Bold indicates maps.

Boxed Text

MAP LEGEND

CITY ROUTES

—Freeway—	Freeway	= = = =	Unsealed Road
—Highway—	Primary Road	→	One Way Street
—Road—	Secondary Road		Pedestrian Street
—Street—	Street		Stepped Street
—Lane—	Lane	)= ==	Tunnel
	On/Off Ramp		Footbridge

REGIONAL ROUTES

	Tollway, Freeway
	Primary Road
	Secondary Road
	Minor Road

BOUNDARIES

	International
	State
	Disputed
	Fortified Wall

HYDROGRAPHY

	River, Creek		Dry Lake; Salt Lake
	Canal		Spring; Rapids
	Lake		Waterfalls

TRANSPORT ROUTES & STATIONS

	Train		Ferry
	Underground Train		Walking Trail
	Metro		Walking Tour
	Tramway		Path
	Cable Car, Chairlift		Pier or Jetty

AREA FEATURES

	Building		Market
	Park, Gardens		Sports Ground
	Beach		Campus
	Cemetery		Plaza

POPULATION SYMBOLS

CAPITAL	National Capital	CITY	City	Village	Village
CAPITAL	State Capital	Town	Town		Urban Area

MAP SYMBOLS

■	Place to Stay	
▼	Place to Eat	
●	Point of Interest	

✈	Airport		Embassy, Consulate	🏛	Museum	🏚	Stately Home
Θ	Bank	❶	Golf Course	🐨	National Park	🏊	Swimming Pool
🚏	Bus Stop	✛	Hospital	✚	Police Station	🕍	Synagogue
🚍	Bus Terminal		Internet Cafe	✉	Post Office	☎	Telephone
⌂	Cave	✳	Lookout	🍺	Pub or Bar	❶	Tourist Information
✝	Church	▲	Monument	⚑	Ruins	𝕏	Windmill
🎬	Cinema	☪	Mosque	✪	Shopping Centre	🦒	Zoo

Note: not all symbols displayed above appear in this book

LONELY PLANET OFFICES

Australia
Locked Bag 1, Footscray, Victoria 3011
☎ 03 8379 8000 fax 03 8379 8111
email: talk2us@lonelyplanet.com.au

USA
150 Linden St, Oakland, CA 94607
☎ 510 893 8555 TOLL FREE: 800 275 8555
fax 510 893 8572
email: info@lonelyplanet.com

UK
10a Spring Place, London NW5 3BH
☎ 020 7428 4800 fax 020 7428 4828
email: go@lonelyplanet.co.uk

France
1 rue du Dahomey, 75011 Paris
☎ 01 55 25 33 00 fax 01 55 25 33 01
email: bip@lonelyplanet.fr
www.lonelyplanet.fr

World Wide Web: www.lonelyplanet.com *or* AOL keyword: lp
Lonely Planet Images: lpi@lonelyplanet.com.au